GUILTY
by
Corruption

The Dark Side of the Sunshine State

G. K. Vega

ISBN 978-1-64492-465-5 (paperback)
ISBN 978-1-64492-466-2 (digital)

Christian Faith Publishing, Inc.
832 Park Avenue
Meadville, PA 16335
www.christianfaithpublishing.com

Printed in the United States of America

Contents

Preface

Have you ever wanted to do something and never got it done because of the numerous amounts of reasons we human beings have? You always had it in the back of your mind and then one day it all comes naturally. This book of my life and the Florida Department of correction has been something I have wanted to tell the world about but just never did. I have lived a painful, hard, emotional life. It is no one's fault, and I do not blame anyone for any of my circumstances. "The Florida Department of Corruption and Fraud" as I call it, has been my temporary housing for almost nineteen years straight. I will provide evidence of my wrongful conviction and mind-blowing events I have witnessed within this horrible place called prison. There will be photos, news articles, motions, expert reports, and much more. The purpose is to show people the truth! Maybe even change someone's life for the better.

I dedicate this book to my mother, Aurora. I understand she had a rough time with me as a juvenile, and I wasn't man enough to help instead of making things worst. As the years go by, I mature more and can only pray that I may have the opportunity one day to make my mom happy. I also dedicate this book to my soon-to-be wife, Zinia. God blessed me with a soul mate, an angel, a truly dedicated woman to whom I will respect, honor and desire for the rest of my life.

Acknowledgments

I was raised in church. I believe in God. And without God's presence in my life, there is no way this book could have been possible.

I thank my mother, Aurora, for having patience with me throughout my juvenile years and as a grown man. Thank you Mom, you are incredibly strong.

This book also would not have been possible without my loving and supporting fiancé, Zinia. Thanks so much for helping with the various drafts of my book and for encouraging me to trust in our Lord God at all times. To stay focused. You are an amazing woman, a gift directly from heaven above. As my other half, you inspire me to express my higher self so that I may touch people through the written word.

My grandparents, Elias and Anna, thank you for never giving up on me! I made many mistakes, and you never judged me. You were by my side all along, never losing hope, and the person who I truly am. I miss and love you both dearly. Rest in peace.

My sisters, Selina and Raquel, although you haven't been there for me as I expected it to be, I still love you with all my heart. My nephew, Jaden and niece, Aliana are beautiful! I pray for the day to be next to you all. I will be home one day soon.

Thanks to each one of my relatives who have prayed for me. I have been incarcerated almost a vicennial. My dream is to bring all our family together. Please stop being strangers!

Last but not least, a big thanks to everyone who has helped me (one way or the other) through this crucial time in my life. This includes, but is not limited to, Elias Junior, Cynthia, Mr. Soler, Jennie, Goyo, Catherine, Alexi, Gisele, Mr. Toro, Celia, Maurice, Lorraine, Richard, Crucita, Ramon, Amada, Nathan, Marilyn, Joshua, Dalniliz,

Christopher, Rosenberg, Harvey, Maria del Carmen, Ian, Janelyn, Johanna, Isis, Lido, Monivette, Xavier, Stephanie, Louis and my appellate attorney, Matthew.

Introduction

In a nation full of detention centers and prisons, it should not be a surprise to you the United States of America houses well over two million incarcerated individuals. The Sunshine State alone has a $4.6 billion-dollar yearly correction budget. With a decrease in mental health programs, reentry, educational courses, and recreational activities in prisons, where exactly is the money really going?

Point blank, you the taxpayer have a right to know the truth. Officials in the government have withheld information that shows you the entire process a human being goes through when judges handout time and end up in prison.

No one made us sell drugs. No one made us burglarized people's homes or businesses; no one made us commit armed robberies, etc. for whatever reason, whether we are guilty, guilty by association or innocent, society has turned a blind eye to the present crisis in prisons. No one truly cares! Because no one cares, officials have taken advantage and frauded in each possible way they can. Why am I talking about corruption when this book is supposed to be a biography, you might be asking yourself? Do not misunderstand me, this book is about my life. Specifically, my life while I was free and my life behind bars. At the same time, this book is about what I have personally seen during this prison tour. It's about different views aimed to help the public make better judgment and therefore vote for better officials. From the outset of my incarceration in 1999, I made a choice to make the most out of my time in prison. I spent hours researching books and was unable to comprehend procedural, substantiated case law. I had no education and little time to file appeals. It was during this early stage in my natural life sentence that I began reflecting on how I made so many incorrect decisions with money and my life. When I was arrested, I had little to show for all the risk

I took day in and day out. I was away from my family. I did not own a home and did not have money for legal representation. I didn't want to go back to my old ways while in prison. However, how was I supposed to fight my case? How else was I supposed to feed myself at night when my stomach hurt for food?

The weight of this realization kept me up many nights. I was anxious and desperate. There had to be a better way to obtain legal help! This book explains more or less the struggle I went through as a child and as I have grown up in prison throughout the state of Florida. Thanks to the education I chose to earn, I have become more alert, mature, and responsible. Recently, while watching the news on prison reform, I became upset because the government talks a good one on TV but at the end of the day, no serious changes are made. When will the mass incarceration stop? I earnestly hope that you will be inspired and moved to action by the information contained within these pages that you'll begin thinking about those in prison who need help and most importantly, those who deserve to be free.

Effective March 4th, 1789:

First Amendment Constitutional Right: "Congress shall make no law respecting an establishment of religion or prohibiting the free exercise thereof; or abiding the freedom of speech, or of the press; or the right of the people peaceably to assemble, and to petition the government for a redress of grievances."

Giovanni's 1ˢᵗ birthday (top left)-Cousins, Irene, Emir,
& Nathan with Giovanni and sister Selina (Top right)-Giovanni
in Ceiba, P.R. (bottom Left)-Giovanni 11 yrs. old (bottom right)

On August 14, 1979, I was born in Lawrence General Hospital. I was
supposed to be born prior to the fourteenth but my mom couldn't
break water. I entered the world via cesarean aka C-section. I am a

favorite to many uncles, aunts, cousins, and especially my grandparents. I was even lucky enough to have two godmothers. But then again, everyone loves babies. Both my mother and father come from Puerto Rican heritage. My father, Antonio, was one in thirteen brothers and sisters. From what I understand, he was a good man caught up in drug use. I'm not going to look down on him or anyone, so all I can write is that I wish he would have never passed away in 1989. My mom is one of four brothers and sisters. Later on throughout this book, you will read more about the good and the bad my mom and I went through. Sometime in 1993, my mom decided to leave Massachusetts and live in a small neighborhood called "Villa Polilla" in Ceiba, Puerto Rico. My grandfather, Elias Sr, was building a two-story cement home and had space for us. "Villa Polilla" in English means "termite ville." The neighborhood was called this way because all the homes were made out of wood at one point and looked beat down and old. It wasn't until Hurricane Hugo hit in September 1989 that people were forced to rebuild in the cement homes. I was enrolled in Maranata Christian Academy, Fajardo, Puerto Rico. There I did prekindergarten and a few years of school.

I remember having an Alaskan wolf dog as a present from my grandfather. One day, my younger sister Selina who is about four years younger than me, picked up a wash rag that belong to my wolf dog. The result was not good at all. The wolf dog bit my sister in the face. Next thing I knew, I was in the hospital looking at my sister hurt and machines all around her face. My grandfather didn't hesitate to pop one from his 357 Smith & Wesson into the wolf dog's brain. The animal was not safe anymore, I was told.

A little time went by and my mom decided to move to Left-Rock City, Queens, New York, with her sister Anita, my three cousins and their dad. The small apartment was on the eighteenth floor. My sister Selina was doing better, and her dad Jose was also staying at my aunt's apartment. My sister, my cousins Irene, Emir, Nathan and I were all enrolled in public schools. Irene is the oldest of all cousins so she took care of us. *Ducktales* was our favorite cartoon. For fun, I would get eggs from the refrigerator, open the balcony, place the egg in the middle of a snowball, and drop it toward people walking by.

Who knows how many people I hit. I do remember throwing the egg snowballs and hitting all types of cars. The car alarms would set off and could be heard all over the housing projects. We couldn't ride the elevator because of the robberies and rapes. So we used to run eighteen flights of stairs up and down every day. Sometimes more than once if we went to the store and bought me the $.25 chips and $.25 juices. Eventually, my mom and Jose rented the first floor of the house in South Ozone Park Queens (Italian section). I went to public school thirteen. Besides all the snow and people getting sliced up and down the street, it wasn't that bad. My mom had a friend who had a daughter that was deaf. They lived out in the Bronx. That deaf little girl, who was my age of ten, became my sweetheart. All I thought about was going to visit her.

In between all of this, my step pops, if it is correct to say, was consuming drugs also. Already a heavy alcoholic, I believe he was on cocaine because the high was an upper. This may have been the reason why he would beat me more times than I can remember. Let's just say that one day, I went to school and blood started to drip down my pant leg. A teacher noticed and called for help. I can't remember in detail, but I think they gave my sister's dad a break. My grandfather found out and within weeks, I was in Ceiba, Puerto Rico, once again. By then, I was bilingual. I wrote, read, and spoke both English and Spanish. I didn't look at it as hard or misunderstanding. I simply went to school and did all of my homework. It wasn't easy, but I got it done.

Life in Puerto Rico for me was good. I loved every single minute of it. I had one pair of shoes for school and church. I had my specific shorts and T-shirt to play with and dirty. We ate at a fast-food restaurant once per month. However, I loved my island, my people, my animals, and my grandparents. Everyone knew each other in my neighborhood. By the time my grandfather had sold his big house and move to a smaller house in Rio Abajo Ceiba, we had a ranch with hundreds of rabbits. Dwarf rabbits that we sold to pet shops, and big New Zealand rabbits for food. We had cows, horses, chickens, fighting roosters, parakeets, a pit bull, and any other animal I could find and breed.

I grew up traveling back-and-forth from the United States to Puerto Rico. I would miss my mom after time went by and ended up with her again. My great grandmother was alive at the time also. Her name was Pilar Guadalupe Fontanez and lived in Berwind section eight housing in Rio Piedras, Puerto Rico, eventually moving near some of her children in Luis Lloren Torres section eight housing in Santurce, Puerto Rico. Every time we visited, my grandfather took his 357 because crime was normal in their housing projects. Murder, drugs, and prostitution, you name it. The worst part to me was hearing gunfire from men attempting to defend their drug spots. Although it wasn't safe, I still would walk around, play with other kids, and go to the store to buy candy every day. I would stay mostly on weekends. My Uncle Manuel had a bodega in the middle of Luis Lloren Torres housing. The store looked like a big prison with bars all over it. I would go to work with my uncle in exchange for milk, bread, and candy. He would also take me to El Comandante Hipodromo in Loiza, Puerto Rico. There we would bet on the horse racing. Back then, Puerto Rico had a famous horse jockey named Alexis who rode on the also former female horse, Vuelve Candi B. In a big race, the Caribbean classic, Candi B got third place behind two horses from Venezuela. I got so hooked, I found out my grandfather had a cousin named Pito Vega who owns a betting agency in downtown Ceiba. Pito would let me get a free ticket, and I would play while learning more and more. One time I had a ticket, and my grandfather put it up in a photo album for us to remember. You couldn't tell me anything about picking horses after that!

Anna Vega Fontanez was my grandmother's name. Her side of the family was mostly known for betting and playing lotto tickets. The rivers that I did my swimming and fishing at, all were attached and flowing downstream from "El Yunke", a natural rainforest located in Luquillo Puerto Rico. Crystal clear, cold waters with jumbo shrimp (freshwater shrimp). I would jump from rock to rock, jump from high rocks into the river, and swim down deep as if I were a fish myself. By the time I walked back home, I was dry. That's how deep I would go into the forest. I remember throwing a rock at a tree with *quenepas*. That's Guinep in English. I hit a beehive, and they flew down and stung me all over my face, chest, and back. I ran so fast that a bull eating grass didn't even acknowledge me. As if the bull knew I was in pain or something. My grandmother boiled water, got lemons from the tree and got some aloe plant. By the next day, the swelling went down, and I was climbing trees already. Some days I would help my grandmother with her garden. She always had different types of fruits or vegetables growing around the house.

My grandfather was always building homes and cages for animals. I learned so much from simply being there next to him. If we weren't building, we were killing a pig, rabbit, or goat. I loved goat milk and the goats themselves. I had a rough time killing the goats but couldn't show a sign of weakness to my grandfather. It was important for me to be on point, same level with my old man. His character was clean cut and to the point. No faking around, get the job done and doing it well. My weaker crying side was held inside most of the time. I had to be strong for my grandmother also because I was the second man of the house. We protected my old lady at all costs. At night, I would cry by myself because I would miss my mom. But I didn't want to be around my mom's relationships, so I sucked it up and let time go by.

We are all different and how we handle circumstances in life. Some of us hold emotions in and keep it moving. While others let it all out, and whatever happens, happens. It is important for parents to realize that their child might look like the mom or dad but at the end of the day, the child is different. All types of things play into the difference. Friends around the child, school environment that seems to change throughout the years, different likes, dislikes and the importance of raising a child with mom and dad at all times. Single parents become involved with work, relationships and without really wanting to, miss out on the heavy situations their child may be going through. Sometimes it's nothing and the child is able to move on. But sometimes the effects can be devastating. I shouldn't have to write about what is taking place around the world right now. You see it on the news, hear it on the radio. Eight out of every ten teenagers that you see on the news for murder, robbery, theft, drugs or prostitution, the juvenile didn't have a father or mother to discipline them properly. Or even worse, they have a mom and dad but were never there through the troubled emotional parts of a teenager's life.

If you're reading this book, and you're a parent, tell your children I love you on a regular basis. Ask yourself one question: are you putting love into action? Anyone can say, "I love you." The Bible in first Corinthians chapter 13:4–8 states in part, "Love is patient, love is kind. It does not want what belongs to others. It does not brag. It is not proud. It is not rude. It does not look out for its own interest. It does not easily become angry. It does not keep track of other people's wrongs. Love is not happy with evil. But it is full of joy where the truth is spoken. It always protects. It always trusts. It always hopes. It never gives up. Love never fails." Do you pick up your child up from school and ask the teacher questions? Do you make sure your child is playing sports or even a musical instrument? Do you know if your child is being bullied or is a bully themselves? Do you take your child to the movies, fishing, and family events? Do you have family dinners and ask your child about homework and school activities? Have you talked about sex and all the horrible sexually transmitted diseases one may catch if not protected?

A good parent doesn't do one of the above, it has to be all done. All the time! Not an easy task yet things that result in a healthy future for that one little mind you say, "I love you too." The truth about me is that my mom tried to raise me right. I was stubborn, hardheaded, and emotional. I figured since I had no father then I did what I wanted to do. The only times I acted right was in Puerto Rico with my grandfather. I was confused and hurt about many things. This is why I don't blame anyone for the decisions I made as a teenager. Years ago, I was upset at certain family members. Now, I no longer hold any grudges towards anyone. I discovered it is better to pray for those who have done you wrong or are presently doing you wrong. Prayer is powerful.

Chapter 2

Age of Twelve (1992)

13 years old (top left) 12 years old with grandparents
in Puerto Rico (top right)

In 1989, my mom decided to leave New York and live in Buena
Ventura, Kissimmee, Florida, with my Godmother Melinda. Shortly
thereafter also separating from my step pops, Jose. I think he was still

an alcoholic. Whether liquor or drugs, either way, he was messing up. We lived with my godmother a little while and then move to St. Cloud, Florida. My mom rented a two-bedroom one-bath apartment on Kentucky Avenue and 10th St. I enrolled in Ross E. Jeffrey's elementary school with my sister Selina. It didn't take long for me to realize we were in Ku Klux Klan land. After school, my sister and I walked a route home with the other minorities because white people would look at us wrong for walking by their homes. One day, after arriving from football practice, a white man attempted to break down our door. I quickly grabbed a knife and told my sister Selina to go hide under the bed. The wood on the side of the doorway broke. I must have scared him off by screaming that I called the police. After the man left, there was a note on the door that read, "You spics get out of town." I didn't even know what "spics" meant. I told my mom but there was nothing we could do. The St. Cloud police department was mostly white people with Ku Klux Klan members or family. Shortly thereafter, one late night I heard a loud boom sound. When I looked outside, my mom's Chevy Chevette that she paid $800 for was in flames. The fire department arrived and did their job. When my mom asked why the car burned, officials explained the radio wires caused the fire. I could not believe the lie a law enforcement officer would say because the car never had a radio. Better yet it never had radio wires. The compartment was empty. We could not afford a radio. I told my grandfather the news, and I was, once again, in Puerto Rico before the end of the month. I felt bad for my mom, but I was never schooled on racism. Up north, I never heard about it besides the Italians not liking African Americans.

In Puerto Rico, we have all colors, shapes, and sizes. The Ku Klux Klan members knew that Hispanics would move in and eventually be a dominant force. And I must say that they were correct. Today, as I write this book, Saint Cloud, Florida, is all Puerto Ricans! I left my mom while she was employed at medieval times, located in Kissimmee, Florida, on west Irlo Bronson Hwy 192. I guess she finally got the point and moved to an apartment on Michigan Avenue in St. Cloud. There apparently more minorities live. But I was still in Puerto Rico, and now I was twelve years old. My life began to change completely. From one day to the other, my neighbor in Rio Abajo Ceiba, named Barbara invited me to her house. She was about twenty-nine maybe thirty years old. It wasn't hard to convince me to meet her at midnight in the first floor of her house. One thing led to another, I was no longer a virgin. I was taking classes at midnight for a while. I no longer played with hot wheel cars or G.I. Joe. I no longer asked for toys.

My grandfather caught on and decided to teach me how to drive. I learned how to drive in a pickup truck Mazda B 2000. I dented the back bumper one time, but other than that, I was a pro. A natural. By then I was in middle school and had my eyes set on a girl named Edna. The bus dropped us off in front of my grandparents' house. I would ask my grandpa for the keys and drive Edna home about 3 miles. I became much more independent of myself too. I started to make and sell cages for animals, selling the rabbits, pigs and goats for money. I would even sell mangos, lemons, sweet peppers, hot peppers, passion fruit, plantains and more. I had to buy myself shoes and clothing. I was visiting church but when my grandfather gave me the truck to go to church, I really went to church. At times I would wander down to the city of Ceiba to stop by and say hi to family members. My father's side of the family also lives in Ceiba. So I had a lot of people to visit. Becoming a bit older now required for me to make tougher decisions. There was a man by the name of Morita. It wasn't hard to know he was doing something other than working. He had a ranch with horses. Motorcycles, limos, and females wondering around. I had to keep it on the down low but I got me a job washing his horses and bikes. To my surprise, I learned how to ride bikes in the hills. I was living okay. Good grades in school didn't have to walk at the age of twelve, fighting roosters for money, and going to church. Everything was fine. Why I decided to leave all of it and go with my mom, I still don't know. Maybe it's because she convinced me that living in a double-wide trailer and more Hispanic community in Kissimmee was better. Turns out S. Hoagland Blvd was a superhot spot for drugs. Especially heroin.

Before I get to the past, know that I am coming from a hustle state of mind already. I had to provide for myself because we were poor in Puerto Rico. We were poor but never went hungry! Anyhow, I was enrolled in middle school and took off from there. I was introduced to the first Newport cigarette, the first blunt of weed, the first thirty-two-ounce old English malt liquor and eight ball, so school faded out slowly. I don't even know how I made it to high school. I was told the schoolteachers didn't want to see my face anymore and passed me to the ninth grade. My mom had been with her boyfriend Ricardo a couple of years by then, and he taught me how to drive standard in a Honda Civic station wagon. I learned quickly. But I couldn't take the cars how I wanted, so I would sneak out at night and meet with my girlfriends. My mom caught me one time as I was coming in through the laundry room and punched me right in the eye. I had to hide for a week while the swelling went down. When I tell you that mom knows best, mom knows best. She repeatedly told me that I would get in trouble with the law if I kept sneaking out in the middle of the night.

Sure enough, I met another teenager my age named Javier. He told me that there were two females, one sixteen years old and the other fourteen years old whose parents left for Las Vegas and wanted to sneak us in while the babysitter was in the living room. I was thirteen years old, so the thought of anyone older was an automatic green light. We rode bikes about twenty miles down to Kings Hwy, through a security gate, down the side of the pond, and right up to their window. We had to be quiet while they gave us macaroni and cheese with Budweiser canned beer. At night, we both got what we went for. Morning time came around, and we left. The following week while having dinner with my mom and sister, sheriff officers were kicking at our front door. To my surprise, they arrested me claiming my friend and I manipulated two older girls into sex. I explained to my mom the truth, and so she hired a lawyer. Depositions were made on the so-called victims. The oldest one said she had been having sex for years, and her mom knew about it already. That she was going to continue to have sex. The one I slept with gave a different statement and expressed that her parents forced her to say otherwise. The case was dropped. But not before my mom spent money, and I caught another ass whopping. I was getting myself into too much trouble.

S. Hoagland Blvd. was full of homes, trailer homes, and apartments. Right about in the middle, there was a Texaco gas station. Still to this day, it is a drug-infested area with no end in sight. I started to hang out with some friends who were older than me by a few years. They were involved in selling any type of drugs available. I had some hustler in me and got my first pound of weed fronted to me. I was sure I made the money first to pay out my debt and did as I pleased with the profit. I bought shoes, clothing, food, and most of the time rented motel rooms. I started to go to nightclubs and meeting people involved in other illegal trades. My mom was not sleeping at night because I would be gone for three or four days at a time.

Throughout all of it, I managed to play baseball. My coach was the father of an Atlanta Braves triple A baseball player. I learned the pitching fundamentals of baseball and most likely would have made it if I wasn't so ignorant and foolish. To make matters worse, I couldn't even practice anymore because my lungs were full of weed smoke and cigarettes. I was drinking all night and skipping school. My mom's boyfriend was also smoking with me. He and I had an okay relationship. We never spent a lot of time together because I was always in the street.

By 1994, my mom decided the trailer home was not going to be good anymore and rented a three-bedroom home in Poinciana, Florida. For those of you who want to know, Poinciana is the other side of Kissimmee, touching with Polk County. Maybe it was because the rent was cheap or maybe my mom thought she could get away from Hoagland Boulevard. It turned out to be a lot of Hispanics and drugs everywhere. The only difference was, there were more homes. My mom landed a nice state job that didn't pay much that was enough to pay the bills. The moving didn't stop me from the hustling. I got me a mobile pager and kept it moving. Poinciana was a town with many homes but only a few stores. It had a Winn-Dixie, Farm store, Fina gas station, Chinese restaurant, movie rentals, a few delis and a small sheriff's office. All the excitement was in Kissimmee and Orlando. My grandfather bought a small piece of land on Pleasant Hill Road. After a few months, he got tired and moved back to Puerto Rico. Turns out, a few years later, a big highway was built and the people were paid a lot of money for the land next to Pleasant Hill Road. My grandfather had a gold mine and didn't even know it. I was going to Poinciana High School. A lot of teenagers were smoking, so I sold weed in the school. I didn't last too long, I got caught and put in jail (juvenile detention center). I received probation and attempted to do what is right, at least for a little while. My mom would have me drop her off at work while I went to school at a GED center. Again people there would smoke, so I sold the weed to them. I ended up violating my probation and was ordered to wear an ankle monitor while it was time to go to a punishment camp.

Stubborn as I was, I was still selling with my mobile pager as a way for people to get a hold of me. I would walk up to the house mailbox and deliver the weed. If I went passed the mailbox the black box would beep and the sheriffs were on their way. I made it long enough and was transported to the juvenile camp. I am not going into detail about it. One can only imagine how those camps are. A lot of yelling, fighting, running, working, patience, and much more. You could do three months or one year in order to go back home. I did it in three months, no problem. At the end, the instructor told me that I manipulated the process and that if he could, he would leave me longer. Back then I wasn't trying to hear that. Now I admit the instructor was right. I didn't learn a damn thing! What I did learn, if anything, was not to make mistakes out in society. Mistakes that would land me in jail again. Before I went to the camp, I bought a 1986 Mazda 626. When I got home, it was in the garage waiting for me. It was standard with tinted windows. My mom told me not to drive it until I got a learner's permit and insurance. You already know I cleaned the car and took it out on many spins.

I was fifteen years old and decided to get a job at the McDonald's in front of old town in Kissimmee. The manager was okay and hired me although I was supposed to be sixteen. Everything was going well. My mom gave birth to my other sister Raquel. I wasn't doing drugs, not selling drugs and at home most of the time. The day that I officially got the job as a cashier in the McDonald's, I was driving Raquel's dad's Toyota pickup truck back home. It was raining, and I had my friend Fernando in the truck with me because he got me the job. A puddle of rain made the car coming down toward me on the other lane, jump out the lane and caused a head-on collision. I swerved but got the truck smashed on one side. We spun in circles until the truck hit a wooden light pole which broke in half and crushed us and the truck. Fernando ate the windshield. The steering wheel saved me somewhat. We were both in pain and bloody. It was nighttime, about 9:00 p.m. I kicked the door open and pushed Fernando through and I followed. A female we knew was riding by slowly watching the accident, and we waved her down. I left the scene of the accident because I had no license and didn't want to go to jail. The state troopers were at my house within minutes. Now everyone thought I was in the woods possibly dead. The helicopter looked for us everywhere. I was at Fernando's house getting medical attention from his mother. On the third day, I called home. To my surprise, my grandfather was there. I guess you already know I went back home that day. It turned out witnesses gave statements that I was not at fault. I got a ticket. Not too long ago, I wrote to the Department of Motor Vehicles, and there's nothing on record—my info is clean! The insurance paid for the truck, which was totaled.

Everything was still going well. I worked from 6:00 p.m. through 3:00 a.m. To make a few extra dollars at night, I would shortchange tourists. People from Asia, South America, and Europe would pay with American express cashier's checks, if the change was $83 I would count out loud the $83 but give them $80. To throw the tourists off, I would give them free fries, ice cream, or burgers. At the end of the night, I counted all the extra money and an average made about $50 to $100. I discovered that a lot of the employees smoked weed, so I started to sell again but more carefully. I use the excuse of working late and would stay out in a motel.

Back then, motels were $20 a night. I met people from all over the world. It was like traveling but staying put in one place. I sold the Mazda 626 and started on the same journey that leads to jail. You would ask yourself, where is Giovanni's other family? Well my Uncle Elias Junior lived in Kissimmee with his wife and kids. I would visit often. Not much more to say about that. My other Uncle Edwin lived in New Jersey with his wife and kids. We would only see him once every few years. Not much to say about that neither. My Aunt Anita had moved from New York to Augusta, Georgia. We would visit once in a while. Everyone was separated by distance. Maybe later on in this book, I can write a little more about my family.

The year 1995 was a fast year. Not only in a bad way but in a good way also. Living in the street is what I wanted to do. As time went by, I felt more comfortable with myself and had the few dollars to provide what I needed. It's like being in a zone, you put your mind to something and sticking to it. Being involved in drug selling is very dangerous, yet you lie to yourself and think that it's all good. I wish that I could talk to teenagers right now. Tell them my many stories and attempt to change a few struggling with similar problems, even older individuals who are living a normal life can learn from people like me. Every day of life is beautiful. Don't you realize, I mean really realize that today you're alive, and tomorrow you can be dead? Millions of us take family, friends, and jobs for granted. It's natural to get caught up in work, sports and hobbies. It goes back to what I wrote in this book, are you just saying I love you? Are you putting love into action?

It is kind of hard to make it all work with our families. The Bible tells us not to judge one another. Yet we often judge our brothers, sisters, mothers, fathers, cousins, and so forth. We first notice wrong in others and only talk positive on their birthdays! That's crazy! But it goes on each day. Some people put the excuse that they stay away from the family drama. Again it's all the same thing. If you stay away, how can you love? By simply saying I love you? By staying away, you're not allowing for things to work out, to get better, to let true love open your heart. I have been in prison almost nineteen years, and can you believe that most of my family don't even know the details of my case? Most of my relatives put it to the side. They think of me from far away.

Anyhow, let me get back to my teenage years for now. I didn't have too many friends, real friends. When you're involved in drugs, fake friends come from all over. People wanting to get high and spend your money. They don't care how old you are or where you come from. Not one time did any adults asked me my age. By the end of 1995, I was dealing with some big shots and staying in some nice places. I had a business associate, a closer friend than anyone else nicknamed Big J. We did a lot of going to the nightclubs, selling, and other illegal things I'm not going to write about. Big J would get so drunk that I had to drive us back home. After a while, he trusted me more and more. I didn't become an alcoholic. I never have because I am a light drinker. I respect liquor and its consequences. However, I started to drink on weekends. Wild turkey, Hennessey, Bacardi and my favorite, Heinekens. I must've driven all over Central Florida and not one time did I get caught driving under the influence. This was because I wasn't driving crazy or anything like that. I lost contact with my mom. From time to time, I would pop up at her job just to hear her mouth about me and "my ways." I wasn't trying to understand everything my mom was grieving about. My mind was in a zone. Headed for self-destruction. Only now I can understand the words my mom would yell out to me. She was right the whole entire time. If only teenagers would do as their parents say, this world would be a much safer place. But I know I might be asking for too much. The time we are living in now is even worse than the 1990s. Society has fallen victim to computers and a very much corrupt government.

15 years old (top)-14 years old with dreams
to become a firefighter (bottom)

Going to take you back to 1996. I was sixteen years old. This was the year I wanted to do bigger and better things although my mind was of a juvenile. The first thing I did was move out of my mom's house. I went half on a two-bedroom two-baths duplex on Amberwood Boulevard in Kissimmee. My roommate was from New York and was in need of help with the rent. To my surprise, people were still knocking on the door wanting to buy drugs from the person that was living there. Apparently, the narcotics team did a raid and took someone to jail. Meanwhile, I got me a job at AT&T and sold weed on the side. The neighbors were an old Puerto Rican couple. The old lady was really nosy and at first I got a little spooked. Turned out, she really was going to nightclubs and liked the nightlife. I didn't allow for her to enter my apartment, and I would cut the conversation short. The less people who know my lifestyle, the better.

I continued to drink liquor, smoke weed, sell weed, and do all types of deals. Drug addicts would sell big screen TVs, house radios, phones, speakers and radios for cars, clothing, shoes, and jewelry. In that lifestyle, you never know what will be available. I wasn't going to school anymore. An old friend of mine was robbing drug dealers and anybody he knew had thousands of dollars in a safe. I gave it a try but it wasn't for me. I stuck with the fast cash. I sat down and talked with my friend, Big J, about moving up in weight. He told me to be the deliveryman of 500 pounds of weed from San Diego, California, a month. The operation was simple. Two Mexican women or men would drive a rental van or U-Haul down to motel in Central Florida. They load the room up and leave the key in the secure area. I would go find a key, look at the area for any suspicious activity, and then go in to weigh the merchandise. Big J would beep me and asked to deliver a certain amount of pounds of weed to different people throughout the day and night. I went to Walmart and bought clear tape and gift wrap. I got boxes, all sizes, from the back of gas stations and would deliver as if it were birthday present. For some reason I thought if I were to be pulled over by the police, and they would not notice. The money I made was good. But it was what we now call *young money*. I didn't have a legitimate plan other than deliver and take care of my customers.

Have you ever gotten sick off liquor poisoning? I bought half a gallon of Bacardi Limon and decided to drink one night. The next day, I felt like I was going to die! Literally, I felt like I was going to be out of commission. My roommate was at work, and the female I was with at that time was at work also. I was able to make it to the house phone and call my mom at work. When she heard my voice, she knew I was bad. She took time off work and brought me chicken soup. I was sick for two long weeks. Don't ever get food poisoning, it's worse than any flu or migraine headache a person can get.

I met more people throughout 1996. One of them was a drug dealer directly from Puerto Rico. He introduced cocaine to me and therefore I started to sell more than weed. It was smaller baggage and

27

more money. My apartment was laid out nice. I carried a German thirty-two seven shot pistol. It wasn't mine, I just had it in case someone got out of control. I had associates with all types of guns, so I never felt the need to be around guns too much. It's not easy to hide guns and cars. It is not good to deliver drugs with the gun around your waist either. Arm trafficking is a charge that will carry more jail time than a sales and delivery or simple trafficking. By 1997, I rented an apartment with my girl at the time. I started to buy more jewelry. When I saw bikes riding down the block, I went and bought a Honda CBR 600. The bike was new, the seller was hooked on drugs, so I took advantage of the price. Then I bought a 1981 white Buick Regal. The car was superclean! I put money in the engine, tinted the windows and added a radio system. If I had the chance, I would get me another Buick Regal. She was my baby! It was then that I started to provide drugs to hustlers on Hoagland Boulevard, Buena Ventura Lakes, and Semoran Blvd, Orlando. I had Big J with all the weed and a new cocaine connects trusting me with enough to make some dollars. On a bright sunny day, two Puerto Ricans stormed apartments and sprayed a tech nine machine gun. Hitting three times a person who was involved in the same activities and I was there that morning, in that same apartment. I was like damn! That could have been me shot up and possibly dead. So I was more careful but was still doing what I was doing.

If I spent time with any of my family members, a few times, it was a lot. I didn't want to bring the attention to my mom or anyone else. I believe people who knew me would run into my mother and more or less tell her what I was involved in. One morning, I was told there was a buyer for five pounds of weed by intersection city around the outside of Kissimmee. I met with the buyer and drove him to Ricky's trailer homes on Hoagland Boulevard, where I had a small stash area within the laundry room. As I was reversing my Buick Regal in front of the trailers, from behind me the buyer pulled out a Rambo knife and demanded I open the trunk. I set the Regal on park and opened the door as far as I could. I couldn't go far as a knife was close to my back. As the buyer was coming out of the car, I ran toward a tree. The buyer followed quickly. I did a U-turn and ran back to my car because underneath the seat I had a small gun with a big clip.

I bought the gun while in Brooklyn, New York, visiting Big J and his relatives earlier 1997. I yelled for the buyer to stop, but he thought I wasn't serious. I ended up shooting towards him and hitting 11 times. Blood was all over me but I hadn't noticed yet. He quickly walked away from me heading down Hoagland Boulevard. Turns out, he walked a half a mile and dropped right in front of some house door. I got in my car and headed to Michigan Avenue where my ex-girlfriend's mom lived. By 5:00 p.m. I was on Central Florida channel 9 News. I left the car on the side of the road parked and close enough to be picked up later. I was on the run, and people started to tell me that the Osceola County sheriffs were looking for me everywhere. I called my uncle in New Jersey but no answer. I collected all the money from everyone involved with my deals. I couldn't go to places where I had been before because the police was out to get me and set up unmarked cars in certain apartments and houses. I ended up going back to my old roommate's duplex apartment where I lived before. I figured the law had no record of me living there because I was a teenager. I rested for days and nights thinking, *What was next?* Meanwhile, the news was flashing in my face accusing me of attempted first-degree murder. I had to make a decision and a good one at the time.

Across the street there was a female named Mary who had two guys visiting her. I was looking through the window and noticed one of the men I knew from McLaren Circle in Kissimmee. I snuck through the back woods and in through Mary's back porch. After a few words, I asked my old business associate if I could pay him an 8 ball of Coke to get my Buick Regal. They both accepted! An hour went by and they came back empty-handed, explaining the car was in Buena Ventura Lakes, in front of Andy's apartment and an unmarked Crown Victoria is down the street watching. I doubled the pay. They accepted. I told them to park the car in front of Mary's apartment and leave her the keys while she had the two 8 balls ready for them. These guys knew what they were doing. They went in a new white Ford Mustang and told Andy to put on a hoodie sweater in order not to reveal identity, jump in the Mustang, and therefore see if the unmarked Crown Victoria police would jump in behind. The plan worked. While the Sheriff's Detective followed the Mustang, one of the guys got in my Buick regal and went the other way. Once the sheriff realized they followed a ghost, they were hot! I let the Buick regal sit in front of Mary's apartment for three nights. I must have looked around the entire area 1000 times for any sign of police. Now it was time to go! I picked up my baby and drove it to the back of the duplex I was staying in. The neighbor did a quick tune up, I got me a Cadillac Fleetwood license plate down the street, put all my money in packs of 1000, hid ten pounds of weed in the trunk spare tire, put a little bit less than an ounce of Coke inside the steering wheel, filled up the gas tank, and I was on Interstate 4 east by 8:00 p.m. I didn't even have a minute to really sit back and think about any more problems I would get myself into if I were to get caught with everything in the car. I'm the first one to tell you today, I was completely ignorant and foolish. I thought I knew it all and didn't know shit! I got to interstate 95 and headed north, wondering how many of my family members may have seen me on TV. When I was tired of driving it was about 4:00 a.m. I parked in front of a motel, ate, and slept. I knew I had a long way before stopping in Clifton, New Jersey, for a few days. Maybe even Paterson, New Jersey, with my family.

I-95 starts to get full of state troopers across the state of North Carolina and even worse in Virginia. They have a reputation of parking in between roads, with trees as their cover and pulling people over. It was early morning, and I was headed up I-95 going well over the speed limit. I flew past one of the state troopers, and all I could hear was the sound of his car engine getting closer and closer. I got in the slow lane, but he scared everyone and got right behind me. I had two choices, punch it and find a place to stop and leave the car behind or pullover and see what happens. I pulled over. The trooper was a tall white man with one of them state trooper hats. He politely requested my license and registration while also explaining I was speeding going over 100 mph. I didn't argue and explained I never had a license, that I had purchased the car from a man with an auto business, which was true. I went on to explain that I was supposed to send for the title and never got around to it because Florida did not go well for me. I gave him my cousin's name, John, his birthday and social. It came out clean. The Regal came up clean too. The license plate, however, came up of a Cadillac. So I explained a friend lend me the plate in order to drive to New Jersey and mail it back to Florida. Since the license plate wasn't reported stolen, the trooper told me that a check of the vehicle would be made. If I wasn't in possession of anything illegal, I could go on my journey. He even told me to be careful in Virginia because they would not give me a chance.

I was happy for one-minute when another state trooper arrived with dark tinted windows. On the side was a white logo that read K9 unit. My heart dropped down to my feet. I was ordered to open the trunk, open both doors and step to the side. I couldn't run, the dog would get me for sure. First, the dog was let loose in the car while I thought about the twenty-two grams of cocaine hidden in the steering wheel. To my surprise, the dog came back out with nothing. Then the dog walks around the car and jumps in the trunk. I knew I was caught right then. Again the dog jumps out the trunk and goes back in the state trooper. I was like *Oh shit*, this is unbelievable. I didn't know what to say. That K9 was placed in his little dog cage and the second trooper left.

But the one that pulled me over told me the following: "I'm going to check the glove compartment and the backseats, after I do so, you may be on the way, Mr. DeLeon." The trooper checks and finds nothing! On his way out of my car, he reaches between the seats and finds my identification card. He looks at it, looks at me, and then softly tells me to turnaround: I was under arrest. When he ran my real name, it came back as an outstanding warrant out of Osceola County, Florida, for attempted first-degree murder. I almost made it! Almost was not good enough. I was booked in Nashville County Jail North Carolina. I refused to talk and was taken to maximum-security old-school cells. Although I was seventeen years old, they still housed me with the adults. The following day, a judge told me Florida has twenty-one days to pick me up with one extension. I knew Florida was coming to get me. This state will pick you up in Alaska for a misdemeanor. They will spend taxpayer's money and go the distance because the people of Florida are blind to the government corruption. All the inmates in the cellblock I was housed in were black. I never saw not one Hispanic inmate. Later, I did find out most white inmates were housed separately. Every day, those men were fighting. They had this code that if you were from North Carolina, you couldn't be with the ones from South Carolina. To me, that was stupid. But they sure did fight.

I made a couple of friends. One was from Alabama and the other came back from prison. I learned how to play chess a little. The TV was outside the bars so we turned the channel with rolled up newspaper. While playing chess one day, an inmate went in my cell and stole my quilt. I guess because it was freezing in that county jail. I saw the inmate from the corner of my eye, going in and stealing my quilt. I silently told my friend, Bama; he then went to his cell and put on his sneakers. I went to my cell and rolled up the orange jumpers to my knees, put on my boots, grabbed my sharpened toothbrush with the razor and stepped out to talk again with Bama. The thief noticed and began to recruit his friends. As he walked around me, I attacked. He had dreads so I grabbed him by the hair, head locked him and dropped back toward the iron bars. His head split wide open as he yelled out a big "ahhh." His friends attacked; they were at least eight. We were only three. I couldn't find my razor through all the fighting. I was pretty messed up! I was full of blood, splits, bumps, etc. My eyes were swollen shut. The officers did a round every hour or so. By the time they came by, there was blood everywhere. The thief was on the floor with a towel over his head. The cut was too open, he was bleeding and hurt. The officers noticed and called for help. I was in cuffs along with several others.

Those so-called gangsters pointed the finger at me when the officers claimed someone would get charged with aggravated battery over the inmate with the staples on his forehead. I didn't say a word. My friend Bama explained the entire story. I was housed in confinement pending investigation. That was good for me because I was hurt really bad. On the twentieth day, I was taken to see the judge again. I was told Florida had twenty-four hours to pick me up or I would be released in North Carolina. Florida had until 5:00 p.m.

the next day. Two agents picked me up at 4:00 p.m., one hour before deadline. The sheriff escorted us to a small airport and officially gave custody to both agents from Florida. While we waited for a small plane to arrive, one of the agents showed me his gun and told me that he would allow for me to travel without leg or handcuffs, and if I decided to run I would get a shot, no hesitation. We flew in a small plane to Charlotte International Airport where I was followed by airport security into a bigger plane with passengers in it. They didn't make a big deal of the issue at hand. Everything was done smoothly, they did not attract any attention.

When we landed in Orlando International Airport, it was a different world. There were Orlando police everywhere. The passengers in the plane became scared. The back door of the plane opened and then I was escorted out as if I shot the president. Florida is known for overdoing police matters! A Department of Juvenile Justice lady was there and had to remind authorities I was a juvenile teenager seventeen years of age. I was placed in the back of the police car and taken into Orange County jail, 33rd St. and John Young Parkway. I stayed there for a few days and was transported to Osceola County Jail, Simpson Road. Because I was seventeen, I was transported again to Lake County Jail, Tavares, Florida, where juveniles were housed. My mom hired an attorney named Winesett. The man was a hippie, I believe he got high. I thought I was going to prison for fifty years because of his appearance. He visited me one time while I was in Lake County Jail, only to tell me to relax; he's on top of everything. In August 1997, I was transported back to Osceola County Jail, housed in solitary confinement for three days while I turned eighteen years old. There was a big chance for me as I had never been in the Osceola County Jail before. On my exact birthday, I was moved to Charlie-Alpha POD maximum. If I didn't go to school with a lot of the men there, I knew the others from the streets. Everyone had seen me on TV and or heard of what happened. Besides the fights and arguing, it went by fast.

On Halloween day 1997, I was called to court unexpectedly. I didn't want to go for a free ride so I refused. The correctional officer told me I had to go, the judge was going to see me. It was the Old

Kissimmee Courthouse. An old red building with a big tree in the front where people say the Ku Klux Klan hung blacks. No Hispanic judges. No black judges. I already knew what I was dealing with, it was no surprise. Osceola is a county that had wood crosses as you came into St. Cloud. A county that knew of the St. Cloud mayor to have a big chapter in the Ku Klux Klan.

I'm going to tell the readers of this book something that I learned is pure truth: white people from up north are not the same, not even close, to most of the white people down south! I was escorted to a judge who was not my assigned judge, the Hon. Judge Roach. God knew what he was doing because she was the only fair judge in Osceola at the time. I was released with a simple word that I would show up in December for my court hearing in front of Judge Johnson. No bond, no nothing. My mom later explained that she'd seen my lawyer "Winesett", walk right out the courtroom with a bright shine around his back as if an angel was within him. I walked out of the Osceola County Jail around 6:00 p.m. Halloween day. I was supposed to go directly to my mom's house in Orlando, instead I went to my girlfriend's house, spent a little time, and hit the streets again. I still can't believe I didn't go directly to my mom's house. That was crazy! The small amount of time I did, the horrible North Carolina experience, the embarrassing flights were not enough for me to calm down. Some people learn quickly, some have to fall many times and learn.

Chapter 4

Last Two Years of Freedom

In December 1997, I was in front of Judge Johnson in regard to accepting a three-year probation plea offer my attorney arranged with the state. The judge enhanced the sentenced to five years of probation and a restitution of $18,000 for the hospital fees of the man I shot. I was forced to report to the probation officers on Colonial Drive in Orlando. I was told to get a job and start to pay $350 a month in restitution. In my mind, I had it all planned out already. I wasn't going to work a $6 an hour job and pay that amount each month, not happening. I was thinking about working and selling on the side. Big J offered a job transporting pounds to his Brooklyn Bushwick housing projects. I told him I would keep it in mind. I landed a job at McDonald's. I didn't want to work there, but I figured it would look good for probation while I did my thing on the down low. On my second probation visit, I asked the officer if I could pay the restitution in four payments and be recommended for early termination of supervised release. Around March 1998, I went to the third probation hearing with a big payment in mind. After thinking and thinking, I finally said to myself, *They can kiss my ass.* I wasn't going to give them a penny more! Within two weeks, I had a warrant for my arrest. I already quit the McDonald's job and was in the transporting business.

The year 1998, although it was full of illegal activities, I enjoyed it well. I bought a Nissan 300 2X, stayed at many motels and hotels, went to nightclubs, and seen hip-hop artists like Ja-rule, Lil' Kim and more. You already know that with fast money comes fast women. With fast women comes fast drugs. I was introduced to ecstasy. Back then, one pill could be cut in half and last all night long. I popped half a pill around 9:00 p.m. and the other half around 1:00 a.m. The pills were called "dirty pills." This meant the pills were mostly heroin. This further meant my body would eventually become sick if I skip a day of consuming ecstasy. I wasn't thinking about stopping anything. I took two trips to Puerto Rico. Both trips I went under other names because of the warrant for my arrest. It was easy to have someone buy a ticket, go with you to the airport, check in, then switch when it was time to go pass the last gate. Security at airports was easy in the 1990s and prior. On my first trip, I went directly to Ceiba, Puerto Rico, with my grandparents. I spent some time with my father's side of the family also. As I grew older, I realized they were not so close of a family. Or maybe because I was never there, I felt out of place. Either way, I went and had a nice time.

My Aunt Natividad Vega had a house in Villa Avila, Ceiba. Behind her house, there was a small creek with freshwater shrimp. I just had to lay my shrimp traps and fish for hours. It is in my blood to go fishing. My sister's dad, José used to take me fishing all the time when I was younger. As I was fishing, I heard a lot of gunfire. Across the grass field into a cemetery, a young man was shooting it out with the police. Apparently he shot two cops and ran across the field to hide, get away. I quickly grabbed my machete and ran toward the back of my aunt's house. I jumped the creek and then a fence. I looked back, and he was about ten feet behind me. All I saw was a big nickel-plated gun while he ran. I reached the side of the door of the house and shut the master lock.

In Puerto Rico, most people in the city have iron bars with locks. As I went inside, I looked through the window and the fugitive was climbing the iron bars, to the roof, jumped to other houses and was hiding in a pigeon house. Police helicopters, motorcycles, dogs, and vehicles were everywhere. They were knocking door-to-door. The code of the street was to quickly dismiss the police when they knocked, so we did that. The fugitive was not caught. No one snitched. It was sad that two cops were shot, but that's how it is when you decide to be in law enforcement. In Puerto Rico, all cops wear a bulletproof vest because of how dangerous the job is. Later that night, I was playing basketball and saw the same man out like nothing happened.

On my second trip, my grandfather was building a house in Rio Abajo Ceiba, Puerto Rico. My Uncle Elias Junior was there helping. So I had to help as well. In the between time, I went out with other relatives from both my mom's and father's side of the family. One night, my Aunt Awilda told me to accompany her to the *fiestas patronales* in Loiza, Puerto Rico. These are carnivals that most municipal counties do once a year. Some are bigger than others. The one in Loiza was dangerous, but I did not know until that night. Like any other carnival, people drink a lot of alcohol and get out of place. And when people get out of place, violence happens. My aunt and I were there for couple of hours when shots were fired in a few angles. We ducked and ran to the car. I couldn't believe how it turned out. My aunt was mad and stopped in the middle of Luquillo, Puerto Rico.

On the side of the road are many kiosks. Kiosks are lined up like a flea market but with wooden walls to separate each food, alcohol, game rooms, and hangout spots. The Luquillo kiosks are famous. On Friday and Saturday nights on the highway, races are conducted. Motorcycles and cars only. The teams take the races seriously. A lot of money is gambled and at times, shootouts happened over all types of different issues. I visited my old neighbors in Rio Abajo Ceiba, who were still fighting roosters. Marcial Sr., that's the father, and Marcial Jr. was the son. They treated me as family, no questions asked. The mom of Marcial Sr., Leonore, grew up with my grandfather. We were all family in those mountain hills. I feel at home when I'm around animals and the farm life. I feel good when I am raising game roosters and riding horses. And with that, I enjoyed my last time in Puerto Rico.

I was back in Orlando. It was the middle of 1998. My old cocaine connect had a black Lexus ES 300 he never used because the car was under his wife's name who in turn was a Kissimmee Police Department officer. The car was basically mine. I had it for weeks at a time. The owner never questioned me. Instead, I would find him and ask him if he wanted his car back. I drove rental cars throughout the day and the Lexus at night. My friend Josie had a black BMW, and we would drive side-by-side down Semoran Blvd., Orange Blossom Trail, John Young Parkway and all over I-4. My mom had an apartment by the fashion square mall in Orlando, and I visited a few times. She was not too happy with my way of living. The visits were short and not too happy.

I met a lot of more people in 1998. I was selling heroin and weed and cocaine if the flip was right. I was called for four pounds of weed and to meet this man called "Flaco," on Semoran and Hoffner in Orlando. As I was going down Semoran, in my 300ZX, I noticed one too many undercover police on the road. I wasn't nervous. Before I could make a left on Lake Underhill Road, I was in custody. My car was parked in front of Popeye's and searched. While I was sitting in the back of the Orlando police car, an officer opened the door and put all my money in his pocket. He left a few dollars in the sandwich bag, to make it "look good." He told me to continue being silent and good luck. I was booked in the Orange County Jail on possession of over twenty grams of cannabis. They attempted to scare me with trafficking but I knew four pounds in the city area was a petty third-degree felony. I bonded out quickly! I didn't even go to the police vehicle in pound to pick up the 300ZX. I allowed the car to be taken. I wasn't worried about anything but the warrant for my arrest on violation of probation. The violation did not come out, I was lucky to be able to bond out very quickly! I didn't know anything about the law, so I talked to a lawyer concerning any prison time for both the violation of probation and the possession charge. He told me I could ask for drug program. I did not show up to the court date because I knew I would be arrested for the violation of probation. I enjoyed as much time as I could.

One night while staying in a motel on US Highway 92 in Kissimmee, I decided to relax and take some pills called Oxycotins. Not knowing what I was doing, as to amount, I consumed too much. To make matters worse, I fell asleep. I had a clear dream with the devil. There was fire all over in a pit of dirt, the devil was orange and red in color with a pitchfork, and a tail with a triangle form at the end. In my dream, I knew I overdosed on the pills, and the devil was telling me my life was over. Automatically, I started to call out "in the name of Jesus Christ." After a few times, I woke up to find the bed soaking wet from all the tears of fear I cried. I got on my knees on the side of the bed and prayed. I asked God that I do not die when I fall asleep again. Now I realized the incident was a sign to let the high times go. I wish I would've realized back then, but like I wrote previously in this book, I was so ignorant and stubborn. I was supposed to graduate high school and become a firefighter. It's still my dream; it's still in my heart. The only thing is, now I am a convicted felon, and I'm unable to fulfill my dream. After all the selling drugs, alcohol, nightclubs, traveling, and spending money, I turned myself over to the Orange County Jail. I was housed in the main building first floor. Quickly I was in front of Judge Mihok. As the lawyers said, I was sentenced to a drug rehabilitation program off Mercy Drive in Orlando called Bridges of America. The place is really good. Disney donates most of the food. Every meal is super! If I could go complete the program right now, I would do it in a heartbeat. With no problem.

In 1998, however, I was not feeling it. On a Friday morning, I got a ride to Kissimmee and was staying with a friend named Leslie. She went to high school with me, and we were cool always. I had to lay low because a warrant was placed for my arrest. Not even two weeks went by before a business associate of mine named Freddy picked me up, gave me a pager, some grams of heroin to sell, and money for a couple of weeks in a motel. I was on my feet in less than two weeks. It was in the beginning of 1999 that I met my connection for weight of heroin. I'm not going to write his name within this book because I believe he is still fighting the thirty years or more he was sentenced to in the feds. But I will write that I made enough money to rent a four-bedroom, two-car garage home in Kissimmee. I bought motorcycles, more jewelry, rental cars, clothing, and ate wherever I wanted. My connection was a platinum customer at the Embassy Suites International Drive, Orlando. He would use the room a day or two, leave it to me for a week thereafter. I started to pop ecstasy pills every night again. This time I mixed it with heroin and snorted it. Not a good combination, not a good drug habit. I kept telling myself that I really wasn't consuming much, and I was okay with the little a day. What I did not realize is that the body becomes adapted to the drug more and more, to the point where if I didn't do some by night, I was sick. And because I had so much of it, I continued to get high as I please. When people start to deal drugs and you reach a certain level, not too big, not too small, you start a hobby.

I was fighting roosters here in Central Florida, so I bought a nice 1981 Mazda RX. All white, black interior. I had a rotary engine expert named Richie Roter do some upgrading. Every chance I had, I put money into the car. I parked in front of an apartment on Royal Palm Drive where a Puerto Rican man was selling bundles for me. The operation was running smoothly, I even met a nice female stationed in the Pensacola Florida Navy. If I had listen to Celia, I would not be in prison right now. Anyhow, I also met another female name Tamara back in 1998 while waiting for the Bridge program. I can't clearly write why I decided to mess with Tamara. She had two kids, a normal job, and nothing going for herself. It wasn't the sex, I think it was more that she didn't mind hiding drugs for me and didn't care whether I sold, consumed, or whatever. When you're trying to lay low, sell drugs and move from point A to point B, you will need all possible locations not to be seen. It turned out that Tamara was a jealous female. I stopped answering her calls or pages on my beeper.

In 1999, I was nineteen years old. A teenager dropped out of high school. I wasn't a victim to anything but my own ignorance. People will blame the neighbors where they grow up. The schools they attended, being motherless or fatherless. Some people were sexually molested as they were growing up and therefore put the blame of failure on the predator. Everyone can come up with one million excuses as to why he or she was not a productive member of society. I hear the excuses all the time here in prison. I'm tired of all the excuses. Excuses get us nowhere!

The year of 1999 was full of illegal activities. I was lucky that another person did not set me up to get robbed or killed. I was lucky to stay away, enough not to get caught up in federal or state indictments of drugs. Believe me, I know plenty of individuals were serving time, heavy time, for conspiracies and trafficking. On a positive note, I did go and attempt to join the Army, Navy, National Guard, or the Marines. No one accepted me. Can you imagine if one of those Armed Forces would have waved my teenage record and educated me fully? Here we are today, where they now allow transgender people serve the country, but they wouldn't pick up a teenager in need of guidance. I'm not writing any excuses, I'm just calling it how I see it. When you're dealing drugs, no matter what level, the devil makes you think that money can resolve all problems. You will think that establishing a business with cocaine money will be okay. You will think that you're doing a great job of providing for your girl and family. The best one of all is you will think that the police will not catch up to you, and you will retire with no problems. I believe that one in every 100 drug dealers will fall back with no law issues. All the rest will eventually end up dead in prison addicted to drugs with loved ones crying on the side praying to God that you will heal. There's absolutely nothing positive about the narcotics game.

On August 14, 1999, I turned twenty years old. My Aunt Marina bought a little cake and sang happy birthday along with my cousins, Jomari, John, and Alexi. I got myself a green and white 1998 Kawasaki Ninja 750. It was the idea bike for me after deciding the 600s were too small and the 1100s were too big. Riding down Royal Palm Drive to my aunt's house, I ran into a sheriff who was stopping people with his own motorcycle. He watched me turn into Flower Lane and park my Ninja. I watched him talking to the lady he pulled over. I sensed trouble. I had no license and the neighborhood was not a clean one. Buena Ventura Lakes, Kissimmee has always been a hot spot for everything, from drugs to prostitution. The sheriffs love to pullover Hispanics. The 1980s and 1990s were a transitional point for Orange and Osceola County, Florida. Hispanics were moving into any community they could find. You know how Miami is known for Cubans? From the west coast of Tampa to the east coast of Daytona Beach, it is now known for Puerto Ricans. A lot of officials were not happy with it! Still aren't happy!

I got on my Ninja and kept my eye on the sheriff through the helmet. The heavyset dressed-in-dark-green sheriff was finishing with another vehicle he pulled over. In order to get back on Royal Palm, I had to turn right or left in front of the sheriff. I pushed my bike back with my legs and decided to go another way around the grass into another side road. As I started to accelerate as quietly as possible, I looked back and saw the sheriff creeping up behind me. I had no choice but to punch it! I'm bending corners in a residential neighborhood. I had a two-block advantage and flying as much as I could. When I reach Osceola Parkway, I looked back again and could not see the sheriff. I did, however, hear the siren loud and clear. I flew past a school and kept it moving. Osceola Parkway was my chance to really get away before the sheriff's helicopter decided to fly over me. I reached Boggy Creek Road, turn right and punch it again. My heart was beating faster than the Ninja was moving. I turned another right on Royal Palm Drive and another right into some apartments. A female name Becky, my friend's wife, was sweeping her porch when I drove the Ninja right through the front door and told her to shut everything down. Sheriffs were everywhere looking. For the time being, I was safe. I walked through the back of the apartments to another friend of mine's house, jumped in his Chevy Impala and was gone. I didn't realize that day could have been my last!

In November 1999, I ran into Tamara again. She was dropping by houses of people she knew I would be at. A few months had gone by since I last spoke with her so it wasn't as bad as before and that's where I went wrong. She was renting a motel room by the week and offered the room for me to use as a stash house. I went by on a Friday morning and found her three-year-old son and two-year-old daughter alone under the blankets. I didn't think anything of it. Tamara always left her children alone if she had to do so. At this specific time, I did not know that in 1997, she had been charged with a felony for leaving her son alone in a house. I did not know she had a record with the Department of Children and Families. I had a Toyota Corolla rental and was serving people throughout the day. It was the afternoon when I was walking up the concrete stairs and found the three-year-old boy hurt and cut on his four head clearly from the concrete. Like a scrape swollen around the area. I knew he opened the motel door and most likely went out looking for any adult. I picked him up and took him to the shower where I turned on the cold water attempting to wake him up fully. I noticed he was getting dizzier and his breathing louder. I went to get a towel. By the time I came back to the shower, he was unconscious. I picked him up again, calling his name, smacking him, attempting to bring him back. I was unsuccessful. I thought about calling 911 right then, but I had a warrant for my arrest. So I called Tamara at work and explained she needed to come by and take her son to the hospital, that he was hurt. I further explained I attempted to revive him in the shower, but he is still unconscious. She was only a few minutes away and therefore arrived quickly. I handed him over to her as she got in her car en route to the hospital. Now I had another decision to make. Either stay in the motel with all the heroin bagged up and guns waiting or leave and wait on her phone call to my cell phone. I left because I knew the warrant for my arrest would land me in jail. I went on with serving clients while waiting for her phone call. I talked to my aunt and explained what happened. I continued to wait for the call. I even snorted ecstasy with heroin at night waiting for the phone call.

Chapter 5

The Beginning of No End

I was concerned for the little boy so I didn't get much sleep that night. I wondered if Tamara would at least call me to give me an update. At approximately 5:00 a.m. the sheriffs surrounded my aunt's house. The police questioned Tamara, and she said Giovanni was the last one in the motel with information. She was not going to admit her children were left alone. She did all she could to keep quiet about her 1997 involvement with the law and Department of Children and Families. The sheriffs knocked on the door, and my little cousin Alexi, around ten years old at the time, answered the door. My cousin Jomari followed. I was in the living room hearing this sheriffs asking for me. Jomari allowed them to come in and look around. I was arrested with no resisting. On the way out the door, in front of my aunt's townhome apartment, one of the sheriffs tripped me while grabbing my head and slamming it toward the ground. The left side of my forehead split open. The sheriff started to kick me around my ribs and stomach area. Again he slammed my head against the ground repeatedly. I could not see from all the blood in my face and the side of my shoulder.

I was taken to the Osceola County Jail sheriff's office where two detectives were waiting to interrogate me. I was told that regardless of the outcome of the interrogation, I was going to jail on a warrant from Orlando. I was obviously still bleeding, hurt, dizzy, and super tired from not sleeping. I believe I took in some of the pain more easily because of how high I was all night. But as time went by, the more I felt like falling out. The detectives did not ask me if I needed medical attention or was I okay. They simply wanted to question me about the motel and Tamara. I agreed to cooperate. But I grew up with the understanding of not to talk to the police, so I kept it short and to the point. "I didn't know what they were talking about, I was not there." Maybe I should've told the detective the truth, but it wouldn't have mattered. The Florida law enforcement and judicial system is forty years back, stuck on racism and malicious behavior. People will never know how deeply corrupt the government is in Florida unless you're an official or have been caught up in the system. The interrogation lasted over an hour and thirty minutes. I kept thinking about all the weight I left hidden in my aunt's house. My cousin John knew if I didn't come back, to call my connection and turn over everything! At times I felt as if I was going to pass out from dehydration. During the midpoint of the interrogation, I requested an attorney. I said, "You said I can talk to a lawyer, can I talk to a lawyer?"

The detective responded, "Do you wish to continue to talk to us about what happened?"

I yelled back, "I just told you, man, I just told you, bro." The detectives ignored the request and continued questioning. For those who don't know the law, allow me to break it down for you: we all have a Fifth Amendment constitutional right to have an attorney present during any interrogation with law enforcement. If we agreed to answer questions, and during the questions you request a lawyer, the detectives must stop the questioning and provide the lawyer immediately.

I was escorted down the hall to the front door of the Osceola County Jail booking. As I came in handcuffed, the lieutenant stopped me from coming in. He got on his radio and requested a nurse to come with the camera. The detective asked what he was doing and the lieutenant replied, "You're responsible for these injuries on Mr. Vega, not my jail." The nurse took numerous photos and wrote down my health condition. She could not believe the detectives didn't request medical assistance. I was then taken into a isolation cell for further observation. As the hours went by, my body was asking for ecstasy or anything that got me high. I was charged with first-degree felony murder without a bond. The Orlando warrant would have to wait.

A few days went by, and I was housed in Charlie-Delta. By then, I was fully withdrawing. I was snapping on everyone that attempted to talk to me because I could not withstand the pain and chills. Back then in November 1999, Osceola County Jail did not provide any type of medication in order to help withdraw. A few ibuprofen was absolutely nothing. I might have slept one hour per day. It was awful! My mom found out through the news or someone told her. I'm guessing she called my grandparents in Puerto Rico and told them also. Meanwhile, it took me two weeks of withdrawing to recover somewhat. My body was weak. I weighed about 160 pounds. I had to withdraw from the Newport cigarettes I smoked too.

As I started to regain my mind and body back, correctional officers I went to high school with started to talk to me. No one could believe I was charged with murder, yet alone of a three-year-old kid. I myself was in the state of shock, confused, and upset. The autopsy was handled by a chief medical examiner of Orange and Osceola County, Dr. Shashi Gore. His conclusion was: "Giovanni caused the death by either hitting or pushing [blunt force trauma]." The three-year-old had bruises in his arm and stomach area so Dr. Gore called it child abuse. To anyone that doesn't know about what truly happened, the TV, and the newspaper would make you believe I was a murderer. This is why you can't believe what the news channel reports on TV when a case is fresh. The police will say anything to make themselves look good and make the defendant look bad. I will show you evidence of such later on in this book.

My attorney was a Puerto Rican from Brooklyn, New York, named Davila. He was under a spell or something, thinking he was the best trial lawyer in Osceola County. Besides following procedures that must be done when a person is charged with murder, Davila didn't do a damn thing. I still believe he sold me out for another case he was handling also. Some medical examiners from Tampa wanted to review the autopsy and testify on my behalf, and Davila convinced me that defense didn't need those doctors. There were witnesses that would have provided valuable information, and Davila did not make a move to find them. I had just turned twenty years old, was a high school dropout, I did not know a damn thing about the law. Anything this Brooklyn's finest lawyer told me, I believed. While I waited the nineteen months to go to trial, the first plea offer was second-degree murder, thirty years. I told him I was not guilty of murder but would take a maximum plea to involuntary manslaughter. No deal was made, I believe my lawyer didn't even forward the message.

I lost my mind, went a little crazy in the county after the thirty-year offer and caught a criminal mischief charge. I kicked the cell door all day until it broke from the cement, and I went out to the dayroom. My Aunt Martina was a second head of classification at the county jail so I didn't pay one cent of the $1100 I was charged with for damages. I knew most of the people coming in and out of the county jail for what some of us call, petty charges. Things like possession, sales and deliveries, battery, driving under the influence, and so forth. The men who stayed for a while were charged with serious crimes like murder, arm robbery, sexual battery, and home invasion.

Like any other county jail, Osceola Department of Corrections was full of fights and everything in between. Like all state prisons and county jails, there were many corrupt officers. The more time went by, the more it got worse. Out of everyone who visited me, my mother, grandfather, and my sister Raquel's uncle named Goyo would help me out with money for food and personal hygiene products. My mom was sad and feeling down about my situation. Most of my relatives probably thought I was high and lost control. No one took the time to ask me what really happened, so how can anyone judge me? Based on police reports?

My lawyer gave me one of the few visits and explained we were ready to go to trial and that I had a good chance of winning the case. He explained the medical examiner, Dr. Shashi Gore, admitted in depositions the concrete stairs could have been the cause of death. What my attorney did not tell me was that Dr. Gore was paid by the county. All his bread and butter was handling cases for the state attorney (prosecutors). There won't ever be a chief medical examiner to take the witness stand and go against the state. What they do is determine if the defendant is poor and can't afford proper representation with proper experts, then decide to move forward or not. If the defense is strong with experts, the medical examiner for the state pulls back and the state offers a plea you won't refuse. If the defense is bogus, the state medical examiner has no one to go against at trial and feels comfortable to hang the defendant. This gets even crazier to which I will write about later in this book.

The last plea offer by this state was second-degree murder, eighteen to twenty-two years. Again I told the lawyer, involuntary manslaughter and give me the maximum sentence for it. I figured, since I was there and if I would've called 911, maybe he would be alive. So sentence me for what I'm guilty of, not what you assumed happened. The lawyer said the prosecution did not accept. I find it hard to believe because during that time that I was waiting for trial, I got upset with a lawyer and asked him to step down from the case. I told them he wasn't doing shit, and I did not feel right with his representation. He responded by saying the judge would not allow for him to step down because we were too deep into the case. That he has been doing a thorough job with my case, and I should feel blessed that he was representing me.

The client relationship I had with the lawyer was garbage at the start and got worse as time went by. If I knew the law back then like I know it now, I would not be in prison. A big 95% of the men and women who get locked up get taken advantage of. Lawyers are lazy in Florida and will trade your case for another they want a good deal on. It's called "juggling cases." They get so many cases that the only way to keep up is to trade with prosecutors. Unless your lawyer has some type of history with the prosecutor and invites him or her to lunch or as they call it "a round of golf." The negotiations take place and if successful, your attorney pays cash for your freedom. The system is a "one hand washes the other" order. No one in the world can tell me otherwise because I have been in prison with former attorneys who have told me how bad the corruption is. I am not writing that every attorney whether state or private is in the game of trading cases. I am only letting you know what happens with the good percentage of them on a regular basis.

Take this for example: an attorney in Orlando making a name for himself takes the high-profile case of "the squirt gun bandit." This sexual predator was squirting sperm on people while hiding in the aisles of Walmart. The man was on camera doing this sick act. The case is an easy one for the prosecution, right? The camera tells it all! I can't mention the lawyer's name but he is now a high-profile lawyer in Orlando. The lawyer went on TV, accepted the case as pro bono, which means for free, did the deal with the prosecution and the charges were dropped. To sum it up, the lawyer wanted advertisement, he knew the predator was guilty but didn't really care. The lawyer paid out of his own money to become a high-profile lawyer. Can you imagine how many families with loved ones locked up call him for representation? I know a lot of more crooked things this lawyer has done, but I'm not going to write about it. I think you get the picture.

Here's a good one for you. The only difference in this case is that the man was actually innocent. Right before I went to trial, the news channels were reporting on a motel rapist. Authorities described the tall black man, middle-aged, waiting for women to go into their rented room and rape them. The predator raped so many women I can't remember the amount. I do remember women all over Orlando in Kissimmee terrified and desperate for the man to be arrested. Even us inmates in the county jail were worried about our loved ones around the area. The door to Charlie-Alpha opens and a tall strong black male enters with his mattress and covers. The man was at least six feet six inches tall. He weighed at least 275 pounds. Everyone quickly identified him as a motel rapist. The question now was, how were they going to beat him up and send him to protection. This was going to take a few days to plan and execute. On the second day, a female high-profile lawyer in Orlando known for representing inmates awaiting death penalty cases went on TV and said she would represent the accused motel rapist. We were like, wow, this dude got super lucky. The female lawyer was good. I thought to myself, she better hurry up and get him out or something before these inmates hurt him badly. On about the seventh or so day, the correctional officer yells out for the motel rapist to pack his stuff, he is leaving. As quiet as the man came in, as quietly he walked out that pod door. We thought he might've been moved to Orlando or something. Sure enough at 5:00 p.m., there he was next to his pretty lawyer on TV. Turns out, the DNA on the victims matched another tall black man and not the one they arrested.

Could you imagine if the inmates would have beaten him into a coma? This is why people must realize that a lot of the news reports on TV are from police officers and have not been fully investigated. The news will convince you of someone's guilt. It is up to you to be open-minded and ask yourself what truly happened or why. Don't misunderstand, as I'm not trying to say that everyone on TV is innocent. There are many who are guilty and must face the penalty. However, don't be like the stereotypes who think if you're in handcuffs, you're guilty. I can continue to write about how many people I've seen with my own eyes walk out of the county jail or prison being innocent. So many that I have even learned to become nonjudgmental.

Chapter 6

May 2001 Trial

By May 2001, Osceola County built a new courthouse right behind the old courthouse. The big trials were to be conducted on the top floor, and I was the first one. That was a minus for me because they wanted to "break the ice" with a win. The judge was black, the prosecutors were white, and the defense attorney and I Puerto Rican. That was another minus for me. Word of advice for those who are going through any civil or criminal trials: if you are white, you can have a white attorney in Florida with no problems. If you're black, go with a white attorney. If you're Hispanic, go with the white attorney. Do not go to trial as a minority with an attorney of your race, not in Florida. You might get good results if you're white with a black attorney. This is something about how the judicial system works in Florida.

When I stepped in the courtroom dressed in long sleeved shirt and tie, I was next to the white bailiff sheriff who was making comments like, "These Hispanics come to the United States to cause trouble." The other white lady bailiff said, "I don't let my daughter date or be around them Hispanics." On the front benches sitting down crying was my mom. That made my blood boil like I have never in my life been so upset. I told my attorney to escort my mom out the courtroom. I could not concentrate with my mom suffering right behind me. The trial began addressing two motions from the defense. The judge didn't even have a copy of the motion and settled for one of ours. That was another minus because the judge knew he would deny anything we raised. The first was a motion called "change of venue." In order to prevail, the defense has to show that the jury has been affected by the news media enough to cause prejudice. That the jury heard of any prior convictions or jail time of the defendant. Basically, that the defendant will not receive a fair trial in Osceola County.

My attorney provided newspaper articles, which stated my prior convictions and clearly talked about me in the county jail serving time. The judge reserved ruling instead requesting the state and the defense question the jury and determine how much information each juror heard or read. Do you want to know how the judge abused his discretion? The prosecutor got up and said, "Your honor, the news reporters contacted me Friday requesting information. I gave it to them and then asked them not to publish it until after the trial because it would taint the entire jury panel." I looked at the prosecutor and said, "It's too late for that, the jury is no good."

The second motion was a Miranda rights violation. My lawyer argued I requested an attorney during interrogation and therefore if the state uses that tape for the jury to hear, it would be in violation of my Fifth Amendment constitutional right and the "*Food from a Poisonous Tree Act.*" Meaning, anything after the interrogation will be regarded as a *due process* violation of a fair trial. The tape was played out loud. Can you believe the sheriff's office messed up the part where I speak about a lawyer? Whatever happened to honest and good work ethics officers? I thought law enforcement was supposed to be a role model in society? My lawyer argued the tape was damaged and should be suppressed. The state argued the damage was nothing! The judge denied the defense motion and proceeded. Saying that he could not hear me clearly requesting a lawyer.

The prosecution was allowed to play the tape forcing me to testify on my behalf. Remember I continued to answer questions during interrogation that I was not there, I knew nothing. All the potential jurors were let in the courtroom benches. There were eighty jurors, and I only saw a couple of blacks. The jurors were by numbers, and I had a copy of their names and where they worked. Numbers one through ten were all white country-style folks. I was like, damn! We began to question the potential jurors. The state found a juror who hated inmates. The man explained his family are sheriffs and that if anyone gets put in handcuffs, they're guilty. The prosecutor would ask that juror's question each time she needed for the other jurors to hear negative comments on inmates. For those who don't know, that is called prosecutor misconduct, bolstering.

While we were questioning them, a female juror got up and told the bailiff she felt uncomfortable around a specific male juror, and she needed to speak with the judge. The bailiff told the female juror to sit down and wait until after questioning. *Vior Dire* is the meaning for the questioning of jurors prior to the trial. The rules were simple at the end of *Vior Dire*. The defendant gets twelve strikes as well as the prosecution. The strikes are used to dismiss jurors you may not want for any reason. Both the prosecution and the defendant can call for (a cause) strike which the judge determines if the juror is simply no good, like the man the prosecutor questioned in order to taint the jury panel (bolstering).

Most of my strikes were used in the front bench alone. These people looked like they wanted to eat me alive. During the picking of the jurors, the prosecutor used "strike" on the black female juror. All because the juror said that "He better be found guilty beyond all reasonable doubt" or she would find me not guilty. The prosecutor began to use her strikes on young male Hispanics. My lawyer objected and argued "racially discriminative" strikes. The judge asked the prosecutor to give a legit reason as to why the strikes on young Hispanic men? She explained the first juror spoke little English and may not understand. My lawyer argued the Hispanic juror answered all questions properly and had no problems with English. The second Hispanic juror, the prosecutor argued, that he seemed as if he doesn't like to babysit kids and would not be a good juror. My lawyer argued both reasons for the strikes were not genuine and in violation of the jurors rights to be free of racial discrimination. The judge denied our objections.

Finally, we had to question the jurors about the media. There were too many jurors that raised their hands admitting to reading about me in the newspaper a day before or on television. Most jurors also admitted they could not be fair and didn't want to be in the trial jury. This was more than enough to move the trial to another county, but the judge denied the change of venue motion and proceeded. Two jurors were brought up to the judge because they had something to say. The first female juror said she was sitting next to a man who was pointing his fingers at me as if he had a gun, stating he would kill me and other foul comments. She said she felt uncomfortable, and the man was disrespectful. The judge asked if she would remain fair and she said yes.

The second female juror explained the same thing. That she heard a lot of foul language, that she felt uncomfortable and scared. She answered she would remain fair if picked as a juror. This incident was another minus for me because the reject judge, by law, had to dismiss the entire jury pool. How on God's green earth will you ever know what the other jurors were influenced to believe? Both the female jurors that came forward to report the horrible juror misconduct, ended up in the jury panel for the trial. Both of them with their brains all tainted from the male juror cursing and pointing his fingers like a gun at me. This goes to show you that judges and prosecutors do not care if they break the law. The prosecutors lie, bolster jurors, hold favorable evidence, and influence a judge into winning a case by all means necessary.

On the first day of trial, I knew I was shit out of luck. I knew my lawyer was trash, and the judge had no type of consideration for the defense. Opening statements began for the prosecution. That's when the prosecutor assumes what happened and why you have been arrested. Basically, their story! The defense does the same thing. The prosecution then calls their first witness. It was one out of the two detectives. This officer of law testified he did not hear me ask for a lawyer, second, he had the balls to testify under oath, he didn't remember me being injured and covered in blood. Third, he testified that he raised his voice at times of the interrogation, but he did not yell. After answering the same from my lawyer. The second witness detective was called. This law enforcement officer testified under oath he noticed injuries on the defendant during interrogation, but felt I needed no medical attention. *Wow*, his partner just had testified I had no injuries, my attorney got the photos that were taken when I came in through booking and allowed for the jury to see how full of shit these so-called law abiding officers can be. One of the jurors couldn't hold it and started to cry when she saw me in the photos all beaten up bleeding. The next witness was an inmate who claimed he was with me in a holding cell for a few minutes, and I supposedly told him I had killed someone. This dirtbag was a nine-time convicted felon who turned out to be one of those snitches working for the state when in times of trouble. The judge allowed him to testify anyway. The inmate was beaten up in the county jail 100 times and still would make it to help the prosecutors. Whenever he went to his court hearings, the first thing the lawyer tells the judge is, "My client cooperated with the state, your honor, give him a break."

The next witness was a former employee with the motel cleaning service. She testified seeing me that Friday, and I asked her for a towel. My lawyer asked her if she saw me in any violent acts or illegal activities. She answered "No." So my lawyer told the judge that the witness had no valuable information. The next witness was a friend of mine that I grew up with. He did not have any information other than that he picked me up that Friday night and was with me for a little while. The next witness was a female who knew Tamara for a while. The female witness was supposed to help the prosecution but instead spoke the truth. She testified Tamara was looking around for me, and she sensed trouble. She further explained there was no way I would hurt any child based on my character or behavior with all the children in her family and neighbors.

The prosecutor hurried up and asked for the witness to step down. The next witness was the motel manager. He explained there were too many Hispanics renting rooms and could not positively identify me doing anything violent or illegal. The next witness was Tamara. She was crying and very emotional. You could tell she was coached by the prosecutor because the answers were not personal, not her at all. The only thing real was her crying. Tamara was not there to witness anything. So all she could say was that she wanted justice. My attorney questioned her about a deal she did with the state in regards to testifying and getting probation for the child neglect charge she was hit with. She did not admit to anything.

The trial moved on. I'm not sure if it was right then or after the next witness, but my lawyer verbally presented a motion for acquittal. My lawyer argued no one seen anything and the prosecution case has been soft from day one. Denied! The next witness was the prosecutor's main witness. Dr. Gore took the stand. He testified, he earned a degree from John Hopkins University and belonged to all types of medical associations. Dr. Gore testified he has over thirty years of experience with hundreds of autopsies under his belt. He went on to testify that the injuries to the child were of abuse and in the hands of me because I was in the motel. My attorney asked him about his prior deposition admitting concrete stairs may have been the cause of death, but he said it was not in his opinion. Dr. Gore played my lawyer earlier and worked it out for the state. That's how all chief medical examiners do it in Florida. That's nothing new! My lawyer failed to investigate all of Dr. Gore's qualifications.

Do you want to know how important it was to investigate this medical examiner? Dr. Gore was not a board-certified pathologist. The standards for the chief medical examiner job were lowered twice in order to hire this Hindu in 1996. You would be amazed on everything I discovered on this nasty sun of a gun, years later. I will write about it later in this book and provide evidence of the corruption the state attorney had with Dr. Gore. When the judge asked my lawyer if the defense had any witnesses, the answer was no. The only one was Giovanni Vega taking the stand to testify what happened. I had no choice but to testify because the prosecutor played the tape which painted a picture of someone not cooperating with the police and denying any involvement. I already wrote what happened earlier in this book so there's no need to write it again. After arguing with the prosecutor I stepped down and walked toward the chair. It was now time to make the jury instructions.

My attorney explained to the judge that the indictment was confusing. The indictment had the elements of a third degree felony murder charge and therefore a third degree felony murder charge should be explained to the jurors. The prosecutor admits the indictment has elements that are not supposed to be there, and she could not fix it while staying up all night. She went on to convince the judge that the jury instructions would be good, and we should proceed anyway. Both my lawyer and prosecutor did their closing statements. When the prosecutor was talking to the juror, she said, "We are here to seek justice for the victim." This was another prosecutor misconduct. The Florida Supreme Court well established that prosecutors may not put into the jurors mind the words of "seeking justice for victim" because you're now forcing the men and women jurors to find you guilty even if innocent. In other words, someone dies, someone pays mentality.

The jurors were given the jury instructions with all the charges they couldn't find me guilty of. The judge read some more instructions, and they went on their way to the juror room. After a couple of hours, a note came to the judge that read, "Can we have the trial transcripts?" The judge ordered everyone back in the courtroom. This no-good lazy judge said the law requires for him to have the witness testimony of the juror's choice transcribed, but that it would be too time consuming. How does someone in their right mind expect the jury panel to deliberate and discuss my guilt or innocence without transcripts of a specific witness? The jurors did not know the law. They have to be able to go back and read testimony in order to better analyze and make a solid decision. This is what happens when you are poor and your lawyer is Osceola County's best and when a judge has no clue as to what he is doing. The jury went back to the room upset because they were unable to obtain the witness transcripts.

A little while later, the verdict came in, and I was found guilty as charged. It was no surprise to me as my lawyer failed to do many things throughout the trial, the judge was incompetent, and the prosecutor was more crooked than the Italian mafia. I was sentenced, as expected, to the maximum penalty of life without the possibility of parole with a side salad of thirty years. This was more pain on my mom and relatives. I was not able to eat or think correctly for at least a month. I had to force a little food and water in order to be alive. For precaution, the county jail houses an inmate on a suicide watch after receiving any sentence of twenty-five years or better. There I was with the mattress on the floor, no sheets, and a green "turtle suit" to cover myself.

My Aunt Martina came by to see me, but that didn't help because she was crying too. A few days went by and I was given the jumpsuit and told to prepare to move to isolation. I requested to go back to the pod I was in, but it wasn't going to take place. They didn't want someone with a life sentence next to unsentenced inmates. So I made a bad choice to make the correction officers, "run it." I attempted to punch every officer that came through the cell door. I was weak from not eating. To make matters worse, they put the two tallest and biggest men first. I had no chance! I was sprayed with tear gas and given a soft ass whooping. I knew too many of the officers and my aunt had the main nurse on alert watching me. Now I was forced into isolation butt naked again. The isolation cell has three air conditioning vents blowing freezing cold air. I was frozen, begging for sheets and or clothing.

The next day, I was transported to the Orange County Jail. While I was being booked in, a male officer confused the pending charge as a misdemeanor possession of cannabis and put a green armband on my wrist. The green armband is called the "Rolex" because an inmate can walk in and out of the county jail to do work details. I kept quiet and waited for my chance. I was going to walk out with any other crew of inmates with green armbands. The officer came back and told me, "I have to change your arm band to red, and you will be going to the third floor main." I was in 3–F for two weeks and then housed in the sixth floor main, 6–C. I met some good men awaiting trial. Everyone with different cases and different circumstances. I even met the Haitian man who robbed the American pawn on John Young Parkway and Americana Boulevard. The sheriffs pulled him over, he shot and killed the first sheriff and shot the second sheriff, who survive but was crippled. The correction officers would search the Haitian's assigned cell all the time. He was retaliated against and I believe beaten numerous times.

I was in front of Judge Mihok shortly after my birthday, August 2001. The prosecutor wanted me to do a year in the county jail and then when finished, I'll be transported to prison. The judge refused to give me county jail time, instead, sentencing me to one year and one day in prison. This sentence would help me be on my way and meet the deadline of appeals. I was done with Orange and Osceola County. Now all I was hearing were more stories of men who did time in prison across the state of Florida. On a Tuesday morning about 3:00 a.m., I was brought down to booking along with two dozen other men. Out of twenty-four of us, more than half were Latinos and remember this was September 2001. I knew a few of these Latinos from dealings on the streets. We were thinking about the ride and when we arrive in prison, it would not be so bad after all. We started to think the stories of prison were not true and prison was going to be like county jail. I'm guessing all of those positive thoughts helped all of us deal with the pressure of going to prison because I'm the first one to tell you we were all wrong!

"PROSECUTOR MISCONDUCT"

SELECTION, JUDGE.

THE COURT: I WILL RESERVE RULING ON YOUR MOTION AT THIS TIME. WE WILL GO AHEAD WITH THE JURY SELECTION. PROCEED AT THAT POINT.

MS. OGDEN: JUDGE, IF THE RECORD CAN JUST REFLECT THAT I HAD SPOKEN TO THIS REPORTER WHO WROTE THAT ARTICLE –

THE COURT: HOLD ON A SECOND.

MS. OGDEN: THAT I HAD SPOKEN TO THAT REPORTER ON FRIDAY, WHO INDICATED TO ME THAT SHE WAS PUBLISHING THAT ARTICLE. SHE HAD ALREADY DONE A PUBLIC RECORDS REQUEST WITH MY OFFICE, AND I HAD SPECIFICALLY ASKED HER NOT TO WRITE THAT ARTICLE AND TAINT MY JURY. AND I WAS TOLD –

THE COURT: THIS ISN'T THE FIRST TIME THAT THIS REPORTER HAS WRITTEN A STORY THAT – RIGHT BEFORE THE DAY OF TRIAL THAT –

MS. OGDEN: THAT SEEMS TO BE A COMMON PROBLEM IN OSCEOLA. BUT I JUST WANT THE RECORD TO REFLECT THAT I DID SPECIFICALLY ASK HER NOT TO.

THE COURT: I UNDERSTAND.

MR. DAVILA: JUDGE, IS THERE ANY REASON FOR MY CLIENT TO BE CUFFED AT THAT TIME? HE CAN HELP ME TAKE NOTES.

THE COURT: ONCE WE START THE PROCEEDING, BY MOTION, I WILL UNCUFF HIM. AT THIS POINT, I DIDN'T KNOW HE WAS

THE COURT: MS. OGDEN, I THINK WE WILL TAKE A RECESS AT THIS POINT. WE ARE GOING TO TAKE ABOUT A FIFTEEN-MINUTE RECESS. BEFORE WE GO OUT, THOUGH, I DIDN'T TELL YOU THIS BEFORE THE FIRST RECESS BECAUSE IT WAS SO SHORT. YOU KNOW A LITTLE BIT ABOUT THE CASE NOW. YOU DON'T KNOW A LOT ABOUT THE FACTS. I DON'T REALLY ALLOW THE LAWYERS TO GET INTO THE FACTS OF THE CASE, BUT YOU KNOW WHAT TYPE OF CASE IT IS NOW, AND YOU HAVE HEARD ME ASKING PEOPLE ABOUT SOME MEDIA THINGS THAT HAVE COME UP IN THE CASE, AND OBVIOUSLY THERE'S SOME ARTICLE IN THE PAPER ABOUT THIS, AND SOME OF YOU ALL HAVE READ THE ARTICLE.

I WOULD ASK YOU NOT TO DISCUSS ANYTHING THAT YOU KNOW ABOUT THIS CASE, WHAT WE HAVE TALKED ABOUT HERE IN THIS COURTROOM AMONG YOURSELVES. THE REASON FOR THAT IS WE DON'T WANT YOU TO FORM ANY OPINIONS OR VIEWPOINTS OUTSIDE OF OUR PRESENCE THAT WE DON'T KNOW ABOUT. AND OBVIOUSLY DON'T PICK UP THE PAPER TO READ THE PAPER.

AND WE WILL COME BACK IN IN FIFTEEN MINUTES, AND WE WILL LET MS. OGDEN FINISH UP HER QUESTIONS, AND THEN WE WILL HEAR FROM THE DEFENSE AT THAT TIME.

WE ARE IN RECESS.

(THE VENIRE EXITS THE COURTROOM.)

(THE FOLLOWING PROCEEDINGS WERE HELD AT THE BENCH:)

MR. DAVILA: JUDGE, APPARENTLY THERE'S TWO JURORS

DO YOU SEE GIOVANNI HERE, RIGHT? ANYTHING THAT THIS GENTLEMAN INDICATED OR SAID WOULD PREVENT FROM YOU GIVING HIM A FAIR TRIAL, AND THE STATE?

PROSPECTIVE JUROR: (273) SAY THAT AGAIN?

MR. DAVILA: WOULD PREVENT YOU --

PROSPECTIVE JUROR: (273) NOT ME. I WOULD BE IMPARTIAL. IF I SAT ON THE JURY, I WOULD LISTEN TO EVERYTHING. HE WAS MAKING ME UNCOMFORTABLE BECAUSE I KNOW HE WOULD NOT, AND I DIDN'T THINK THAT WAS FAIR.

MR. DAVILA: OKAY. THANK YOU, MA'AM.

THE COURT: THANK YOU, MA'AM, FOR LETTING US KNOW THAT. WE APPRECIATE THAT.

(PROSPECTIVE JUROR 273 EXITS THE COURTROOM.)

THE COURT: DO YOU ALL WANT TO STRIKE HIM FOR CAUSE? THAT'S MR. MICHAEL SMOLIK?

MS. OGDEN: THAT'S FINE.

MR. DAVILA: THAT'S ABSOLUTELY FINE, JUDGE.

THE COURT: I HAVE LEARNED THAT THERE'S NO SENSE IN ME BRINGING HIM IN HERE TO SCOLD HIM, BECAUSE HE COULD CARE LESS BASED ON HIS OUTBURST HERE IN COURT. BUT MY CONCERN IS THAT ALSO ONCE WE TELL HIM TO LEAVE, I DON'T WANT TO MAKE ANY COMMENTS OR OTHER OUTBURSTS. I THINK THE OTHER JURORS WERE MATURE ENOUGH TO UNDERSTAND HE'S JUST ACTING SILLY. BUT I'M GOING TO TAKE A RECESS AT THIS TIME, AND IF YOU ALL WANT TO PUT MR. VEGA UP, I

THE COURT: DEFENSE HAVE ANY OBJECTIONS TO THE JUROR IN SEAT NUMBER FIVE?

MR. DAVILA: JUST ONE MOMENT, JUDGE.

(PAUSE IN PROCEEDINGS.)

MR. DAVILA: SHE'S OKAY, JUDGE. SHE'S FINE.

THE COURT: STATE, SEAT FIVE?

MS. OGDEN: ACCEPTABLE.

THE COURT: STATE HAVE ANY OBJECTIONS TO THE JUROR IN SEAT NUMBER SIX?

MS. OGDEN: NO, YOUR HONOR.

THE COURT: DEFENSE HAVE ANY OBJECTIONS TO THE JUROR IN SEAT NUMBER SIX?

MR. DAVILA: YES, JUDGE. WE OBJECT, PEREMPTORY.

THE COURT: OKAY. SECOND STRIKE.

STATE HAVE ANY OBJECTION TO THE JUROR IN SEAT NUMBER SEVEN?

MS. OGDEN: WELL, AS MUCH AS I WOULD LOVE TO LEAVE MR. MARRA ON, I THINK IT WOULD BE AN APPELLATE NIGHTMARE. SO I WOULD MOVE TO HAVE HIM STRUCK FOR CAUSE.

THE COURT: DEFENSE HAVE ANY OBJECTION?

MR. DAVILA: NO, JUDGE. I GLADLY JOIN WITH HER. I WILL STRIKE HIM FOR CAUSE.

DEFENSE HAVE ANY OBJECTIONS TO THE JUROR IN SEAT NUMBER EIGHT?

MR. DAVILA: JUDGE, I BELIEVE HE STATED DESPITE THE

MS. OGDEN: JUDGE, I WOULD MOVE FOR MR. CASTRO TO BE STRUCK FOR CAUSE. HE INDICATED THAT HE ONLY UNDERSTOOD PART OF WHAT WE WERE SAYING.

THE COURT: DEFENSE?

MR. DAVILA: JUDGE, I THINK HE SPOKE ENGLISH FAIRLY WELL. I DON'T THINK THAT'S GROUNDS FOR CAUSE. HE INDICATED HE UNDERSTOOD. HE ANSWERED HER QUESTIONS.

THE COURT: STRIKE FOR CAUSE.

SEAT 21, DEFENSE?

MR. DAVILA: YES, YOUR HONOR. WE STRIKE.

THE COURT: YOU ARE GOING TO STRIKE?

MR. DAVILA: YES, SIR. THAT'S SEVEN, I THINK.

THE COURT: OKAY. STATE HAVE ANY OBJECTION TO THE JUROR IN SEAT 22?

MS. OGDEN: YES, YOUR HONOR. I WOULD STRIKE NUMBER 22.

THE COURT: STATE'S FIRST STRIKE.

SEAT 23.

MR. DAVILA: JUDGE, EXCUSE ME. I HAVE TO OBJECT AT THIS POINT, BECAUSE IT'S CLEAR THAT THE PROSECUTOR IS GETTING RID OF ALL THE HISPANIC MEN IN THIS CASE, JUDGE.

THE COURT: WELL, YOU HAVE GOT TO ARTICULATE MORE THAN THAT. WHAT WERE YOU TRYING TO TELL ME?

MR. DAVILA: I'M SAYING SHE'S USING HER CHALLENGES IN A DISCRIMINATORY WAY, AND SHE'S USING THEM TO GET

MY FAMILY IS IN LAW ENFORCEMENT, AND THEY ALL SAID ONCE YOU'RE ARRESTED, YOU'RE GUILTY, AND THAT WAS THE WAY I WAS BROUGHT UP.

MS. OGDEN: OKAY. AND I UNDERSTAND THAT. BUT WHAT I'M THINKING OF MORE OR LESS ALONG THE LINES -- SAY IT'S A TRAFFIC ACCIDENT, OKAY, WHICH HAS NOTHING TO DO WITH THIS CASE. I'M JUST MAKING THIS UP. THERE IS A CAR ACCIDENT. YOU GO TO INTERVIEW ALL THE WITNESSES. NOW, EVERYBODY IN THIS CAR ACCIDENT HAS BEEN IN JAIL AT SOME POINT IN THEIR LIFE. ARE YOU GOING TO BE ABLE TO LISTEN TO THEIR TESTIMONY TO DETERMINE WHETHER CAR A HIT CAR B, OR CAR B HIT CAR C, OR BECAUSE THEY HAVE ALL BEEN IN JAIL YOU'RE JUST NOT GOING TO LISTEN TO ANYBODY?

PROSPECTIVE JUROR: (172) HONESTLY, I WOULD RATHER HEAR IT FROM AN INDEPENDENT WITNESS. BECAUSE LIKE I SAID, I WAS RAISED THIS WAY. YOU HAVE BEEN TO JAIL, DONE TIME, YOU'RE GUILTY, AND THAT'S ALL THERE IS TO IT.

MS. OGDEN: OKAY. AND I UNDERSTAND THAT POSITION, GUILTY AS TO THE OFFENSE THAT THEY MAY HAVE COMMITTED. BUT WHAT I'M TALKING ABOUT IS IF THEY'RE TALKING ABOUT AN INCIDENT THAT'S TOTALLY INDEPENDENT OF WHATEVER THEY'RE CHARGED WITH..

PROSPECTIVE JUROR: (172) I CAN SAY IT THIS WAY. MY COUSIN IS A CORRECTIONS OFFICER FOR THE STATE. AND EVERY ONE OF THEM IS INNOCENT. BUT ACCORDING TO THE WAY

Chapter 7

Entering the Jungle-Orlando, Florida

Central Florida reception center is located off the beeline expressway in Orlando, Florida. It is by far, way different than the county jail. After going through the razor wire fence, the transport bus arrived in the sally port. We all exited the bus and lined up in the sally port next door which was full of officers. We were told to strip butt naked. At the same time, everyone lifted up their testicles, turned around, bent down and coughed a few times. Let me tell you, this was toward the end of September, and it was cold. Especially when the sun hasn't come up yet. The officers were warm with jackets and hot coffee in hand. Every command was done by yelling. Some Latinos did not understand or speak English. This was the perfect opportunity for the officers to slap, punch, and kick any inmate who didn't understand the command or better said, verbal order. Not all, but a good majority of the officers abused their authority and used excessive force Monday through Friday. You will not find an inmate who came in through CFRC back then and tell you no one coming off their transport bus did not get physically abused. If the inmate defended himself, they would handcuff the inmate, as always, then take the inmate to a corner where the cameras can't see and break bones within the inmate's body.

Unfortunately, and it's saddens me to write that some inmates have not made it and died from the injuries. Don't worry, I will show you proof as I write this book. As we were all standing side-by-side in our boxers now, a sergeant had a box with homemade knives in it (shanks). He explained to everyone that some of us would be running into problems with other inmates and it would be wise to grab a knife for protection. Although I did not have any "beef," I didn't think twice to go up and grab a knife. Before I could put my hand in the box, the sergeant took out his handcuffs, ordered me to turn around, then had another officer escort me to confinement. Classification let me out the box a couple of days later. I had to go back to transfer and receiving to deal with the same sergeant. I received a special treatment. My weight was taken, vital signs, personal information questions, bald head haircut and bedroll were all done quickly. I was given the housing assignment and on my way I went. As I walk toward the bravo dormitory, the recreation yard was open with a small square building, which turned out to be the canteen. The yard had basketball courts, softball, all types of games, and men hanging out, smoking cigarettes.

By the time I walked across the side of the yard, I talked to several different people I knew from Orlando and Kissimmee. The first thing I asked for was a shank. They laughed at me, told me to go put up my bedroll and hurry up back to the yard. Back in the county jail, I was selling cigarettes but not smoking. So I wasn't about to start smoking in prison neither. The reception center yards are much different from the permanent prison yards. Some inmates that have been down a while will be fishing for weak-minded fresh meat. In between, violence may happen, even rapes. Some inmates will join gangs for fun or for protection. Some inmates figure they will pay for protection and be okay. I myself am not a warrior/Mike Tyson. But I will never allow for anyone, including officers, to take advantage of me or hurt me. I will use all necessary force to ensure my well being. I am, however, a laid-back individual who stays away from all the drama. I stay away from other people's business, and I will walk with respect.

The reception process lasted almost two months. I did a test for my education level. The mental health counselor spoke with me, classification spoke with me, the medical department spoke with me, and I was done. I asked the classification officer to follow the law and keep me in Central Florida. This nasty lady sent me to Jackson correctional institution in Malone, Florida (the panhandle). The transport bus Took fifty-one of us to Lake Butler reception center. What is now named, Regional Medical Center.

We were housed in the west unit, better known as the wild, wild west. And no, it wasn't that bad on the inmate violence. The triangle, which is Union County, consists of regional medical center, Florida State Prison and Union Correctional Institution. Union County and its surrounding counties are still today full of Ku Klux Klan members. Where else can a Klan member get a job? Do you think someone in the city will put up with racist behavior? The Klan members are bred from children to hate minorities and eventually get a state job with the Department of Corrections. These hateful malicious officers would kill inmates with no problem. They hate people with gold teeth and hate anyone with any type of charisma to themselves. From the minute I got off the bus, I felt the negative vibe. These rednecks were yelling at us and looking for someone to beat up. They spit in inmates' faces and threw away personal property just to have a laugh. This is the place where construction workers found human bones from inmates the Klan members killed. The same place where the FBI has repeatedly raided and arrested officers for excessive use of force and murder. Before closing Lake Butler reception center and leaving town residents jobless, the state made it a reception medical center. A simple way to keep the spirit alive! I kept my mouth shut and moved along quickly. One day while waiting in line for the canteen, an officer showed us a clear bubble-gum-like jar, plastic, which had broken teeth all in the bottom, about a quarter full. Most of the teeth had gold around it. He explained proudly and loud, "This is what we do here in Lake Butler, Florida." He shook the jar like it was loose change.

My direct appeal went to the fifth District Court of Appeals in Daytona Beach, Florida. I was assigned appellate counsel to handle the initial tier review (my appeal of the trial errors). The lawyer's name is Noel, and he is still today handling appeals. These assigned by the state lawyers are mostly full of cases. There is no way they can do a good job on all the cases. So they find a trick in the law and file what is called a, Anderson v. California. This advises the appellate court you have no issues to raise. In turn, the appellate courts grant the Ander's brief and deny your very important direct appeal. This is exactly what happened to me. I found twelve grounds that would have given me a new trial, and this appellate lawyer claims I did not have one ground on the face of the trial transcripts. I didn't know anything about the law back then, yet I knew this lawyer was full of shit. I didn't know what to do.

The detectives confiscated a lot of money from me when I was arrested in 1999, and I was awaiting the hearing. All of a sudden I was picked up and transported back to the Osceola County jail. The same judge who handled the trial and sentenced me said that drug dealing events were testified during the trial, and I had no employment receipts to show I worked for the money. He authorized $750 and told me if I appeal, I would get nothing. My lawyer who represented me in the trial looked at me dumbfounded. He told me to take the small amount and run with it. I knew I was in the wrong so, back to prison I went. Back in Lake Butler Reception Center, I started to learn a lot of things from inmates' actions and officers' actions.

One of the first things I noticed is prisoners in Florida are not united. If any type of incident breaks out, they transfer each inmate to one different prison across the state. There are well over fifty prisons, so go figure that one out! The officers, most of them, they know the system is soft. They get information from inmate snitches and manipulate inmates into hurting each other. I learned we have all worked for free within the prison system. Cutting grass, food service, electricians, plumbers, carpentry, construction, janitors, computer programmers, paralegals, medical assistant, librarians and God knows what else. Could you imagine the millions of dollars it would cost the state if they were forced to pay companies to handle all of the above?

I heard that in the 1980s and 1990s, the Department of Corrections were feeding inmates okay food. An inmate would get real meat and a fair portion. When I came in, this was not the case. Breakfast trays are so disrespectful I don't go to breakfast at all. Would you get up at 5:00 a.m. to 6:00 a.m. to walk down to our dining hall full of inmates who haven't brushed their teeth, to get yelled at by officers, only to get a tray of watered-down oatmeal, two small pancakes the size of waffles, syrup that will make you shit in five minutes, and sometimes an apple? The best breakfast tray was on Thursday. A combo of two biscuits sometimes the size of half a dollar coin, cream beef that I am not sure how they cooked it up and potatoes. If you asked me, I believe the only real food on the tray were the biscuits. Some people will eat anything and therefore have no problems with what is given to them. Years later, you see them in wheelchairs all messed up or on six hundred pills for their health. How can you drink juice that if you spill it on tile, and try to bleach it but still not be able to get the stain out? How would someone go to medical and allow for a nurse to inject you with the flu shot? Do you know how many times I have witness inmates receive the wrong medication?

I quickly learned to be careful and not take any medication or eat any food or juice. The state employees in Tallahassee do not give one inch of care for any inmate in the system. They do not care about any relatives or even if an inmate educates himself. Tallahassee folks know some inmates will be content with TV, a honey bun, and another inmate to have sex with. Some of them lie down and don't fight their cases in appeals courts. New laws come out, and the inmate is so institutionalized, the two-year window to appeal flies right by them without even knowing.

Chapter 8

First Blood—Malone, Florida

JACKSON C.I. 2002

I arrived in Malone, Florida Jackson Correctional Institution toward the end of 2001. They inventoried our property and gave us our housing assignment. I was housed in hotel dorm wing three cell 114 upper. My new roommate was nicknamed Bo-legs. He had been in the system some years out of Jacksonville, Florida. The man turned out to be alright. The institution ran like this on a daily basis: breakfast at 5:30 a.m. to which I didn't go and still do not go to this very day. 7:00 a.m. count. 8:15 a.m. all scheduled callouts, work call, chapel, recreation and canteen. At 11:30 a.m. everything shuts down and back to count we went. But the counts went very fast. By 12:15 p.m. one dormitory at a time was released to lunch, recreation, or canteen. It was your choice. By 1:30 p.m. chapel and all other call-outs were called. At 3:30 p.m. we went back to the dormitories. By 4:15 p.m. it started again. If it was summer, we could be out at recreation until it became dark. The old school officials really knew how to get an inmate tired and to bed nice and early.

Most chaplains throughout the system are looking for paycheck. Not surprisingly, they are former correctional officers. Employees go from food service, to officer, to classification, to chapel, to fired and back at another institution starting all over again. The chapel at Jackson back then didn't allow for too many activities to happen. He would limit other volunteer chaplains from bringing inmate cookies, religious books, or even a writing pad. He would give us a problem about gold chains with a religious emblem or medallions. I had to write a grievance in order to have a vendor send in my gold cross with chain. Classification was one of the most unprofessional racist people I have ever met in my life. These people wanted me to wait five years in order to submit a transfer to Central Florida. Each time I asked, I would be threatened with confinement. They would skip by inmate progress reviews in order to not deal with the inmate issues.

Progress reviews back then were every three years. So imagine waiting three years only to be told you already went to progress review and if you ask again, confinement. I knew then that I had to start hustling and pay a lawyer to handle my business. One day and early 2002, I was speaking in the yard with a friend I knew from the streets named Jock. This guy had a hard time getting along with people. He would get into fights all the time. He was still gang related and not attempting to change. He explained to me that weed and crack moved good at that specific institution. That I only had a certain amount of time to continue my appeals, and he knew the best paralegal there. We agreed even if I started to hustle, I would not make it on time to hire a lawyer from my appeals. I ended up paying $500 to the paralegal. Big mistake! But at the time, I did not know about the law and felt it was the right thing to do.

Neither my mother or any of my other relatives were going to help me with money to hire the appeal lawyer. I'm not sure at what stage my mom was in her relationship; however, she was far apart. I had to beg for a visit and beg for a few dollars in my account. I guess she got tired of so much hope she gave me as a juvenile. Anyhow, I did not have any time to waste. I did what I did best, hustle. I met a good friend named Morejon. He had just came out of super max security and Florida State Prison for attempting to blow up the front of the Dade correctional with explosives. You can't blame him for attempting to leave, he was in since the 1980s and was old. We had one thing in common, to hire a lawyer to get us out of Jackson correctional. In May 2002, I learned how dangerous it can get in a prison.

One inmate along with his "Daddy" stole a book of stamps and a pack of tops, loose tobacco from the locker of a Mexican inmate. The Latinos didn't even know the Mexican inmate until he went out to recreation at 1:00 p.m. asking for help. It was a bad time to steal anything from my Latino at Jackson. The entire South America was there. This was not including Cubans and Puerto Ricans. A few Latino gang members wanted to take out the thief who was playing dominoes among his friends. By 3:00 p.m. a few of the Latinos walked over to the domino table and asked for the pack of tobacco and book of stamps back. That thief rejected the deal claiming he did not give a shit. Yard closed at 3:30 p.m., then we had count and then the yard re-opened again. By 5:00 p.m., I was on the West side basketball court playing with my friend. As the inmates entered the yard, I felt trouble. The Latinos were preparing for war. Silently, they dug out the ground every shank available. I can't believe some people did not notice. The officers were on alert because one of the thieves feared for his life and checked into protection. He told the officers everything that happened and what may happen at any moment. Officials really did not care if we killed each other or what. To them, it was another chance to use force and beat inmates unconscious.

I was dribbling the ball when I heard a loud gunshot. That AR-15 or it may have been an M-16 assault rifle spooked everyone. The officer yelled numerous times for inmates to drop down to the ground, but no one paid attention. The riot began with Latinos stabbing that thief at the domino table. It quickly became a black vs. Hispanic fight that lasted a long time. Inmates of both races got stabbed, hit over the head with steel horseshoes and any other physical injury you can think of. The officers all ran out to the yard attempting to stop the violence but were completely unsuccessful. They had to call back up from other prisons around the area. It looked like a royal rumble. A big royal rumble. You could smell the blood. Soto, Hernandez and I, used the fence to protect us and faced front to any incoming action. We escaped with minor injuries. By the time officers gained full control of the riot, it was nighttime. We were all lined up along the fence, hands on the fence, our backs to law enforcement. I could hear the helicopter on its way and the sirens of ambulances. Knives and weapons were all over the ground close enough for the inmates to grab if needed be. We were taken in to the dormitories ten at a time. But not before we were stripped search in front of a camera and asked gang-related questions. The pressure was on any Latino inmate. They kept on accusing me of being a gang member. After a few minutes, I was escorted to my assigned dormitory where everyone was locked down. At around 2:00 a.m., what must've been sixty officers were going cell-to-cell picking Latinos to put on the bus and transfer. I was hoping for the free ride but was not lucky. A few hundred inmates were transferred, and I was not one of them. I had to continue my time at Jackson.

Things happen in prison. Rapes, robberies, killings, assaults, stabbings, battery on staff members, and stealing. In some places more than others. Jackson Correctional had violence because there are always going to be knuckleheads starting trouble. What the prison failed to provide was education. They only had a GED program to those short in time. If you had fifteen years or more, you were denied educational classes. I quickly realized if the state throws inmates into prison and do not allow for the inmates to seek education, it is a recipe for destruction. Most inmates will become better criminals, and the state of Florida loves the revolving door they have caused. I started to lift weights, run, play sports, and do all the exercises you can think of. I was in good shape. I had to do something with my time while my connection started to supply once again. A few officers were terminated, and they became cautious about doing anything.

Summer went by quickly. I continued to work out and receive visits from my female friend. My 3.850 post-conviction motion was done and ready for Osceola criminal court. I thought the motion had good grounds but in all reality, it was straight trash. What else could I do at the time? None of my relatives stepped up to help me.

The year 2002 was coming to an end. Morejon told me the connection was ready and we could start with cocaine. I moved around little by little, as smooth as possible. The old man explained to me that only those who lay low last in the drug game in prison. The problem we started to encounter was that the customers were cooking the cocaine into crack. They started to break into lockers in order to get food, shoes and personal property in exchange for money. Most of the money ended up in my hands and out to my savings. It didn't take me long to have the money for a lawyer to handle my transfer, I was smart enough to also put a nice amount in my inmate account.

I was picked up by correctional officers one day and housed in confinement under investigation. My name was coming up regularly, so I cooled off for two weeks. It wasn't that inmates were talking about me, it was the dirty urinalysis test some failed and then pointed the finger to where the drugs came from. I got out of confinement and quickly paid a lawyer out of Tampa, Florida, to get on Tallahassee classification and get me south. A couple of months went by and my classification officer at Jackson called me up to her office and ordered to speak with me. She told me that it didn't matter what type of lawyer I had, I would not be going anywhere. I kept quiet and in my mind I said, *This bitch will transfer me one way or the other*. The lawyer did a phone conference and told me to stay out of trouble because he was close to getting Tallahassee to approve my transfer. I told the lawyer to hurry up. Jackson correctional was too far from Orlando, and the officers were beating inmates in the confinement dormitory.

I personally saw officers take out inmates in stretchers with a black sheet over the body after spraying gas and using excessive force.

One specific officer who is now dead, Kirkland, was just starting back then and was the devil in disguise. This man would stand in the middle of the prison and get horny from taking property from inmates. If he didn't like the inmate, he would handcuff the inmate and personally escort to confinement where his buddy officers were waiting to spray gas and kick the inmate to sleep. The violence at Jackson was climbing. A colonel named Ham came in to fix it up. He got rid of many officers, mostly black officers, and transferred 400 inmates. I still wasn't lucky enough to transfer! I watched as 400 new inmates came in. Can you believe that half were homosexuals? The rumor was that Jackson became the AIDS prison of the panhandle. There were so many homosexuals they had their own basketball and softball team. They would lay in the yard feeding each other ice cream. I knew it was time to go and now!

The year 2003 went by fast. The 3.850 motion was in the Osceola courts and I was waiting for the lawyer to get me away from Jackson. One night, I was called up to the front of the prison in order to see a man delivering a document from the state attorney's office of Osceola Orange County. These sorry no-good officers wanted me to testify against Tamara and her case. First they forced her into my trial and now they wanted me to turn on her. Respectfully, I told the man I was not agreeing or signing anything. I explained he made the long trip for nothing. That I may have a life sentence but I will never have the name "snitch" on me.

Years later, through one of my attorneys, I found out she got off her case because the state needed me to proceed, and I refused. Maybe getting good results from her case was not good enough and later ended up in prison anyways on other different drug trafficking charges. Halloween came around, and it was freezing cold up there in the Florida Panhandle. My classification officer called me up to her office, and I went carefully. This lady was super upset Tallahassee called her and asked why she hadn't put my transfer in. I kept my cool and only answered questions. When she asked me where I want to go, my heart raised 300 mph with excitement. I requested Martin correctional and Bell Glades correctional. Within two weeks, I was approved to Martin Correctional. When I told my mom, she was happy but still gave me one last visit at Jackson because my grandfather wanted to see me. It was my sister Selina, her husband, George, my grandfather Elias Senior, my mom and her husband Richie. Everyone came in okay to the visit park. While we were eating, a redneck officer ordered for Richie, my grandfather, and I up into the search room for questioning. This hateful, malicious officer accused my grandfather of being under the influence of alcohol. My eyes opened wide like an animal and before I snapped, my grandfather grabbed me by the wrist and told the officer that he does not drink alcohol. I opened my nostrils and breathed in. Then another officer was walking through and was asked if he smelled any alcohol on my grandfather's breath. The officer said no! So we went back to the table but not before I told the officer he was in violation for taking my family in the inmate search room. Furthermore, he harassed my family and me. After my visit I went back to my cell and wrote a letter to the lawyer I hired for the transfer. I explained the cameras caught everything and that the female officer continued to harass throughout the visit. I still don't know what the lawyer did but the warden called me up to his office to apologize. I did not see the officer ever again at Jackson. They most likely moved the officer to the inmate work camp.

In April 2014, I was awakened at 3:00 a.m. and on my way to a transport bus, "Bluebird." I was happy to leave that hellhole. When I got the chance, I looked at the files and found out I was not going to Martin or Belle Glade correctional. Better yet, I was on my way to the best private prison in Florida, South Bay Correctional facility.

South Bay, Florida

SOUTHBAY C.F. 2004

The trip was a quick one because I was happy to leave the panhandle. I went to Lake Butler Reception Center, Central Florida Reception Center, and finally South Florida Reception Center. South Bay Correctional Facility looked like a big county jail from the front.

On the inside, it holds 1900 inmates with huge dormitories and rec-reation yard. A group of seven inmates arrived that morning and were searched by all African American correctional officers (females). I didn't see the officers take anything from any inmate. They just wanted to make sure we didn't have any weapons or cell phones. South Bay Correctional, a private prison, provided the inmates with personal hygiene products, different public phone system, different food, different canteen and basically different everything. I was given my housing assignment, Alpha dormitory 107 upper. The minute I walked in the quad, I couldn't believe what I was seeing. It was a different world, everyone was doing time relaxing. The officers didn't harass you or scream at you just to be nasty. If you needed tissue, you could get it. They had satellite TV with DVD movies each weekend. Because the phone system was different, I could not call my family and let them know where I was. I had to turn in a new phone list. However, that night, a Hispanic inmate allowed for me to call home from a cell phone. They also gave me food while my money trans-ferred over from the state system. South Bay has big cells, air-condi-tioned and clean showers. You could paint your room and wax the floor. I could not believe I was there! All the officers were black! The warden, assistant warden, assistant inspector, a few sergeants, and a few officers who were white, are barely around to be seen.

They offered certifications in small engines, computers, car-pentry, culinary arts, commercial driver's license, and horticulture. You could earn your general education diploma also. They did talent shows every holiday. The chapel was great! All types of volunteers from all types of religions came in with books, food, and even pencils and paper. The visitation park was a place where you could really enjoy your loved ones. Really! Vending machines sold $2.50 items like if you were at a pharmacy or something. I didn't see any officers harass any of the inmates or their families. If you did something out of hand, like kiss too much, the officer would pull you to the side after the visit and ask you to keep it to a minimum. No big deal! The officers at South Bay were respected way more than the officers in any state prison. Yes, there was corruption. But there is corruption in all state prisons too. Would you rather do time in a prison with rehabilitation that is serious or in a state prison with nothing? In a state prison with Ku Klux Klan officers who come to work miserable wanting to use excessive force?

I, the author of this book, can honestly write that I earned my general education diploma in three months. And it took that long because I had to wait for the Palm Beach education department to schedule a test date. At Jackson, I couldn't even attend school. I then took computer classes, life skill classes and began to earn an Associates Degree out of Ashworth University. I still owe them money for the psychology books. Education made me more mature! I changed completely after I started to feel good about my accomplishments. Gov. Scott at one point attempted to privatize many prisons; however, it didn't work out. Old school officers complained that they would be out of jobs. Reason being, private institutions stay away from employees with misconduct records!

I settled in really good. Within a half year, I had some education under my belt, friends and family visiting me on a regular, a cell phone and began to make a lot of money selling heroin. People paid in cash so it worked out even better. I had to start saving for lawyers because the 3.850 motion was denied on all levels of the appellate system. With no release date, no appeal motion with the court, what was I to do? Lay down and wear it for the rest of my life? Here I was in 2005 and no one in my family, still, did not offer to help with a good appellate lawyer. Some inmates will give up and commit suicide. Other inmates will give up and turn gay. Others will be satisfied with the small portions of food the state prison provides, a cup of coffee here and there, a basketball game or two, homemade wine once in a while and a visit from a family member whenever the relative feel guilty and visit. I am not that type of person. I will never give up! I needed money, and money I got!

First thing I did was hire a private investigator from Lutz, Florida, named Dwyer. The old man was a former FBI agent of twenty-five years. He read my transcripts to see what he could do. I paid him $2,500 and another $2,000 to find what he said might be a potential witness. I am assuming the private investigator had a lot of cases because he took a while to start. At South Bay, so much went on that with the bad memory I have, I can't write about everything. The facility is a little world within a world. But then again, every prison across the United States of America is its own world. While I was at Jackson correctional, I was placed in confinement under investigation a couple of times and never caught a disciplinary report.

I got my first disciplinary report at South Bay coming out to recreation one morning. All inmates were coming out to the dorms with their shirts untucked. So here I am with my shirt untucked walking pass a redbone female sergeant. The lady told me to tuck in my shirt, and I looked at her like she was dumb. Then she raised her voice at me, and it gave me the green light to curse her out to the point that she called for backup. I was housed in confinement and delivered a disciplinary report. The disciplinary hearing team of officers that consisted of one classification officer and one high-ranking regular officer, sentenced me to thirty days in confinement.

I did fourteen days and got out only to be housed in alpha dormitory again. I now had to walk by this sergeant and see if she would retaliate. The lady sergeant called me to the office station and asked me if I was okay. I apologize for the foul language and explained I did not like for anyone to disrespect me like I am a chump. I further explained all inmates were walking out to recreation with their shirts untucked, and she singled me out. The look she gave me said it all. She was out to get money from inmates she thought were hustlers. The sergeant had other inmate snitches who would point out those that were involved with any type of moneymaking operations. A friend of mine got her off my back. It all worked out great because the same sergeant left me alone for the two years or so while I was at South Bay. I could walk by her with contraband on me with no worries.

Out of all the prisons I have been to, South Bay has been the only one where I felt as if time went by fast. There I sipped on different hard liquors on the weekend and watch movies of few days after being released in the movie theater. When my mom gave me a visit, she knew I was in a better place. On her way in through the front of the visit park, the officers treated the relatives with respect. It is so much better when the family feels comfortable about visiting us. In state prison, there will always be a sorry-hating male or female officer in the front of a visit park ready to turn our relative away for clothing that's too tight or a clothing color that is see through.

The years of 2004 and 2005 were somewhat alright and what made them even better was the New England Patriots won back to back Super Bowls. You know I was born in Lawrence, Massachusetts, and therefore I love the Red Sox, Bruins, Celtics, and Patriots. On the college football, my team is the Florida State Seminoles. I dreamed a lot about going to Fenway Park and watching my baseball team play. I have never been to any sports Arena or field to feel the enjoyment of cheering for the team I like. In Puerto Rico it was always horses, fighting roosters, and fishing. Don't get me wrong, I love my island. But I would really accomplish one of my dreams of being there taking photos and maybe even obtaining autographs. Calling my family up north, my cousin, I stumbled upon a female friend named Cynthia. We would talk over the phone and a couple of months later she flew in to meet me in person. Everything went well. She moved from Massachusetts to Palm Bay, Florida, because she had relatives there also. I met her three daughters, son, mother, aunt, and cousin. May God bless her with all her lovely family. They treated me with respect and gave me much love.

The private investigator contacted me and advised he found out the last known address to a Hispanic male named Reyes. I could not remember for the life of me who this man was. The private investigator explained the location was in Merritt Island, Florida, and the witness had several phone numbers and home addresses. He also advised I hire a criminal lawyer who can help me file any motion needed when the witness was found and questioned. I wasn't going to hire any lawyers until I knew for sure we had something solid. I continued to save more and more money. Cynthia helped me by investing my money and other things. Or better said, we helped each other.

Too many things that I did, and I don't even know the statute of limitations for each one. I'm not going into details. I'm never going to be proud of my past illegal activities, what I can be honest and write is, I have done it for myself when needed to do so. I started to deal with a lot of cell phones. I always kept two for myself sold the rest with chargers and/or anything else you may want with your cell phone. The hard liquor drinking became more and more. Not that I would drink a lot at one time, but I was drinking a little bit more often. I have never been a heavy drinker. I get tipsy with a little alcohol, especially if it's strong liquor. I would share a lot of the bottles with friends, so we would watch movies and eat popcorn. We watched movies until 5:00 a.m. One of those nights, I had a special half-gallon of peppermint schnapps. It was the first time, and the drink was smooth. I overdid it with an ecstasy pill. I overdosed! My body was there but my brain was not. I could barely see or talk. If I lay down, my brain would automatically pass out as if I was going to die. My roommate was nervous. I didn't want to declare a medical emergency then get a urinalysis done and be in confinement for a while. What I later found out was that my body totally shut down from dehydration. Between the alcohol, ecstasy, and hydroxycut I was consuming to exercise, it took the life out of me. Don't even ask how I made it and was back to normal in three days. All I can say is God was not ready for me yet!

In July 2006, an inmate had a family member call the institution inspector to report that I was selling heroin, cell phones and liquor. My cell was searched and all the inspector found were tomatoes, onions, and raw eggs. The next day, the inspector searched the entire quad and the public phones. One of his assistants opened the public phones and found a few chargers and bagged up heroin. They left, and I took a loss. But I thought as long as they don't get anything on me, I am good. By lunchtime I was in handcuffs and on my way to confinement. While I was being escorted, I offered $1,500 cash for the inspector to overlook the situation and release me without any disciplinary report. The answer was no. The inspector attempted to freeze my inmate account and confiscate over $7,000 but was unsuccessful.

Money orders were coming in as I was in confinement, and the inspector again attempted to confiscate with no success. The inspector didn't know I had someone paid, right next to him. The determined inspector attempted to have a prosecutor press charges for introduction of heroin into the facility and trafficking. Again he was unsuccessful. While I was in confinement, I had the public phone buy an extension cord, rolled up to the food flap. I was using the phone all day every day. I told Cynthia to call a lawyer in Tallahassee right next to the Department of Corrections.

The attorney scheduled a phone conference with me quickly. The agreement we made was that he would deal directly with the warden. Have the investigation dismissed and any disciplinary reports on the way. I also want to transfer to Belle Glade's correctional in the same West Palm Beach. The lawyer charged me $6,500 and I told Cynthia to go into my savings and pay him immediately. While the lawyer was in talks with the warden, the inspector made sure a possession disciplinary report was given to me and found guilty as soon as possible. Not even 24 hours after being sentenced to sixty days in confinement, a paper was slid under the cell door, which I picked up when I woke up. It was a notification that classification was recommending me to close management one, the highest level of punishment besides supermax. I picked up the phone and screamed at the lawyer through a three-way phone call. I demanded my money back. The lawyer agreed after a couple of phone calls but only gave me back $6,000 and I wasn't mad.

By October 2006, I was transported in a van to Charlotte Correctional Institution. At that specific time, Charlotte House closed levels one, two, and three. The institution also had a mental health unit. On the way there, I was a little nervous because close management is mostly knuckleheads who don't care and are constantly doing stupid things. I heard stories about Charlotte, but one can only believe half of what people have to say because lies are everywhere. On the van was a young man who was also on his way to Charlotte Close Management. We were talking about how he took a cup of water, put bleach and lotion in it, cooked it in the microwave, and threw it on another inmate for being slick mouth. I did see the victim prior to me being housed in confinement. To sum it all down, the victim was black with white pinkish spots all over his neck and face from the burns. The man will look like a cow for life!

Certificate of Completion

This is to certify that:

Giovanni Vega

has successfully completed a minimum of 120 hours of training in

LifeSkills/CLN

On September 17, 204
Co-sponsored by South Bay Correctional Facility
and The Florida Correctional Privatization Commission

L. Lewis
Acting Program Director

Michael Bryant
AFA Program

SOUTHBAY CORRECTIONAL FACILITY 2004-2006

Palm Beach County Health Department

Certificate of Completion

Giovanni Vega

has successfully completed the following course
provided by the Palm Beach County Health Department

HIV/AIDS-Awareness (4 hours)

Coretha Smith
Facilitator

HEALTH

May 14, 2004
Date Completed

SOUTHBAY CORRECTIONAL Facility
2004-2006

DEPARTMENT OF EDUCATION

State of Florida

This Certifies That

GIOVANNI VEGA

having satisfactorily completed all requirements of law and standards prescribed by the State Board of Education, thereby demonstrating satisfactory evidence of educational competence, is hereby awarded this

HIGH SCHOOL DIPLOMA

and is entitled to all the Rights and Privileges appertaining thereto.

In witness whereof our names and the seal of the State Board of Education, Tallahassee, Florida, are hereto affixed, this the

2nd Day of November, 2004   Diploma Number: 200090522

John L. Winn
COMMISSIONER OF EDUCATION

Murray Cordell
FLORIDA GED ADMINISTRATOR

Certificate of Enrollment

Issued To:

Giovanni Vega #X12646
Po Box 7171
South Bay Correctional Facilit
South Bay, FL 33493-7171

Date of Issue:
05-22-2006

Issued By:

Ashworth College

Degree Program:

Associate Degree Program in
Psychology

Approved By:

F. Miller Mills

Student Number:

AC0615989

SOUTHBAY CORRECTIONAL FACILITY 2004-2006

This place has the same setting as Central Florida Reception Center. Every inmate there was accused and found guilty of some type of infraction. This includes, but is not limited to, assaults on other inmates or officers, attempted escapes, attempted murder, participating in riots, drug trafficking, cell phones, multiple positive urinalysis results and sexual battery. Some inmates didn't have any type of disciplinary history in years but were leaders of gangs. The officers at Charlotte, most of them, were unprofessional, malicious, and wanting to use excessive force. You already know the typical Southern Florida "Klan" mentality. I was housed in fox dormitory. The cellmate I had was super dirty and apparently gave up on bathing. I knew right away I could not do a level three behind the door with someone so nasty and me being so clean. A couple of days later, a Cuban man nicknamed "Pistola" offered to help by having the officer move me to his cell and also gave me a job cutting hair, feeding level one and two and three. I didn't have to sit in the cell all day long. I did, however, take a few hours to continue with my college courses. After working for about a week, I got comfortable and started to sell top cigarettes better known in close management as "keys." Every so often, I sold weed. The money coming in was nothing compared to South Bay, but it was money. Mostly through money orders and Western Union.

There is not one single institution in the United States of America where an inmate cannot convince an officer to make some money. They can be white, black, or Hispanic, it doesn't matter. They can be a rookie officer, inspector, or even a high-ranking official. 85% of the correction employees will either start smuggling at the beginning or wait until retirement is near. The ones that never smuggle most likely killed an inmate and committed a sin anyway. This place has become so bad in all aspects of corruption, only the federal government can save the state from continuing to fall apart.

Close management level three authorizes one shower every other day, two hours TV every other day, and recreation in a cage three or four times a week. You can use the phone after each shower and get a shave. No razors, only hair clippers. I was lucky that the state classification didn't accept the recommendation of level one and instead approved level three six months. This meant I could be released back to general population quicker. But first I had to make it through all the bullshit of close management. Fights would happen all the time. Officers would get assaulted and although very few, some inmates would get raped. One morning, a lieutenant was walking around to make sure all inmates have their bunks made up neatly. She kicked the door of a famous inmate known for drama. "Make your fucking bed right now, inmate," she yelled.

The man got up from his bunk and screamed back at her, "When I catch you, I'm going to kill you, bitch." The female lieutenant left without any further action. The next few hours, all we would hear were the sounds of a breaking heater. He was making a shank and the drama was going to follow. I was looking up toward the second floor when his cell seemed to be sparked up on fire. You could not see in through the window of the door. I automatically thought he burned himself alive. The dormitory sergeant was a pure asshole so he got what was coming for him. The sergeant stood in front of the burning cell, unable to look in and hearing the inmate screaming, he got on the radio and ordered the cell door to open. Flying out came a ninja! The inmate covered his head with a T-shirt only leaving his eyes open to be able to see. He held the shank against the sergeant's throat standing from behind him in order to have control. "You're my hostage now, anyone come up the stairs, and I kill you," the inmate threatened. Within minutes the entire shift of officers were standing by the front door of the quad wanting to burst in and take control of the situation. The warden and captain were doing the talking from the first floor. Smoke filled the quad and the inmates started to kick the doors unable to breathe. Officers handcuffed and escorted the inmates to all the recreation cages, two per cage. I don't know how, but we spotted the news antenna parked toward the trailers in the back of the institution. The hostage drama ended in less than one hour later with a deal you won't believe but was the safest. The inmate was escorted to a van, untouched, uncuffed with the promise of a trip to Florida state prison maximum management. The officer was saved, that's all that mattered. After a long vacation, the sergeant came back to work as nice and respectful as a person can be. It took a near death experience to learn how to be humble.

Did I tell you about the kitchen at Charlotte? Rats, mice, spiders, and flies run around like they are in the woods. On a dinner tray came a roach with the sticky salad. The beans were super dangerous too! You could break your teeth from small rocks within those beans. They didn't care how the food was served. The idea was, serve the tray no matter how dirty it maybe. Food service has been an easy way for directors to fraud. They submit to the regional office a certain amount of money needed to feed the inmates. Then when they get the money, a small amount of food is ordered, allowing for "some people" to put money in their pockets. When inmates go to the dining hall and pick up the tray, the amount is short or even missing a portion. I will write more about it later in the book. Right now, it's all about Charlotte.

The visit for a close management inmate level one were behind glass, once per month with one call per month. The visits for close management inmate level two was every two weeks behind the glass, one phone call per week. Close management level three was contact visit for two hours, every other week and the phone a few times per week. I used the phone all night long because I was an orderly (worker). I was promoted as an orderly and was able to walk to other dorms that housed inmates in general population, the other half close management one and two.

Through the back door, I negotiated with a new connection in population. He was giving me twenty packs of top cigarettes for $100 Western Union and I would turn around and sell three packs for $50 Western Union in the dormitory I was housed. It added up pretty good. I had to strap up like a suicide bomber on my way back because if the officer searched me thoroughly, I was fired. I had those guys smoking good in close management. It was good because an inmate would smoke a cigarette and lay back to relax. When they got high, they didn't even want to look out the cell door. So I was doing the officers a big favor at the same time by keeping most inmates settled and relaxed.

But with all the selling comes the snitching. I woke up one morning dreaming officers would search my cell. I got up and had about a dozen "keys" top cigarettes, ready to go down in a hole in the wall that once upon a time had a fire extinguisher. I heard "four times coming through the front." When I looked out the door, it was the search team. I got on the toilet and pushed each one through with all of the pack of rolling papers. The room was clean. I was strip searched and threatened. I laughed. Underneath my bunk was a big white laundry bag full to the top with AA batteries, cookies, deodorant, saltine crackers, squeeze cheeses, peanut butter squeezes, chips, writing paper pads, envelopes, snickers, M&Ms, and honey buns. This was payment from people for weed and tobacco. My boss would let me pick up all the food people owed to me as we passed out food trays and picked up the trays. I made a big deal out of it because in close management level one and two, we could only order five food items per week. And level three, we could order ten food items per week. How can one have so much at one time? I kept a close eye on my surroundings.

In prison, sometimes it's hard because we all have the same routine. These dudes will smile in your face then turn around and tell any officer what you may have done or are doing. The worst part about it is that they do it for free! I couldn't go to sleep at night knowing I told on someone. It would be like the end of the world for me. It's unbelievable how some grown men hate that you're making money to support yourself.

My job in the other dorm fell apart. Not that I messed up or got caught. I simply quit one day because one of the officers was spitting on the sheets in the laundry cart. I explained he was putting my life in danger, and I was not down with those types of actions. I kept the job in my dormitory and made the best of it. A lot of times inmates were beaten by officers while in handcuffs and my work partner would write down the names and number in order to contact the family and notify the incidents.

We weren't just doing negative things, we did positive things too. I helped out plenty of people who were struggling and very hungry behind the door. It is in my heart to help others. But if I feel the person is a slick no-good bastard, I will bypass. I do not associate with those who are constantly attempting to lie to others, steel or manipulate people to fight one another.

I had my all-black Timberland boots I bought at South Bay Correctional Facility. One officer told me to take my boots off saying I got them from another officer. I couldn't believe the accusations! Then the slow-minded officer explained he was going to write a disciplinary report. Not even three hours later, I called Cynthia and asked her to contact the lawyer in Tallahassee and have him call the warden and fix the problem. I told her to pay him $300 for the call. I never went to any disciplinary hearing or heard from the officer. The warden didn't even allow the officer to come around my assigned dormitory. Nine out of ten officers think every inmate is broke, has family that doesn't care or no family at all. This mentality is what gives them the green light to use excessive force and kill inmates. Officer misconduct has been around so long that it will take a God movement to slow it down a great deal. We are praying that everything falls apart and builds back up much better. We are praying for a lot of rehabilitation in order to change lives and help upon release.

I caught a disciplinary report for another issue. I failed to follow a verbal order. It was still very cold in early 2007, and I was tucked under my blankets sleeping at 7:00 a.m. The officer went by, looked in, and then behind my back wrote the disciplinary report. I was found guilty and housed in disciplinary status. I did about three weeks and was back in normal close management. What I did not know was the management board extends any sentence in close management when the inmate is found guilty of any disciplinary report. I was extended three months more.

Shortly after going through all the nonsense of extending the stay at Charlotte, I got myself into another mess. The dorm sergeant told me to give him the "keys" I have hidden in my shoes. So I did what he asked me to do. This sergeant put the cigarette packs in his pocket and told me who snitched on me when and how. It was the same man I was eyeing all along. I asked for a fight between me and the man as soon as possible. The only place was in the sally port.

The sally port is the hallway between the front of the dormitory and the quads. This sergeant locked the hater and me on one side and locked the other inmate workers on the other side. This way no one got jumped. My friend Pistola had a shank on him and was ready to stick the hater but couldn't come through the back door. We fought three rounds. When finished, the sergeant made us shake hands and reminded us of no medical assistance for the time being. When the back door finally opened, I told Pistola to put the shank away and chill. I was busted up good. My nose was bleeding, knots all over my head, cracked lip, and a lightly swollen eye. The one thing that messed me up was that in the mix of action, I hit the steel on the side of the plexiglass window and got a decent concussion. I had ice in a t-shirt to bring the swelling down. When I made it back to the cell, I knew I got worse because I could not lay down. The same thing that happened to me at South Bay happened to me right then and there. I would pass out cold if I lay my head down. I had to sleep with my back against the wall for two nights. I still went to work and continued my regular. The hater quit the job after all the inmates were calling him names. Pistola kept looking at the hater wrong, and he decided to ask for a move to another dormitory. I could have decided to stick the hater myself and get boosted to close management one. Then do two years or better at Charlotte dealing with the same foolishness. I was ready to go back to general population, not extend my stay again!

Around the start of 2007, I hired the law firm of Davis and Stephenson. I gave a lawyer $2,500 dollars to review my legal documents and familiarize himself with the case. We agree to present newly discovered evidence after the private investigator found the witness and gave a statement under oath and notary. So I gave him $5,000 more. I had plenty of money saved up with Cynthia and a good amount in my inmate account for emergency. The witness stated he showed up that Friday morning of November 1999 to the motel where I was at. He went on to say that Tamara, before leaving in her car, was spanking her child a bit too aggressively. He observed all this while parked in a motel parking looking up toward the second floor. In conclusion, Mr. Reyes explained I would pay him to drive my rental cars around town in order to handle my business.

When Stephenson, my lawyer, reviewed the information he explained to me that's something bigger and better came up. Dr. Gore was barred from performing any autopsies in Florida because cases he was found guilty of negligence for. So we held back on the Reyes statement. I gave Stephenson $3,000 to hire another private investigator and find everything possible on Dr. Gore. I did my own research on Google and was amazed on how many news articles came up on Dr. Gore. This so-called medical examiner testified falsely in numerous cases dated back to when I was a kid. The district state attorney knew back in 1996 exactly who they were hiring. A non-board-certified experienced doctor who was willing to fully cooperate with the state no matter how down and dirty he needed to get.

The Medical Examiner's Office was under investigation from 1995 through 2002 for the flip-flopping of evidence and hundreds of murder cases. And this shit continued for seven years while prosecutors knew about it and kept quiet. I fell in 1999 and lost trial in May 2001. What does that mean? It means the prosecutor knew Dr. Gore's office was being investigated and allowed for him to testify against me anyway! Can you imagine if I would have known of this investigation? My trial lawyer would have told the jurors all the corruption and Dr. Gore's testimony would have been no good. No jury in their right mind would've found me guilty.

Remember when the jurors were deliberating, they requested the trial transcripts and the judge refused to supply the transcripts of any witness because it was too time-consuming? The jurors were not convinced of Dr. Gore's testimony. Not providing the jury with the witness transcripts results in a court's abuse of discretion. Judges make jurors upset all the time. It is a court tactic used to help each other. A lot of the judges, lawyers, and prosecutors have lunch together, do family barbecues together and have sex with one another when possible. They will catch feelings and will railroad your ass over the next law officials. Quickly! I know this for a fact, no one can tell me otherwise.

A good friend of mine who is one of the clerks of courts in Jacksonville, Florida, we have spoken in the past while she ate in the judges' chambers. Even the judicial assistants are crooked! A lot of the times, a judge will know your lawyer has meet all the requirements by law to obtain relief, but still deny you in order to keep that prosecutor happy. These people don't give a rat's ass about human life or how you may have grown up. The Florida Justice System is years back in time. Do not think that I'm upset because I'm truly past that emotion. The reason I'm writing this book is because I want to show the entire world of my wrongful conviction and how the Florida government is full of corruption and fraud. I have a first amendment constitutional right to do so.

I finally was released from close management in May 2007. It felt good to get away from that trap. In a couple weeks, I was transported to S. Florida Reception Ctr. where I ran into Pistola once again. He had a female officer working for him. My get-out-of-punishment present was an ounce of weed. I didn't have to spend any money from my inmate account and was able to move around like I wanted to. Throughout the years, the laundry department throughout Florida corrections have become nasty, and they penny-pinch all the clothing. We would get new sets of clothing every six months. Today, you will be lucky to get one set brand-new. Most of the time you have to pay an inmate to wear new boxers, T-shirts, pants and shirts. "Blues." You even have to pay to have your clothing pressed in order to feel comfortable in front of your family at a visit. You would think the corrections department encouraged and provide inmates with new clothing. So we could look presentable in front of the public eye. The truth is year after year it gets worse. Between the budget cuts and the fraud, the inmates are left to resolve in violence due to living conditions. Start voting for officials who will make a change.

"WITNESS STATEMENT"

I, ~~Iris Soto~~ Iris Soto (Initial IPS), am making this statement freely and voluntarily. I am requesting that this statement be written for me because I cannot write well in English, but I understand and can read English.

I know Giovanni Vega and used to lend him my vehicle from time to time in 1998. I remember with clarity the morning of Tamara Torres' child's death and the months (Initial IPS) afterward. That morning I went to the Budget Inn between 8:30 am and 9 am to the best of my recollection. I picked up Giovanni Vega and he drove me to work. I returned to the Budget Inn around 11 am or 11:30 am to the best of my recollection. I saw Giovanni Vega and the two children, picked up my keys and left.

Initial IPS

(1)

96

Later that day I heard that the baby died.

A few months later I was in the Orange (Int. I.P.S) County Jail and I ran into Tamara Torres. Tamara told me that Giovanni said the baby fell in the shower and was hurt. Tamara said she went home to the hotel and the baby was alive on the bed. Tamara said she did not call 911 or any other emergency number but instead picked up the baby and drove the baby herself to the hospital.

Tamara told me that she knew Giovanni Vega did not kill the child. Tamara said that she should have called 911 because she thinks she contributed to the death by not calling for help right away.

Initial
I.P.S

(2)

97

Giovanni Vega looked after those children everyday and never had any problems. Giovanni told me that the baby fell in the shower and he immediately called Tamara Torres, the mother, who said she would be right there.

No attorney ever contacted me before, although a Detective Brown did contact me a couple of times via telephone, but never followed up. I never had the opportunity to make a statement in this case.

I am making this statement because I believe an injustice has occurred. I do not believe that Giovanni Vega would have intentionally hurt that baby.

Initial
IPS

(3)

I swear or affirm that this statement is true and correct to the best of my ability and I understand that making a false sworn statement would constitute perjury.

Iris Soto POB ~~████~~

11/7/07
Date

Osceola Corrections Depart
Inmate IP# 15107

(4)

Chapter 11

Evidence of Malicious Guilt

I'm going to step out the prison system for this chapter and provide some, not all, news articles concerning the corruption between Dr. Gore and the prosecutors. I can write a story and paint a picture like anyone else can in a book. However when you read for yourself what was taking place, only then will you actually believe what I have been put through. Seeing is believing, right?

Remember how I explained Dr. Gore was barely hired in 1996 after commissioners were refusing to accept his degree from India? The district state attorney at the time pushed to hire Gore as chief medical examiner so aggressively that the standards for the position were lowered not once but twice. The district state attorney knew his prosecutors would obtain higher conviction rates with someone agreeing with the state 100%. Can't lose like that, can you? Gore gets the $169,000 a year and does illegal private work on the side. It was a win-win decision for both parties. Who cares about men and women going to trial attempting to prove their innocence! The Orange Osceola State Attorney's office was on a mission to show the public, Disney World and the Legislature branch, "we are a zero tolerance judicial circuit of Florida."

There are news articles that speak about how the Orange-Osceola Medical Examiner's lost bullets, blood, hair, and other evidence in murder cases without informing police, prosecutors, public defenders or defense attorneys. Specifically in 1994 and 1995. You're asking yourself how does it relate to Giovanni Vega and his case? The Medical Examiner's Office continued its corruption until the news broke out in 2002, that's how! They kept it quiet as long as they could. Do you know how many convictions were obtained in seven years with the testimony of this fraudulent, non-board-certified pathologist? I was locked up in November 1999 while the corruption was still taking place. I went to trial in 2001, well before the news threw the medical examiner's office to the public in 2002. The prosecutor who handled my case knew all along about the corruption with the Medical Examiner's Office and Dr. Gore, yet she kept quiet. That is withholding of evidence favorable to the defense! In many cases like this, people are compensated millions of dollars because of the severity of prosecutor misconduct.

To make this even more interesting, in early 1999, Dr. Gore testified in a murder case which years later was overturned on the amount of lies found in Dr. Gore's testimony and autopsy report. Mr. Yurko was released from prison after a hearing in front of Judge Lawson. The now Florida Supreme Court Hon. Judge Lawson stated, "One can hardly maintain public trust in a system of justice if you let stand a conviction obtained through reliance on an autopsy that is later thoroughly discredited." For those of you reading this book asking yourself how on God's green earth does Orange-Osceola County get away with all this corruption, allow me to explain 1996 was not the beginning. Look at the news articles in the New York Times stating Dr. Gore can be sued for removing a dead person's eyes for transplant against the mother's wishes. The article is dated 1988, when Gore was an assistant medical examiner in Orange County. Dr. Gore's record of misconduct dated back so far, his only option was to work for the district state attorney.

In August 2002, Dr. Gore was caught and accused of doing private work on county time. Prior to this mess, Gore was accusing the Deputy Chief medical examiner of the same stating, "That really upsets me, private work is allowed only on your own time", said Gore. How do you accuse your assistant of misconduct and a week later get caught doing the same thing yourself? All I can say is, *wow*. A month later, September 2002, the deputy chief medical examiner accuses Dr. Gore of misleading the court with false testimony. I already knew that Dr. Gore was full of shit when he testified against me in 2001. So that's nothing new to me.

In 2002, Dr. Gore faced discipline for the second offense in two months. Once again, Gore was getting paid by the county while getting paid for private work. This man did a fantastic job at making money by any means necessary. I guess it was part of the deal when Gov. Chiles appointed Gore chief medical examiner followed by Gov. Bush years later. The problem turned out to be the Florida Department of Law Enforcement medical examiners Commission office, are the only ones with the authority to terminate Dr. Gore. How does the FDLE run the medical examiners commission? I'm still trying to figure it out. But what the truth is, and get ready for this, if the FDLE arrested Dr. Gore for any of his hundreds of infractions, Dr. Gore would not last five minutes in the county jail. Do you know why? He would automatically snitch on all the prosecutors he infected/botched the autopsies for.

Orange and Osceola County Florida would have been the delinquents of the United States of America. Could you imagine dozens of prosecutors being arrested for working with Dr. Gore way back since the 1980s? Not going to happen. The only way all this corruption would have exploded to the maximum was the FBI stepping in and rounding up all who were involved. Unfortunately, we live in a society where certain law officials conducted themselves above the law. Florida, since before I was born, has always been above the law. In January 2003, the Yurko case blew up, and Dr. Gore was put under pressure. Record showed Gore listed a baby in an autopsy report as a black infant when in fact both parents are white. Gore listed incorrect measurements of the body and the most puzzling discrepancy in the autopsy report was his opinion on the internal organs. "I removed the anterior part of the entire chess bone and then removed the heart, lungs and all the organs," Gore testified. However, shortly after the victim died, the organs were donated! Earlier in this book, I already wrote Yurko was released and the opinion the judge gave.

In August 2003, Gore announced he was ready to retire because of old age. "There is no problem, nobody is forcing me out," Gore stated. The truth was the state opened an investigation concerning Gore's work ethics. The Medical Examiner's Office was also cleaning up the scandal of all the mishandled evidence and hundreds of cases. If you asked me, it was thousands of cases.

By October 2003, the public was demanding Gore shouldn't wait to step down as chief medical examiner. By then, too many cases were popping up and officials were doing nothing about it. The sad part about it was, is and always will be, the public is so busy living life, no one really knows how corrupt the government can be. In January 2004, the newspapers were now demanding Dr. Gore to be removed from office immediately. In February 2004, a state board barred Dr. Gore from performing any more autopsies. It was the strictest discipline ever taken against the chief medical examiner in Florida. The state medical examiners commission ruled Dr. Gore committed too many errors in a case, which sent a man to prison for life. No it wasn't me, not yet anyway. I didn't even know all this stuff was happening until 2007 and beyond. The prosecutor never informed me their expert witness was a fraud. Maybe in another state, they would abide by the law and release prisoners when things like this happen. Not in Florida.

There are also news articles concerning a similar state expert scandal in Massachusetts. Not being racial or anything like that, but Dr. Gore and the expert in Massachusetts are both of Hindu descent. I'm just saying! I come to prison and find out one of the most crooked psychiatrists in the history of the Department of Corrections is of Hindu descent. Again I'm just saying! Is that like saying Trump is crooked! Everyone knows our president is a law-abiding citizen who always tells the truth and does what is best for our country, not his investments, right? It's all a coincidence! Last, I will also provide the actual Florida Department of Law Enforcement legal document conclusion on Dr. Gore's discipline. After reading eleven chapters of this book, do you feel I can get at least the benefit of the doubt and be given a new trial? Hold that thought, there's a lot more to go, a lot of information to read and discover.

"COMLAINT AGAINST DR. GORE"

STATE OF FLORIDA
MEDICAL EXAMINERS COMMISSION

MEDICAL EXAMINERS COMMISSION,

    Petitioner,

vs.

Shashi B. Gore, M.D.

    Respondent.

CASE NO. 04-1

Discipline b, MEC

ADMINISTRATIVE COMPLAINT

The Medical Examiners Commission files this Administrative Complaint against the Respondent, Shashi B. Gore, M.D. The Commission seeks to impose discipline upon the Respondent based on the following allegations:

1.   Respondent is the Medical Examiner for District Nine and was appointed to that position by means of a Gubernatorial Appointment. Respondent's current three-year term of office ends on June 30, 2004.

2.   The actions of the Respondent in the death investigation of Infant Alan Yurko through its documentation and Respondent's trial testimony did violate the provisions of §406.075(1)(l), Florida Statutes, in that Respondent exhibited *Negligence or the failure to perform the duties required of a medical examiner with that level of care or skill which is recognized by reasonably prudent medical examiners as being acceptable under similar conditions and circumstances.*

3.   This Administrative Complaint is issued pursuant to Sections 120.569, 120.57, 406.02(4)(c), and 406.075, Florida Statutes. Any proceedings concerning this Complaint shall be conducted pursuant to Sections 120.569 and 120.57, Florida Statutes, and Chapters 28-106 and 28-107, Florida Administrative Code.

WHEREFORE it is alleged that the Respondent, Shashi B. Gore, M.D., is guilty of violating Section 406.075 (1)(i), Florida Statutes.

NOW, THEREFORE, the Medical Examiners Commission hereby complains against and alleges that disciplinary action should be taken against Shashi B. Gore, M.D., as provided in Sections 406.02(4)(c), and 406.075(1), Florida Statutes, for the reasons set forth above and in accordance with the Election of Rights Form and Explanation of Rights Form attached hereto and incorporated herein.

BY ORDER OF THE MEDICAL EXAMINERS COMMISSION THIS 17th DAY OF FEBRUARY, 2004.

STEPHEN J. NELSON, M.A., M.D.
Chairman
Medical Examiners Commission

CERTIFICATE OF SERVICE

I HEREBY CERTIFY that a true and correct copy of the foregoing has been sent by express mail this 18th day of February, 2004, to Shashi B. Gore, M.D., at the District Nine Medical Examiner Office, 1401 Lucerne Terrace, Orlando, Florida 32806.

VICTORIA G. MARSEY
Program Administrator
Medical Examiners Commission

Lost, Mishandled Evidence May Mean New Appeals

Reprinted with permission from:*Florida Prison Legal Perspectives*Vol. 6, Issue 6; ISSN#: 1091-8094

ORLANDO

Stunning revelations of forensic evidence missing from or mishandled by the Medical Examiners Office for Orange and Osceola Counties, located in Central Florida, shocked public defenders, defense attorneys and Floridians during October and may lead to a wave of new post conviction appeals by dozens or even hundreds of criminal defendants who are still in prison.

According to a report that was only recently released, during the mid-1990s, specifically in 1994 and 1995, the Orange-Osceola Medical Examiner's Office lost bullets, blood, hair and other evidence in murder cases without informing police, prosecutors, public defenders, or defense attorneys. Chief Public Defender Bob Wesley noted that at least 26 cases from 1994 and 1995 may be involved after he reviewed the 66-page report that was written in 1995 but that didn't surface until this September.

Among the findings of an in-house report were missing evidence lists and logs; bags and boxes of evidence in hundreds of cases that had been cut open or had their seals broken; bones, teeth and skulls without identification of any kind; and missing money and drugs, along, with missing bullets and tissue scrapings from under murder victim's fingernails.

"From a forensic standpoint, I was shocked," said Orange County sheriff's Sgt. Robert Corriveau, who was lent to the Medical Examiner's Office in 1995 to supervise an inventory after it was found the evidence stored there was in total disarray. He described what he found as a legal nightmare. Many evidence bags were ripped open or unsealed, there was no way to know how many cases had been cross- contaminated.

A further revelation that recently came to light is that Dr. Shashi Gore, who has run the Medical Examiner's Office since 1996, lacks board certification as a forensic pathologist. Worse, none of the other doctors there are board-certified forensic pathologists. Orange County officials who had knowledge of the massive problem 7 years ago but who kept quiet about it, and prosecutors who claim they only recently learned about it, are now claiming it's really no big deal. Others are saying different.

Carol Gross, office manager for the Medical Examiner's Office in 1995, said, "This put our credibility at high risk."

Joe DuRocher, Orange-Osceola chief public defender in 1995, said, "There is no question in my mind something as significant as this investigation should have been revealed to the public defender's office."

More than just murder cases may be impacted by this now-revealed fiasco. Insurance cases may also be affected. However, Orange County officials have stated they do not intend to review the 1994 and 1995 cases further without specific request from attorneys or law enforcement.

The following statement has been made by the Ninth judicial Circuit Public Defenders' Office:"Defendants and inmates who believe their cases may be affected by the controversy at the medical Examiner's Office should consider consulting an attorney. Assuming the fact that evidence problems exist(ed) at the Medical Examiner's Office, and that these problems were not previously disclosed at the time of trial or plea, an inmate might seek the advice of an attorney to discuss: (1) whether evidence in their case was mishandled, mislabeled, contaminated, lost or destroyed by the ME Office; (2) whether favorable exculpatory or impeachment evidence was suppressed related to the ME Office; (3) the general reliability, credibility, and competence of work performed by the ME's Office; and (4) whether they have a remedy, e.g. petition for writ of habeas corpus and/or motion for post-conviction relief under Florida Rule of Criminal Procedure 3.850."
[Sources: Orlando Sentinel, 9/30, 10/2, 10/5, 10/6, 10/11/02;
Ninth Judicial Circuit Public Defenders' Office]

FDLE

| Florida Department of Law Enforcement

Guy M. Tunnell
Commissioner | Medical Examiners Commission | P.O. Box 1489
Tallahassee, FL 32302
(850) 410-8600
Fax (850) 410-8621 |

February 4, 2004

MEMORANDUM

To: Stephen J. Nelson, M.A., M.D.
        Chairman, Medical Examiners Commission

From: Jon R. Thogmartin, M.D.
       Probable Cause Panel Chairman

Subject: Report of Probable Cause Panel reference Complaint against Shashi Gore, M.D., M.P.H.

In response to your memorandum of January 20, 2004, the Probable Cause Panel was convened on January 30, 2004 at 1:30 PM at the Florida Department of Law Enforcement Regional Operations Center in Tampa. All assigned members of the panel were present: Mr. Lane Rees, Mr. Robert Dillinger, and Dr. Jon Thogmartin. Also in attendance were members of the Commission staff: Ms. Vickie Marsey and Mr. Jim Luten. Staff members had already mailed the panel members a notebook of their findings and reference materials upon which they based their conclusions.

The first order of business was the election of a chairman, which Dr. Jon Thogmartin accepted. Next the panel reviewed the statutory reference, which established this panel as well as the procedures, which the panel and the Medical Examiners Commission would be following in these proceedings. Staff members then reviewed the reference material they had previously forwarded.

After extensive discussion the panel voted unanimously on the following:

> Probable cause exists that Dr. Shashi Gore has committed a violation of s. 406.075(1)(i), Florida Statutes, which states: *(1)A medical examiner may be reprimanded, placed on a period of probation, removed, or suspended by the Medical Examiners Commission for any of the following: (i) Negligence or the failure to perform the duties required of a medical examiner with that level of care or skill which is recognized by reasonably prudent medical examiners as being acceptable under similar conditions and circumstances.*

> The panel recommends whatever action, sanction, or penalty that would preclude Dr. Shashi Gore from performing any autopsies until June 30, 2004 when his appointment as District Medical Examiner ends. The Panel notes that it considered that fact that Dr. Gore has announced his intentions to retire as of this date, and that a Search Committee is being formed to identify a District Medical Examiner. The Panel also acknowledges Dr. Gore's long service in District 9, and allowing him to remain in his position as District Medical Examiner would only be intended to ease the transition to the new District Medical Examiner.

The panel approved the following report, which summarizes its findings as it addresses the twenty-five (25) enumerated concerns that the complainants had forwarded to the Medical Examiners Commission and to the Division of Medical Quality Assurance of the Florida Department of Health.

Committed to
Service - Integrity - Respect - Quality

ORANGE COUNTY GOVERNMENT
F L O R I D A

February 11, 2004

Stephen J. Nelson, M. A., M. D.
Chairman
Medical Examiners Commission
State of Florida
Tallahassee, Florida 32302

Re: Complaint against Shashi B. Gore, M. D.
        Alan Yurko case (Date of Death 11/27/97)

[handwritten:] Dr Gore agreeing to stop performing autopsies

Dear Dr. Nelson:

In consideration of the above matter, I would like you and other respected members of the Commission to know a few things below:

A.   I would stop performing autopsies with immediate effect from 2/13/04.

B.   While unpending the "pending" cases, I will consult with the Deputy Chief Medical Examiner and the Associate Medical Examiner. All pending cases will be thoroughly studied and evaluated in conjunction with the above doctors.

C.   I will restrict my activities primarily in completing the paperwork and finalizing my cases and the cases of other physicians.

D.   I will concentrate on the administrative duties and look after the investigative duties primarily.

E.   To prevent further recurrence of typos, misprints, or oversights, I have made it mandatory that all autopsy reports be checked twice for the accuracy before the reports go out.

Under these conditions, I request the Commission to consider the plan, which is laid out as above. I assure you that these reparative steps will go well ahead. We all want to make our Medical Examiner system efficient, accurate, and empathic while serving the citizens of our community.

If the Commissioners have any other useful suggestions, I would certainly implement those to improve the performance of the office.

Thanking you for your attention.

Sincerely,

Shashi B. Gore, M. D., M.P.H.
Chief Medical Examiner

DISTRICT NINE MEDICAL EXAMINER
Serving Orange & Osceola Counties
1401 Lucerne Terrace ▪ Orlando, FL 32806-2014
Telephone (407) 836-9400 ▪ FAX (407) 836-9450 ▪ e-mail: http://www.citizens-first.co.orange.fl.us

G. K. VEGA

ISSUE NUMBER – 1: FINAL ACTION ON ADMINISTRATIVE COMPLAINT AGAINST DR. SHASHI GORE. Dr. Nelson announced that the Medical Examiners Commission needed to take final action on the Administrative Complaint issued against Dr. Shashi Gore, the District 9 Medical Examiner. He pointed out that the packet contained copies of the Administrative Complaint which had been signed by Dr. Nelson on February 17, 2004; the Election of Rights which had been executed by Dr. Gore on March 11, 2004; and a letter of March 17, 2004 from Dr. Nelson to Dr. Gore in which the terms of Dr. Gore's probation were reviewed in detail. Dr. Nelson remarked that this arrangement would also allow for a clean transition for the newly appointed District 9 Medical Examiner when that person takes over subsequent to Dr. Gore's retirement. Dr. Nelson then noted that each Commission member at the meeting had received a copy of a letter from Dr. Gore, dated March 29, 2004, in which Dr. Gore acknowledged that he understood and agreed to follow the terms of his probation as summarized in the March 17, 2004 letter. The contents of these two referenced letters are as follows:

March 17, 2004

Dr. Shashi Gore
District 9 Medical Examiner
1401 Lucerne Terrace
Orlando, Florida 32806

Dear Dr. Gore:

This letter is to notify you of the receipt of your executed Election of Rights Form in Case # 04-01 by the staff of Medical Examiners Commission (MEC) on March 15, 2004. It is acknowledged that you chose Paragraph 3, which reads in part:

> I DO NOT ADMIT the allegations of fact in the Administrative Complaint, but hereby AGREE TO DISCIPLINE proposed by the Medical Examiners Commission Probable Cause Panel, to wit: PROBATION UNTIL JUNE 30, 2004, BASED ON YOUR CESSATION OF PERFORMING AUTOPSIES AND OTHER PROVISIONS LISTED IN YOUR LETTER OF FEBRUARY 11, 2004 TO DR. STEPHEN J. NELSON AS CHAIRMAN OF THE MEDICAL EXAMINERS COMMISSION (SAID LETTER BEING HEREBY INCORPORATED INTO THIS DOCUMENT AS EXHIBIT A), ALL SUCH ACTIONS ON YOUR PART BEING EFFECTIVE ON FEBRUARY 13, 2004.

In order to avoid any misunderstanding and to clarify the terms of your probation, I have attached both your letter of February 11, 2004 as well as the draft of the minutes of the February 12, 2004 Medical Examiners Commission meeting. It is clear from the minutes that it was the intent of both the Probable Cause Panel and the Medical Examiners Commission in its entirety that you remain "*out of the morgue*" and refrain from initiating any new casework activity until such time as your appointment as the District 9 Medical Examiner ends on June 30, 2004. Since you were not present at the February 12th MEC meeting, all of the details delineated for your probation might not have been known to you.

However, as you know, we have spoken on several occasions since the meeting and I have also spoken with your attorney about the fact that your probation covers not only you refraining from performing autopsies, but it also precludes you from initiating any new casework. Examining bodies at crime scenes and performing external examinations are also precluded because these are activities that may logically lead you to subsequently certifying these deaths.

Chapter 12

Bowling Green and Perry, Florida

I arrived at Hardee Correctional in June 2007. I had all my property from the private South Bay facility. Two pairs of Nike shoes, the Timberland boots, colored pencils, sunflower seeds, shave or haircut clippers, my nice gold necklace with charm I upgraded, black-colored boxers, sleeveless T-shirt, G-Shock watch, gold ring, cologne bottles, Pro 35 headphones, Sony digital radio, nice sunglasses and my mouth full of gold teeth with diamonds. While I was at South Bay, my cellmate knew the dentist, and I was able to pay cash to have my mouth done correctly.

The property sergeant at Hardee was a Filipino who was a dirty, slime, scum bucket. His thing was, take any property from an inmate to turn around and give it to his snitches for information. This sergeant personally searched my property. First he told me I couldn't have any property from a private facility on his compound. I called his bluff! He started to throw away damn near all my property in the garbage can. My blood boiled more and more as he just went through my personal belongings while laughing about it. I remained calm and thought I have plenty of money and can hustle everything he threw away back. Then he said, "Give me your necklace!" We fell out with words. I'm not going to write about it but will tell you that I ended up threatening the sergeant and being placed in confinement. He promised to make my life miserable as long as I was at Hardee. The captain, however, ordered him to put all my property in the bag and put it away pending the outcome of the investigation. The sergeant never wrote a disciplinary report. He knew he was wrong.

I was in confinement trying to figure out how I can transfer somewhere else. A good friend of mine was in general population and I paid some stamps to deliver him a "kite" explaining I needed his help in order to be transferred. My friend never received the "kite." The institution classification team told me I was playing games, and they were going to transfer me somewhere in the panhandle where all my property will be taken away. I was at Hardee for exactly 3 weeks. I got on the transfer bus with all my property and the Filipino sergeant looked like he wanted to beat me up. To tell you the truth, if the regional director's office was not inspecting that morning, the sergeant would have handcuffed me and beat me. So I was blessed. I would have reported it to the FBI, but it's better not to go through all that bullshit if you can avoid it.

I was on my way to the panhandle. Destination: Taylor Correctional Annex. We were a group of about fifteen. The procedure when inmates arrive at a prison is to be strip searched and search your property. There were three rows of chairs, five on each row. The chairs were right in front of a wall opposite side of the tables where your property is searched. We were told to sit down, face forward, and wait for your name to be called. If we looked back and get caught, suffer the consequences. As we stared at the wall, young female nurses would walk by shaking their butts in order to cause someone to crash. The officers knew these nurses would be fishing so they kept a close eye.

My name was called, and I was searched by a halfway civilized officer. The property he didn't let me keep, I was able to send home. I told him I would file a grievance and appeal certain items, which a few weeks later I was able to get back. None of the fifteen of us looked over and sweated a female nurse. What did happen was something I will never forget. A Cuban inmate was arguing with the officers searching his property about some sunglasses. About seven officers escorted him, handcuffed to a secluded room, and beat him unconscious. The poor Cuban's head was cracked open. It took staples to hold the wound together. I was housed in Lima dormitory. Every prison is different so Taylor Annex had a lot of bad and a thing or two good.

At the visiting park, officers harassed. The medical, dental and pretty much every other department was pathetic. I was even denied my request to continue the college courses. I was in Ku Klux Klan land once again. The use of force on inmates was a regular. My work assignment was inside grounds which meant I was going to cut grass with "Flintstone" lawnmowers. They believed in slaving inmates. We would push the Flintstone lawnmowers from 8:15 a.m. through 11:30 a.m. Stop to eat lunch and continue from 12:30 p.m. through 3:30 p.m.

No one in the state of Florida has been sentenced to hard labor. If this were the case, the sentence would have to be a lesser one. Yet inmates work for free in Florida. A normal sentence will be finished when you complete 85% of the sentence. On average, an inmate gets ten days gain time per month. Technically, inmates work and earn those ten days. What I have found out is the time an inmates earns in months or years, is now at times being supervised. For example, if you get a 20 year sentence under 85%, you'd do 17 years under the 85%. The remaining three years they want to put you on supervised release. This means some inmates will end up doing 100% of their sentence when the federal and state law required 85%.

I have seen so much neglectful action by classification officers it is a damn shame. They come to work with hateful hearts, like to see inmates down and will go out of their way to make the sentences hard and difficult. I'm not saying all correctional officials are this way, but the truth is there are more bad than there is good. Just like one bad apple spoils the others, so does a hateful officer reflect on the few good officers. It's always been this way.

I started to see around and get to know the movement. Even in Klan land, money talks, so I started to deal with a Mexican named Tank. This man was a tall, strong Mexican. Like a Mexican you would see in California prison documentary or something. Tank put me down with a white inmate who knew the officers that were about making money. We started to flood the prison with weed at first. Then came to find out cocaine and heroin moved fast also, so we sold a little bit of everything. I met a heavyset inmate whose brother owned half of the Tallahassee auto auction. I was buying cars directly from the half owners and then paying the one hundred dollars to have vehicles delivered to Orlando. Once in Orlando, Cynthia would pick up the cars and drive them to Palm Bay. I asked my mom if I could park a couple of cars in her driveway and the answer was no.

So I continued to handle my business on my own. My lawyer Stephenson had me transported to the Osceola County Jail in September 2007. I was in front of Judge Morgan requesting for the sheriff to handover all the evidence in my case as well as the medical examiner's office. While in the county jail, I called my Aunt Martina and arranged visit through a glass window. She had a friend at her house named Cathy who also offered to visit me. After the visit, Cathy and I stayed in touch through phone and letters. She lived in Kissimmee with her son Christian. Meanwhile, I was transported back to Taylor Annex Correctional Institution.

It was now around November 2007 shortly after my Boston Red Sox won another world series. I was housed in Lima dormitory again. I did not waste any time to make money and continue to pay for my lawyer. Stephenson explained I would need at least $10,000 to have a medical examiner to review the autopsy in my case. I already had plenty of money saved and had vehicles as assets. Lawyers can be expensive and therefore I was not going to stop the hustle. Cathy began to visit me in prison. She was born and raised in Colombia. Very nice, respectable woman who comes from a religious family. I did not tell Cathy how I was getting money but knew that one day I would have a lot of explaining to do.

Things got a hot at Taylor Annex, so I needed to exit. I had my lawyer contact the Department of Corrections in Tallahassee and scheduled an appointment with a psychiatrist. A couple of weeks later, I was in front of the doctor asking me how often officers beat inmates at Taylor. The doctor said if I told her the truth, she would see to it that I am transferred closer to Orlando. When I got back to Taylor, I did not tell anyone I was on my way to another prison. I collected most of my money and only sold to those with cash in hand or same-day Western Union. The Lima dorm sergeant was getting tips from her snitches that I was involved in illegal activities. She would search my assigned cell with no success. She would pull me over and pat me down to see if I had any shanks or cell phones.

The sergeant lady had a husband who worked in the midnight shifts. I already knew there would be a day he searches my cell at night. Instead, the sergeant man comes into my cell and asked for my new Cherry porno magazines. He told me if I lied I would be on his bad side. I reached in my locker, took some folders out, and handed him the yellow envelope between the folders. He took my magazines and didn't say a word. I didn't know what to do. Someone told this redneck about my porno magazines and who knows what else. I began to think way too much and knew I had to remain out of the spotlight because my transfer was any day. At about 11:30 p.m. that very same night, the sergeant calls me up to the officer station, asked me to open both doors and come in. I refused. I explained it would look bad if I'm in the officer's stations talking to him. I asked the sergeant to say whatever he needed to say through the flap. When he got up, all 300 and more pounds of him made me nervous. He walked toward the flap and said, "I know what you do and how you do it. But I like how you move. Here's your porno magazines back. I have eyes everywhere."

I knew there was big trouble in Little China! It was only a matter of time before officers paid me a visit I was not going to like and may very well end up in violence. When it rains, it pours. Seems like things happen on top of the other. Can you believe the very next day, an officer decided to put on his white Ku Klux Klan mask or whatever it's called in the officer station so all inmates can see him. I was like, "Oh shit." I could not believe what had taken place. It blew my mind at a time where I am trying to figure out what to do about the night shift sergeant, the officer with the mask was fired. Some black inmates became upset and slashed with a razor the faces of other white inmates. The violence was stopped quickly. I got woken up at 3:00 a.m. and was out of that hellhole a few days later. It could not come at a better time.

When I looked at the file and saw Tomoka Correctional, I felt blessed. I knew I would be closer to my mom in Sanford. Not that it was a big deal because my mom visits me once a month even if I am five minutes down the street. I have never been a priority number one or two or three for my mom. As I have grown older, I just accepted it and moved on. I've been doing things on my own since I was young anyway. I had a lawyer to pay and at the time, this is all that mattered. I thought my sister Selina would drop by to see me now that I was close to Orlando also, but she never showed up. I have never been important to her neither. It is what it is. Some families are close, and some are not. There is nothing one can do but move forward. Besides, I was not missing any visitations anyway. I've always been blessed to have friends visit me and asked how I'm doing.

Chapter 13

Daytona Beach, Florida

TOMOKA C.I. 2008

I arrived in Daytona Beach on January 3, 2008, my sister Selina's birthday. Tomoka was not a bad prison at all. Besides a few unprofessional officers, the rest were respectful and attentive. At the time, it had softball, basketball, big soccer field, tennis, flag football, and quite a few interesting programs. Blind services, which is reading books on a recorder for people around the world who are blind but are able to hear. Masonry, which is the building of homes with cement blocks and brick mailboxes. We could go to the institution church with our family every first Sunday of the month. The officers didn't bother any inmates or relatives in the visit park, and the wait for the family was thirty minutes to an hour.

Tomoka was not at a level of the South Bay CI, but it offered enough to keep us busy. That's the way things are supposed to be anyway. I settled in quickly. There were too many Puerto Ricans from Orlando and Kissimmee. I knew it could mean trouble because it is always one who causes a mess for all the others. I also knew a lot of people from Orlando, not just Puerto Ricans. I guess you already know I started to hustle once again. And let me tell you, there was money to be made in there at the time. I'm not going too much into detail, but in one month on average, I would make at least $4,000. If it was a good month, $5,000 or $6,000. This wasn't including all the cars I was still buying from the auto auction and reselling. Not including gold jewelry I bought and resold. Not including a couple more flips I had friends doing for me on the streets.

My lawyer was paid in full and Stephenson even told me he would do a trust account with all the extra money I gave him. This way he could do work, charge the account, and send me the work receipts. I hired the former deputy chief medical examiner of Orange Osceola to review the autopsy and provide his conclusion, Dr. Anderson. First, my lawyer had to go back to court several times and request for the judge to order the Medical Examiner's Office to release the entire autopsy documents, photos and other forensic results. They gave us a hard time. For some reason, they didn't want for any other experts to look at the first results by Dr. Gore. The medical examiner charged $500 an hour with a $2,500 retainer on average. I ended up paying a total of $9,300 for Dr. Anderson's opinion.

One day, an inmate was snorting depression pills (Wellbutrin). It makes people feel as if high on cocaine. The inmate got up and walked over to drink in the water fountain when his eyes rolled back, and he fell like a tree headfirst against the concrete floor. His forehead split wide open, blood was pouring out like a river. The officer called medical, and the waiting game began. Can you believe the nurse showed up twenty-eight minutes later?

I was housed in bravo dormitory. This was a two-man cell T building which inside looked like small housing projects. It is the dorm where Tomoka has always liked to house gang members, inmates with serious mental health issues, those who stay in and out of confinement and any other type of disciplinary history. Classification will also house inmates with life sentences. We were offered Spanish Bible study on Wednesdays. The pastor was allowed to bring in all types of Caribbean food on Christmas. The deal was you attend church on the regular, you feast for December 25th.

Not bad compared to how nasty and small portioned the food is served within the Department of Corrections. I was taken to the captain's office numerous times for urinalysis test. At 3:00 a.m., 6:00 a.m. and during counts. My cell would get searched, and the officers would never find any major contraband. On the other hand, inmates were dropping like flies with dirty urinalysis results and possession of narcotics. The institution staff went into panic mode. The K9 dogs would help with the searches more and more.

As we walked toward the recreation yard, searches would take place. Some inmates were found overdosed on the heroin and brought back to life. I was to the point where I did not want to go to the recreation yard because so many Puerto Ricans were living wild. They were stabbing, robbing, consuming drugs and circling up, talking up gossip like women. I had a $100 piece of heroin to deliver one evening around 6:30 p.m. As I walked toward the yard, all of a sudden the officers started to run everywhere screaming at all inmates to go back to their assigned dormitories. I felt a bad vibe, a very bad and unusual vibe. I handed the piece to the client and walked fast back to bravo dorm.

We were placed on lockdown immediately. Fire engine trucks and ambulances were on their way, and it was not looking pretty. As I looked out of our cell windows, dozens of rapid response team officers were marching toward all the dormitories with search equipment. We needed to find out and fast. One officer, upset and confused, explained a female officer was killed. I couldn't believe what I heard and automatically, I knew we were in for some heavy searches where a lot of my property will be taken and thrown away. By nighttime, the prison was full of all types of ranking correctional officers and Florida Department of Law Enforcement detectives. The lady apparently was stabbed twenty times or so, left butt naked for dead. At first I thought it was an escape attempt. But when I found out who it was, I couldn't help but think negative. The suspect had a history of sexual battery on record. Why this female officer was left alone with a predator, I'm still trying to figure that out. So much for the Florida Department of Correction motto, which states, "We never walk alone."

Several female officers quit within days after the murder. I don't blame them for doing so. We were searched Monday through Friday, 5:00 a.m. to 5:00 p.m. for a total of three weeks. Every day, a group of officers were brought in from the surrounding prisons. The assistant secretary or the secretary of the corrections department at the time was on TV with the Volusia county state attorneys promising to have the suspect on death row and be put to death within six months. The public, not knowing the law, must've been happy of the promising lies. Truth is, a death penalty case can take years to uphold in Supreme Court. Most death penalty cases are reversed to life sentences.

Here we are, ten years later, as I write this book and the accused was found guilty, sentenced to death and is still at Florida State Prison appealing. I have learned the Department of Corrections does not care about its employees. They paint a good picture of honor and all types of bullshit to make the officers feel special and wanted. At the end of the day, the inmates decide whether the officer goes home or not. Anything can happen at any given time around here. Even someone with a year left can have an emotional drop and simply take out an innocent bystander.

If you're reading this book and you're saying to yourself the percentage of assaults on officers is low, think again! Have you ever worked for a company where incidents happen but the supervisor is never told of the incidents? Or the supervisor finds out of the incident and turns a blind eye? The corrections department is full of incidents that never make it to the news. Incidents that never make it to supervisors. This is a place of secrets. A place of lies and deceit. There is a Department of Correction's annual report stating deaths, budgets, assaults on staff, and other lies for the public to think things are running smoothly.

A few months later, it was an early Sunday morning, 7:30 a.m. I was showering getting ready for a visit. When I looked out the shower window, I saw what turned out to be braided sheets made into ropes. Three inmates were climbing the fences. The last one couldn't make it and therefore all three climbed on the roof of bravo dormitory and sneaked back into their assigned cells. A sergeant just arriving on shift spotted the ropes and called for help. We were locked down again. The rapid response team started the searches again. Questions were asked, no one snitched. The FDLE was back in the crime scene. Once the news was involved, to satisfy the public once again, two black, two Hispanics and two white inmates were chosen to be placed in confinement under investigation. The administration knew they were wrong, but at the end of the day, we are nothing but numbers.

I was one of the Hispanics dragged in handcuffs and leg irons to confinement. I could not believe my luck. Out of all people, I get accused of attempting to escape. Once I was placed in the confinement cell, my roommate had a cell phone. I quickly called my lawyer and explained the situation I was in. After two weeks of refusing to answer questions, all six of us were released back into the general population in bravo dormitory. As we walked toward the dormitory, officers were escorting six other inmates: two blacks, two whites and two Hispanics. In less than five days, 400 inmates were transferred to other prisons and 400 new inmates arrived. I was not transferred! I didn't want to go anywhere. New people meant new money.

I started to give Cuban Eddie most of the heroin to sell because my name was mentioned too much. I had a feeling I would not last long if the drugs were causing inmates to crash. I was picked up by the captain and major. They told me I would be placed in confinement pending an investigation after searches in delta dormitory revealed syringes full of heroin. I had a couple of inmates pointing the finger at me. I was really upset because it was the beginning of November 2008 and the holidays were around the corner. I did November, December, and January and most of February in confinement. In the last week of February, I was labeled a security threat and transferred to Everglade's correctional institution in Miami, Florida. I was only at Tomoka ten months in general population and almost four months in confinement. I made the best of the ten months. Even while in confinement, clients were sending Western Union confirmation numbers for money owed. I was sad to leave Tomoka, Daytona Beach, Florida. But sometimes you have to do what you have to do in order to have a fighting chance of freedom. Remember that my attorney discovered the corruption and he was not working for free.

Chapter 14

South West 187th Avenue, Miami, Florida

I was told to pack my property; I was being transferred. I couldn't be any happier because I was reaching the four months in confinement. It was time to say goodbye to Daytona Beach. After placing handcuffs and leg irons on me, I was escorted from the confinement unit, Echo dormitory, to the transport bus. It was about 8:30 a.m. and there was movement of inmates all over Tomoka. I nodded my head to those I knew and didn't acknowledge any inmates who were trash. It was a bittersweet feeling. I didn't want to leave but at the same time I was glad to be out of confinement. I passed through Central Florida reception center in Orlando and was at South Florida Reception Center within a few days.

If any politicians want to see for themselves how nasty, dirty, horrible, lazy, unprofessional a prison can ever be, go to any dormitory in South Florida Reception Center. The cells are broken down completely. Some toilets may work, others don't. Some lights work, others don't. The windows are broken to the point that anyone could go right through it and be next to the dormitory. You won't get anywhere unless you hit the fence, but that's crazy. Bugs would fly in the ceiling; mosquitoes were as big as a small wasp. The food was terrible. Rats all over the dining hall along with roaches. The bathrooms looked like you went down into a septic tank. Shit everywhere with greenish mold. The only two things SFRC had were the officers didn't harass in the visit park, and they weren't going to use excessive force unless you got completely out of hand.

I got to Everglades Correctional in the last week of February 2009 and felt a big difference. At Tomoka Correctional in 2008, there were a few Hispanic and black officers. The majority was white though. Everglades was all black and Hispanic officers with a few, very few white. Again there wasn't any serious harassing. I found out that some black officers were beating inmates, but it wasn't on the regular. Those officers were eventually fired. The chapel was super great at Everglades. Every day, volunteers from all religions would come in to preach and counsel inmates. They were allowed to bring snacks and religious materials. The visitation was once every week, odd or even, Saturday, Sunday. I'm guessing they did it that way because a lot of families visit regularly.

One would think the corrections department would have the inmates build a bigger visiting park like they have inmates build everything else for free. It goes to show you the government only does what it is convenient for them. So much shit talking about how much officials care but when it comes down to the truth, it's nothing close to their claims.

I was housed in delta dormitory. I moved my way around the prison to see what was what. Come to find out there were numerous inmates working with the inspectors on a daily basis. These snitches would give information and the inspector made sure they were not transferred anywhere. You already know they were doing it in order to stay close to home in Miami! A Haitian friend of mine was working with the female officer and explained to me what exactly was going on. I needed more time before I began to hustle again.

Right before I left Tomoka, classification had suspended my visiting privileges for one year. My mind was focused on how I could obtain a reversal through the grievance process and start to get my visits again. To make matters worse, my assigned classification officer at Everglades was a black lady with bright neon orange hair who had a history of attempting suicide. This lady felt I should not get my visits back ahead of time. She sure was wrong! One thing I learned in all the years of being imprisoned is you don't write a grievance on any official complaining about petty things. It will never work! High-ranking officials will cover for the officer no matter how wrong he or she may be. What you do is, wait and see where the officer commits a serious misconduct. Sleeping, excessive use of force, fraud, the destruction of state property and anything else that they will have no other choice but to suspend or terminate the officer. Through an inmate from Caguas, Puerto Rico, who worked in the classification building, I was told my classification officer would throw away inmate request forms and grievances. Most of the time, anyone could walk in her office and find the paperwork balled up in her garbage can. The lady felt as if she could get paid and do little work.

There was something wrong with the dining hall, and I couldn't determine what it was. The portions of food were too low while Hispanics and blacks were employed for food services. That combination was not adding up. Usually when a minority is in charge, usually, the food will be somewhat close to its standard. I never did find out what exactly was happening until one day the feds came to arrest the food service director for fraud. I was not surprised but instead a little sad that a person can cut the portion of an inmate meal and pocket money on the side. The old trick in the book: the warden gives bonuses to directors who keep cost of food low! A bonus based on starving an inmate.

On my way to the recreation yard one day, a Hispanic inmate decides to sneak into a dormitory, stab another inmate into vegetable status, and then sneak back out to the yard on time. You might've said it was like being a hitman for the mafia or something. I mean this dude not only went in a dormitory unassigned to him, unnoticed, but he walked back out of the dormitory unnoticed. The warden was an older Cuban lady. She ordered a transport bus that holds 51 and made it to be filled up with nothing but Hispanics. I was not one of the chosen and thank God for that because the bus was heading all the way up to the panhandle. The men were upset because they were all paying for actions committed by someone else. I'm sure you heard about the saying, when it rains it pours?

Not even a month later, someone called in that there was a bullet and a gun in the prison. That was not fun at all. We all were on lockdown again. The Miami-Dade SWAT team were on the roofs of the dormitories watching while all inmates were escorted back and forth to the dining hall. They all watched the correction officers conduct a thorough search of the prison. The reports of a gun or bullets are handled seriously because sometimes they will find what they're looking for. In this specific case, nothing was found except for shanks, drugs and cell phones. One day I was talking to Cathy over the pay phone, and she explained that an inmate from Tomoka using a cell phone I left behind, called and told her I was going to the visit park to see different women. She automatically called him a frog, which for Colombians that means snitch. She went on to explain he was a chump for snitching and if he called again, she would call the prison and do the same to him. This goes to show you how hateful and jealous people can be. I have never been the type to hide what I do and don't do from my girl. She understood different women did different things for me on the streets, so how else could I plan and execute? Certain things one can't talk about over the phone, only in person. It's not like I was kissing up on someone other than my girl neither. These women friends of mine were getting paid out there. I wasn't dealing with scary soft women. They were strong hearted and dedicated who knew how to blend in the streets when they needed to do so. No drama ever happened to any of them. At least we all worked together the right way.

Day in and day out, I watched so-called gang members walk directly to the inspector's office and sit in the office, talking, for hours at a time. I watched those same gang members get caught with drugs, cell phones and not do any confinement time. In this Florida prison system, anything goes. There's no unity, no respect and definitely very few attempting to educate themselves. It was bad when I came in and now it is worse. Society has change so much that when men come into prison, their way of living is really messed up. They walk around with no morals, no dignity and no plan in life. This young generation has been raised to accept homosexuality and therefore walk around prisons like predators hunting sex. It's sad! What will make anyone laugh are inmates who act tough and hard, but they allow oral sex from another man. When confronted, they say it's not being gay. Don't people know that pitching or catching is the same game? It's all homosexual activities!

Speaking for myself, I believe in man and woman marriage only. I do not respect homosexuality. However, I do not go around pointing fingers and judging. We all have to answer to God one day, and we all have to worry about our own problems. One day, I went to the barbershop for haircut. There was a young, slim Puerto Rican man cutting hair claiming he knew what he was doing. What made me stay away from him was how openly he was talking about doing business. I caught a bad feeling and didn't answer directly to any comments he was making. A few days later, as I walked through the center gate toward the dining hall, the officers posted up on the wall a news article reporting on an officer who was set up with marked bills, and two ounces of cocaine. Not surprisingly, it was the slim Puerto Rican barber. I'm not sure as to whether he is working to get time cut off his sentence or if he does it for free. What I do know is his actions were and will always be slimy! Again this goes to show you how these men are thinking and acting. It's disgusting!

In the early 2000s, many prisons across the United States began experiencing cell phone contraband problems. Don't get me wrong, it's absolutely no problem to us. For officials, as they claim, inmates can handle drug transactions, threatening victims and escape. In an attempt to scare inmates of ever owning or using a cell phone, inmates with short sentences who were caught with a cell phone were charged with a third-degree felony, punishable by up to five years in prison. When Everglades correctional sent the first one to a Dade County Courthouse, the judge told the prosecutor, "Don't ever bring such a case to my courtroom again." The judges are flooded with serious cases and have no time to handle a cell phone charge made up by the Department of Corrections.

From time to time, I hear of someone going through the same thing but only in places where it's secluded. Places where the courthouses are not full of cases and have nothing else better to do. I have been a subscriber to the *USA Today* newspaper for many years. I enjoy reading news from around the world and the United States. I also love all types of sports. I was reading the front page of the newspaper about a famous, well-respected medical examiner professor named Dr. Douglas R. Shanklin. I called and got his address at the University of Tennessee Medical Center. I wrote to Dr. Shanklin a short to the point letter. I explained the medical examiner Dr. Gore botched the autopsy in my case, and I have been sentenced to life because of the corruption. About three months later, in 2009, Dr.

Shanklin called my lawyer Stephenson, asked for $1,000 and the autopsy report. Stephenson agreed! But Dr. Shanklin said clearly, "If he has nothing wrong, I will not waste my time." This meant if he did not see any negligence within the autopsy, he would back away quickly. I instructed Stephenson to start the process with Dr. Shanklin while we waited for Dr. Anderson's autopsy report. If Dr. Shanklin requested more money, he would be paid in full immediately. I was worried because Dr. Shanklin only charged a $1,000 fee. I was waiting for him to come back and asked for $10,000 later. Maybe even more.

So now I had a lawyer and two medical examiners working on my case. I also had another private investigator at my lawyer's request, to go out and find another witness who came forward to the sheriff's office but was turned away. These Florida sheriffs only want to know bad things about you. Anytime a person has something good to say about you, not all, but a good amount of sheriffs will either throw away the statements or not collect the statements at all. While everything was going on with my case, I decided it was time to strike a blow at the classification officer about getting my visits back. I got a carbon copy request form. That is, white on top, yellow in the middle and pink at the bottom. The department did away with carbon copy request because supposedly it no longer can be afforded. I wrote, "I have submitted several requests in regard to my visitation suspension and have received no answer. Please do not throw away my request forms and allow for a review of my visits." What the classifications lady did not know was I filed a grievance directly to the warden and Cathy e-mailed the warden about the classification lady misconduct. It worked!

In less than a week, the assistant warden approved my visits once again and suspended the classification officer. Once the neon orange-haired lady came back to work, she had me transported on a van to South Florida Reception center where I waited to be transferred to Clermont, Florida, Lake Correctional Institution. It all turned out good for me because I got my visits back and my first blow, I didn't have to go far for a second blow and Clermont, Florida, is close to my relatives and Kissimmee, Orlando, and Sanford. I was going to put the inspector general's office on Everglade's classification for not wanting to approve my visits but God made it work out. I was kicked out of Everglades correctional in September 2009. The only thing that hurt me a little was that Cynthia was upset at me and decided to fall back on her help. We talked during a visit and couldn't come to an agreement. Cathy had a Dominican friend in Jacksonville named Jane Lynn who stepped in to fill Cynthia's shoes. Jane Lynn was not at the level Cynthia was in, not even close, but I did teach her a thing or two, and we made money together. The problem was Jane Lynn worked a nine to five and could not fully dedicate time. But again, we made it work. Everglades was a waste of time for me because I did not hustle. All the money that came in from March 2009 through September 2009 was made out in the streets, not in prison. I took the good with the bad and kept it moving! I always heard about Lake Correctional and how it was running. There I was, on my way to Central Florida.

LAKE C.I. 2010

We headed out to Lake Correctional early in the morning. There wasn't too many of us, maybe fifteen. As the bus went through some parts of Orlando, memories would come to mind. I turned on my radio, was back and forth listening to 102 jams and Rumba 103.1. My favorite music is salsa but I listen to a little hip-hop also. The choice in music comes from living up North and in the island of Puerto Rico. Most of the music I listened to is old school. For some reason, the new generation just can't sing or rap anymore.

Lake correctional was established in 1975. The rumor is that prior to 1975, it was an immigrant workers camp. I'm pretty sure it was! The prison is built on a hill with what's classified as a lake in the middle but looks more like a big pond. There are turtles, ducks, and gators. Many years ago inmates would go fishing in this pond-looking lake. Inmates swam and hang out by the water. All of that did not exist when I arrived September 2009. Although I did see plenty of inmates take officers on high-speed chases and dive into the lake in order to get rid of the contraband. The searching of our property was quick and easy. The officers were a good mix of whites, Hispanics and blacks. I guess it was because the warden was black too. I was housed in echo dormitory. I met my roommate on some dangerous terms because I walked in the cell, and he was getting ready to run down the stairs and stab someone he had a fight with. I placed my property on the top bunk and didn't unpack until my new roommate was done. Blood was all over the quad as both inmates stabbed each other and argued. After a while it was over with. The blood was cleaned by other inmates, and it was like nothing happened. The wounds were stitched with homemade needles, alcohol pads and triple antibiotic ointment.

The building was a butterfly-style dormitory. Four quads, each housing about fifty-six inmates. Almost everyone had a cell phone. There were so many, at one point, you could buy a used one for $75 in canteen food. There was plenty of liquor, so I started to drink on the weekends. My assigned classification officer was a nice, professional middle-aged lady. She handled all her responsibilities and even answered all request forms quickly. We could go to the law library every day, and the recreation yard was open daily too. The officers were not into beating inmates, which is always a plus. Lake Correctional is one of the biggest, if not the biggest mental health hospital for inmates.

The most expensive inmate in the state of Florida was an inmate with my last name. The story on this mentally challenged kid housed in the hospital was that he originally came into prison with a few years sentence. Another inmate stole from his locker a few hygiene items. A Hispanic gang put pressure on him to handle business, and he killed the thief. A judge gave him an additional life sentence for the murder. The results were devastating. He lost his mind completely. The medical helicopter would land at Lake numerous times a month in order to save this kid. He was opening up his stomach, the intestines would come out like worms. He would cut against the artery vein and bleed to death. Medics brought him back to life over and over again. The prison doctors and nurses just wanted him to die already. The price tag to maintain him was $140,000 a month. Sadly, there are other inmates, lost souls just like him, at the hospital always. Inmates who got lost in the system. They don't have a family or their family doesn't care.

Right before I arrived at Lake, another murder occurred. Two inmates, one serving a life sentence and the other with around six months left to go home, broke into an older man's locker. Do you know what was stolen? A honey bun! When the older Hispanic man found out who did it, he killed the first one he could get his hands on. That turned out to be the young male with six months left. Can you imagine what his family felt when they finally were notified of his death? While I'm on the subject, when an inmate dies in the Florida Department of Corrections, the families of the victim sometimes get notified a week later. These nasty officials will spoil evidence if they have to in order to cover all tracks. It doesn't matter if it's inmate on inmate or officer on inmate violence. By the way, the accused murderer is on death row now. For a honey bun! Some people want the respect at all cost!

Don't think of me wrong, but I started to hustle again. It wasn't by choice, it was by demand. Dr. Anderson finished the autopsy report, and my lawyer was ready to file. I paid another $5,000 for the newly discovered evidence motion and had to set aside $3,000 in case the court set a hearing, and Dr. Anderson would come in to testify his conclusion. Then I had to pay another $1,700 to the private investigator the lawyer recommended because the private investigator found the witness. The old lady, under oath, explained she told a detective in my case she had information to give on my behalf. But the detective did not follow up with obtaining the statement and forwarding the evidence to the prosecutor.

The lady said she knew Tamara. She went to say that Tamara spoke to her and explained she was forced to attend the trial. That she had a feeling I did not harm anyone. I had a conversation with my lawyer, Stephenson, and was anxious to file both new witness statements. Stephenson convinced me that the medical examiner corruption was a "home run." That I shouldn't worry about the new witness's statement until we had the results from the motion he was preparing.

In November 2009, my beautiful mom gave me a visit for Thanksgiving. This was such a surprise that I told everyone else not to visit that Thursday. My mom would visit me every few months and got a little better with once a month visit. But never did my mom visit on any holidays. I am not going to mention my sisters or the rest of the family because they visit when their guilty conscience have built up so much that it's time to stop by. Anyhow I enjoyed spending Thanksgiving with my mom. I always enjoy every single visit with my mom even when we don't agree on certain things throughout the visit.

My grandfather passed away toward the end of 2009. The news of him having cancer made me upset that I wasn't able to be out to help him pull through. This was the man that raised me. I did everything I could to help him, each time he accepted my help. I forwarded Western Union to him, gave him a Chevy Malibu 2001 in great condition with low miles, clothing, shoes, and jewelry. I still felt it wasn't enough but at least I did. I represented! Most of my relatives really didn't help like they were supposed to. People were living their lives and not worried about anyone else including family.

My grandfather was not the easiest person to get along with but no matter what I respected him and loved him unconditionally. He left behind a companion who was not my grandmother but at least the old lady helped with washing clothes and all the little things women do around the house. Some of my relatives didn't agree with the lady, none of them stepped up to help. It's easy to point the finger at others and judge. When it comes time to sacrifice and be there for someone, people make 100 excuses to justify themselves.

In the beginning of 2010, I received a letter from a Dominican female who lives in Spanish Harlem, New York. I wrote back and requested her number. I explained I was in a relationship and could not start with anyone else. I also was sincere about my hustles, and she understood. Rosa ended up renting an apartment five miles down from Lake correctional. She was not a bad person. Being raised in New York helped her to be smart in the things I needed her to do there in the streets. We made plenty of money together. I believe she might still be using some of the hustles I taught her. After all, she grew up poor and understood the struggle. My attorney was working on the motion and that is all I had on my mind.

I wrote to the American Civil Liberties Union in New York and express my concerns with the Florida Justice System. I received a response stating they don't accept criminal appeal cases but would take the time to read through all the information I mailed. I gave up on them quickly. The response was not what I was looking for. I must have written to 1000 different organizations, lawyers, and doctors about my case. Some lawyers didn't have a license to practice in Florida. Some doctors stole my money. Thousands of dollars at a time. I just kept making money and putting it into good use.

At Lake Correctional, snitches would get knocked out all the time so I was able to move around more freely. I was able to take more risk. Many people were hustling at Lake, some big with the quantity and other small. Cash money moved around good also. With a lot of drugs and contraband in a prison, comes a lot of drama.

One morning during 7:30 a.m. count, the sergeant in echo dorm conducted a count allowing the cell doors open. This way he didn't have to come back in the quad after a count and lock the cell doors open. As the sergeant walked around counting, he ran in a cell demanded an inmate to hand over the cell phone. The shocked inmate jumped from the top of the bunk and faked as if he was going to hand the sergeant the cell phone. Instead, he threw the cell phone out the cell and into the first floor knowing another inmate would grab it quickly. All of a sudden we heard fighting. The sergeant and the inmate we're going blow for blow and moving out of the cell into the top tier. When I peep out of my cell, I was like, "Oh shit." The sergeant's feet were halfway across the railing and getting ready to be dropped from the second floor to the first. I knew that if the sergeant landed on his head, he would die. The officer in the officer station came out running, leaving the station alone. If he didn't, the sergeant would have dropped like a stuntman in a movie. This was no movie though, this was a life or death situation. The sergeant made it out alive with some bumps and bruises. The inmate got beaten by a group of officers and escorted to a van. Destination: Florida State Prison Supermax housing.

I had to hide my cell phone while the doors were still open so I walked across the quad and gave it to my hold down man. As I walked back, a white shirt majors spotted me and came running into our quad. He handcuffed me and sat me down on the bench. The major ask me why I was walking from one side to the other while everyone is supposed to be on their bunks sitting. I answered short and simple. I was going to take a shower before the search team came, and we would be unable to shower. He didn't believe me and left me handcuffed behind my back for hours. I just kept quiet. The search team never showed up but all of us were locked down for the remainder of the day. My shoulders were burning up from all the hours of pain. The major came back that afternoon and said he knew the cell phone was in the quad and in twenty minutes there better be a cell phone in the middle of the day room. Not even two minutes later, a cell phone slid across the floor and under the TV. When the major came back, he was satisfied and left. What the major didn't know was that the cell phone he had in his hand was a spare, used for parts only.

I met a young Cuban man called Primo. He was locked up at the age of fifteen for arm robbery and was almost done with the twelve-year sentence Broward County gave him. This kid was the exception of the young, ignorant generation coming into prison. He was respectful, humble, and was willing to educate himself as much as possible. Primo is heavy-handed. A knockout artist like Tyson back in the old days. He was training with an older Puerto Rican man from New York who had mixed martial arts experience. As the months went by, he got better and better. He was taking the MMA training very seriously. It was a good thing because he kept out of trouble. He was occupied mentally and physically. As I write this book, Primo is fighting out of Hollywood, Florida, and is a top prospect in mixed martial arts. Last time I heard from him, he settled in with a female and were expecting a baby. Whoever said all inmates don't amount to anything upon release are wrong.

The problem in Florida is that there is no rehabilitation and therefore most inmates come back to prison. This system is designed and will continue to be designed with the intention that inmates come right back to prison. If inmates were educated with certifications and degrees, less inmates would come back and the government would be forced to close prisons. If prisons close, there are less jobs for the country folks in the Ku Klux Klan which are unable to work anywhere else. Then the Republican Party would lose votes. I am not a Republican or a Democrat. I believe both are full of lies, corruption, and don't care about the American people.

However, the truth is, Republicans go to the extent when it comes to keeping men and women in prison. Conservatives will lock you up and throw away the key. Liberals will give a second chance. We don't have to go far to see right now what I am talking about. Who came out of Alabama and was appointed attorney general by Trump? Google and read on his history. When the United States Supreme Court Justice passed away, why did most people want Obama to elect the next justice? So that liberals could dominate the Supreme Court and pass laws that would result in preventing mass incarceration. The United States houses the most inmates in the world. California, Texas, and Florida have the largest amount of incarcerated individuals within the United States. California passed a law, which considers the age of twenty-four or less, a juvenile. Texas passed a law allowing inmates to file habeas corpus motions if the forensic evidence in the case was botched. That means I would be free right now in Texas and California.

Florida refuses to raise the juvenile age and continuously denies motions arguing mishandled forensic evidence. The new "game" Florida has implemented now is barring inmates from filing motions of post-conviction relief. Enough said! It is sad that all good things come to an end, right? Some people like to eat too much and become overweight. Some people like consuming alcohol too much and become alcoholics. Some people like running too much and end up with bad knees. Some people like having different sex partners and end up with a sexually transmitted disease. I was too comfortable at Lake Correctional. Under the circumstances, that is! There was a newly built prison in Live Oak, Florida, named "Suwannee." This hellhole of a place, consists of work camp, main unit and annex. It was time to open up the annex! Word got around Lake Correctional that 150 inmates were going to be transferred to Suwannee. We didn't know when but we were told sooner than later. A couple of inmates at Lake who snitched for the administration gave tips on who were the ones "flooding" and "causing trouble" around the prison.

On October 10, 2010, fifty inmates were shipped to Suwannee. I was not one of them but on the same Monday, my name was seen on the next transfer list. My heart must've came out my butt when I found out. I had a half-dozen people call central classification in Tallahassee to stop the transfer and leave me close to home. It didn't work!

On October 13, 2010, I was on my way to Suwannee. I hid my cell phone and about 100 OxyContin pills. The head of classification sent a memo to Suwannee warning we might be traveling with all types of contraband. Nobody cared. We did not know what Suwannee was about, and we were not leaving anything behind. By the way, remember the inmate who set up the officer at Everglades Correctional with marked money into ounces of cocaine? He arrived at Lake a few weeks before my transfer to Suwannee and quickly set up a female, a girlfriend of another inmate. The low life scumbag said he needed someone in the streets to go pick up two ounces of cocaine with his money. The poor female was arrested on the spot.

(Note from the author) from start to finish, I intend to be fully honest with all the stories within this book. I will also attempt to provide clear and convincing evidence in order to back my comments and arguments. This will be accomplished with court documents.

Forensicdimensions

November 16, 2009

To:
Christopher Stephenson, Esq.
Attorney At Law
Davis And Stephenson, P.L
227 N. Magnolia Avenue
Suite 101
Orlando, FL 32801

From:
William R. Anderson MD

re: Collado, Xavier (FL v Vega)

At your request I have reviewed the file relative to the death of Xavier Collado and have the following observations and opinions.

The analysis of this case included review of the medical records as well as the autopsy photos, autopsy report, microscopic slides and ancillary studies. It is my conclusion that several significant issues are evident relative to the initial review and forensic analysis by the original medical examiner involved in this case, and I have concluded that the original autopsy report is not scientifically sound and draws an erroneous conclusion based on recent advances in medical science, which I discuss below.

Until recently, the concept that a relatively innocuous 'short distance' fall could result in death was often unrecognized by medical trauma investigators, including many medical examiners. This was the predominant medical opinion in 1999, though shortly thereafter a series of articles began to populate the medical field and it is now understood that a 'short distance' fall may be a reasonable cause of death when certain medical evidence is apparent.

The difference in mechanism between a high-velocity impact injury resulting in diffuse neuronal axonal injury—as in a homicidal assault situation—and a lower energy situation in which a moving head impact caused a subdural hemorrhage with subsequent increased intra-cranial pressure related brain injury, was often not appreciated and consequently mis-diagnosed before approximately 2001.

A number of studies in the literature over the past several years have addressed the issue and have shown that relatively benign moving head injuries can result in the same type of injury we see in this case—specifically a moving head impacting a stationary object or

1630 Bridgewater Drive   Heathrow, FL 32746   (407) 333-3512

137

Collado, Xavier (FL v Vega)
11/16/09
pg 2

surface with resulting accumulation of blood in the sub-dural space—a space occupying lesion with subsequent brain compression[1,2,3,4]

This appears to be the case in the above-listed case in which the medical examiner interpreted the brain injury as a high velocity process, and described as not being consistent with a lower velocity process, despite the fact that the mechanism of death is consistent with a 'mass effect' resulting from a subdural hematoma.

Specific histological tests have been available, for a number of years, to aid in the microscopic analysis of the brain tissues in order to determine the presence of absence of a high-energy diffuse axonal injury. These Immunological histochemical studies—which were not performed in this case prior to the final determination of the mechanism of death—can be critical factors in making the differential diagnosis between inflicted and accidental head trauma.

The omission of these studies represents a significant departure from accepted forensic medical practice which, had they been done, would have supported the diagnosis of a low-impact, probably accidental, injury in this particular case.

The medical examiner indicated that he was unable to determine the ages of any of the contusions although no microscopic analyses were done of the areas of injury. It is possible to determine differences in ages of injuries in many cases through the changes that occur in the tissues secondary to the body's physiological responses to injured tissue—often quite helpful in determining differences in ages of injuries.

The failure to collect and analyze these tissues again reflects a serious deficiency in the analysis that led to the final conclusion as to the manner and mechanism of the death. It is clear that the timing of the injuries is a critical component of the analysis required to determine the manner and mechanism of death, and how specific injuries relate to the death—or conversely whether they were consequential to that death.

This determination of age of injuries may also be critical in associating or excluding specific individuals as having access to the victim when the injuries actually occurred.

Certain injuries, such as the area of tearing in the frenulum of the upper lip were considered as a sine qua non in the diagnosis of intentional abuse for a number of years. Careful scientific analysis, however, has determined—and reported in the literature—as being a very non-specific finding, simply indicating that some type of trauma has taken place, often no more sinister than an accidental fall. This development in medical science has occurred since 1999 and is a torn frenulum is no longer regarded as direct evidence to intentionally inflicted trauma.[5]

Although the medical records indicate that the child had a significant abnormal elevation of the white blood count upon admission—indicating that the injury had been on-going for a significant period of time prior to admission—there was no explanation of these

1630 Bridgewater Drive   Heathrow, FL 32746   (407) 333-3512

Collado, Xavier (FL v Vega)
11/16/09
pg 3

findings by the medical examiner in either his autopsy report or case notes. This is important in the timing of the injuries and should have been an integral part of the analysis, although it appears that these records, if reviewed at all, were not addressed— again constituting a departure from accepted forensic practice.

A recent study released in February 2009,[6] by the National Academy of Sciences has indicated that in many cases, testimony by forensic scientists is based upon suppositions not supported by objective scientific evidence and theories—too often being anecdotal based upon unsupported supposition rather than hard data. This is certainly the situation in this case.

1630 Bridgewater Drive   Heathrow, FL 32746   (407) 333-3512

Collado, Xavier (FL v Vega)
11/16/09
pg 4

In view if these significant deficiencies in the analysis that led to the conclusions to which Dr. Gore testified in this case and the newly discovered changes in medical science, it is my opinion that the findings do not pin-point any time frame as to when the injuries may have occurred or how they occurred, and consequently should not be used to single out any particular potential perpetrator, and also do not exclude, for the reasons listed above, accidental trauma as the manner of death.

It is my opinion that, based upon the available forensic data, it is absolutely reasonable that Xavier Collado died from an accidental fall and that the conclusions based upon the autopsy examination performed by Dr. Sashi Gore is not scientifically sound and not based upon principles of reasonable scientific and medical certainty — often even ignoring information available to the scientific community at the time of the evaluation.

It is also my opinion that, if a competent medical examiner preformed the autopsy of Xavier Collado today, she or he would reasonably not opine with any reasonable degree of medical certainty, that Xavier Collado's death was the result of a homicide to the exclusion of other probable mechanisms, including accidental trauma.

1. Plunkett, J. Am J Forensic Medicine & Pathology 2001: 22 (1-12)

2. Denton, S.: Am J Forensic Medicine & Pathology 2003: 24 (371-376)

3. Howard, M. British Journal of Neurosurgery: 1993: pp335-365

4. Donohoe, M. Am J Forensic Medicine & Pathology 2003: 24 (239-242)

5. Maguire, S., Hunter, B. dt al:, Arch Dis Child. 2007;92(12):1113-1117; doi:10.1136/adc.2006.113001

6. Strengthing Forensic Sciences! n the US. National Academy f Sciences Report; twww.nasonline.org/site/DocServer/Forensics Report.pdf?docID...

1630 Bridgewater Drive   Heathrow, FL 32746   (407) 333-3512

William R. Anderson MD

curriculum vitae

autobiographical sketch:

MEDICAL SCHOOL:

University of Miami School of Medicine
Miami, Florida
MD 1968

RESIDENCY TRAINING:

Strong Memorial Hospital
University of Rochester School of Medicine
Rochester, New York
1968-1970
Anatomic Pathology

Duke University Hospital
Duke University School of Medicine
Durham, North Carolina
1973-1974
Cardiac Pathology
Clinical Pathology

University of North Carolina Medical Center
University of North Carolina School of Medicine
Chapel Hill, North Carolina
1974-1976
Forensic Pathology
Clinical Pathology

BOARD CERTIFICATION:

American Board of Pathology
1976
Anatomic & Forensic Pathology

1980
Clinical Pathology

Chapter 16

Swantanamo Bay

Live Oak, Florida

SUWANNEE C.I. 2013

Fifty of us arrived at Suwannee Correction at around 8:30 a.m. As the bluebird backed up into the sally port, we noticed about thirty officers with every different metal detector device you can possibly think of. I knew it was going to be a very long day. The searches were thorough. The officers spoke country. Out of thirty, maybe three were there to do the job and not mistreat us. The rest, well, let me just explain I had no idea I was once again in Ku Klux Klan land. Everyone made it to the dormitory without any complications. The

Suwannee Annex has ten dormitories and each one was closed except for the one where they started to house us in. We were 150 moving all around all over the prison with no problem. I was surprised with everything there! The food was hot and a decent amount. New clothing, new mattress, new cells, new bedsheets, and we were asked what type of work assignment we wanted. There might have been a few black officers but they mostly turned out to be okay. The visitation was great! I could wear my shoes to visit park and overall the officers respected the visitors. The only bad thing at that time was all the gates within the prison. Going to visit, I had to go to a total of eight doors/gates. There is a big guard tower in the middle, and the recreation yards are super small.

This is one of the reasons why Suwannee was named "Swantanamo Bay." Just one reason! All good things come to an end, right? Buses started to bring in inmates from all over the state and by June 2011, a new warden arrived. We called the warden "No neck." This was because he walked around with no neck to his body. It's hard to explain, but he looked like his shoulders were pushed all the way up to his neck. Within one month, about 80% of the officers we're transferring to work at other prisons. But not before warning us how bad Suwannee was going to get. This warden had a plan of harming, killing and mentally breaking down inmates. To do such a thing, he had to scare off the good officers and bring in his made-up team. His main man was the colonel. The officers were what we call "reject officers."

At Charlotte Correctional, a black inmate was killed by officers so the ones under investigation ended up at Suwannee. At Florida State Prison, another black inmate was dropped down the stairs, killed while handcuffed to the back. These officers under investigation ended up at Suwannee. At Mayo Correctional, another tortured but not killed. All the officers in that investigation were sent to Suwannee. Most female officers chewed tobacco in their mouth, "dip." The Suwannee Annex quickly became a mafia of officers down with the "program" of emotionally, physically and mentally killing inmates. Believe me when I tell you that there's way too many incidents and deaths to write in this book about Suwannee.

Around that time, the Department of Corrections had a new secretary, and she came in pretending to put a stop to officer misconduct. Arrests were made here and there. But nothing close to how it should have been handled. They needed to terminate officials from the top to the bottom. You kill a snake by the head, not the tail. The officers formed "cliques" or better known as teams. On each shift, these teams were out to beat inmates. The colonel specifically requested for classification to arrange for "trouble" inmates to arrive each week in order for his officers to be able to discipline harder. We were known as "pieces of shit" to the colonel and all the teams he influenced mentally. An inmate by the last name of Jimenez was caught one night with a cell phone. Jimenez did not argue, resist, or even say a word. Upon being housed in confinement, different shifts took turns spraying Jimenez with "gas." All of his personal property, sheets, and clothing were taken. He was left with a mattress, butt naked in freezing cold weather. The confinement unit has air-conditioning, so cold, the officer walked around with jackets in the middle of the summer.

One day, we lined up to go eat in the dining hall. If caught talking on the way there or back, we were told to return to the dormitory and denied food. These decisions would cause for inmates to be angry and then give the officers a reason to use excessive force. One inmate was caught talking. He refused to go back to the dorm. The officers beat him down so bad, they left all the blood on the concrete like a murder scene or something. When we went by, the officers would yell out to us, "This is how we do it here."

The visitation park was very small, and they made it even smaller by putting gates outside. We were harassed on every angle. The officers would harass visitors every weekend. Visitors were told to change clothing on a regular. One female sergeant told me I couldn't kiss my girl in the mouth. Then she told me I couldn't hold hands. I guess the sergeant felt she was above the law and started to tell visitors inappropriate comments. After a few weeks, she was moved to the laundry department. The colonel replaced her with another female sergeant who was just as bad. It was hard to find a civilized officer because the employees had to be down with the "program" or work somewhere else.

With all the pressure and abuse in the hands of all officials, come retaliations, assaults on staff. While most inmates would not hit back, some would. The violence escalated and escalated. We were on seven-day lockdowns at least every other month. Sometimes sooner! There was an officer nicknamed "Tight shirt." This was a young country boy on steroids in his mid-twenties. From the minute he came into work, he put his lunch bag up and go search inmate cells. When the inmates said anything, he would use excessive force, most of the time leading to a broken bone!

One evening, "Tight shirt" comes to work happy as can be. What he did not know was an inmate was waiting with a long needle-like shank ready for Tight shirt to search his cell. Like clockwork, Tight shirt put his lunch bag up in the officer station and began his rounds. To make sure his cell is searched, the inmate smoked a cigarette. The minute Tight shirt ordered for the inmate to exit the cell, the shank went flying into Tight shirt's neck. The other stab hitting the steroid-juiced-up officer in the arm, thrown up used as protection. The shank dropped to the floor and a fight engaged. Now Tight shirt had the advantage because numerous officers swarmed in to assist. To save his life! The inmate was handcuffed and beaten as usual. When the paramedics arrived, the inmate was reported to be suffering from broken ribs, broken teeth and God knows how else officials beat him. Let me tell you I do not like violence. But sometimes things have to happen in order for the truth to come out. After a rare investigation that took well over a year, "Tight shirt" was terminated for the use of excessive force one too many times. This officer's termination did not in any way slow down the teams engaged in misconduct.

Chicken night has always been the best meal within the corrections department. Some kitchens cook it crispy while others don't cook it well at all leaving pink all in the middle of the chicken. Suwannee became horrible with food portions and the quality of the food. I knew for sure the warden had to be frauding out of the kitchen. If any inmate complained about the portions, officers would house them in confinement with disciplinary reports made up of false accusations.

It was a rainy evening. The male sergeant named "Cockeye" was directing traffic. One inmate decided to turn around and walked back to the dormitory because he did not want to get wet and eventually sick. The sergeant screamed to get back in line. The inmate expressed his concerns and continued to walk. Cockeye pulled out his gas can and sprayed the inmate on his back. Have you ever seen a tree get cut down and fall toward the ground? That's how Cockeye looked when the inmate turned around and knocked him out cold. The tower immediately called for help. The inmate did not resist as the officers were kicking and punching on him while handcuffed. We were placed on lockdown for another seven days.

Swantanamo Bay became somewhat of a turning point for me. I hustled a little bit, stopped after realizing I had to find a way to get transferred. I sold my cell phone and maintained clean. The money on the streets started to slow down little by little. Cynthia moved to Ohio. Her boyfriend influenced her to steal my part of the funds. Rosa moved back to New York and did the same thing. Jane Lynn kept strong for a minute but decided one day she did not want to end up in jail. All I had left was my girl, Cathy. I could only ask her to do little things here and there because it was not in her DNA. Cathy was the model delicate type of female. Don't get me wrong, she was dedicated. But definitely not someone to do business deals with people on the streets.

I became desperate. My lawyer was asking for thousands of dollars while he filed motions and battled with the courts. Who was going to help me now? I never did have anyone to help me anyway. Dr. Anderson's conclusion was extremely favorable to my case, and I had to continue paying. I fell out with my family. I found out my mom's husband was making negative comments about how I made my money and all the things being brought out there in the street. Here I am, drowning to death in prison with no help, and my own family staying aside while making comments. It just didn't make any sense. I had classification withdraw my sisters and mom from my visitation list. I did not accept any correspondence from my mom. I told my girl to limit the information about me to my mom, not to ever give her the phone if I call and she is around. I had a long talk with Cathy and explained I wasn't in my right state of mind. I was worried and felt the obligation to continue to help Cathy and have enough for my lawyer. I separated from Cathy and advised her to move with her brother in Long Island, New York. I was rolling on fumes with the money. I could not spend on canteen items as I regularly did. Things just fell apart for the time being.

Another inmate a few cells down from my cell kept on asking me to read a Christian book titled *The Purpose Driven Life*. He was asking me every single day. Sometimes I would look at him with the mean face not wanting to be bothered. One morning, I decided to write my attorney, asked him to contact the news channel about my case and provide Dr. Anderson's conclusion explaining my innocence. Central Florida channel 9 News reported on my case. I was hoping for a thorough investigative report on the corruption with the Medical Examiner's Office and the prosecutors. What I learned is that the state controls a lot of what news channels report on. For example one news channel will talk bad about our president while the other talks good. I continued to worry.

The motion for newly discovered evidence was in the Osceola Courthouse pending. I started to lose faith in my lawyer after realizing he was not an appellate expert. There was nothing I could do but move forward with Stephenson. He was too deep into the case. The awesome book, *The Purpose Driven Life* was offered to me once again. I started to read and became addicted. I gave my heart and soul to God again. I was praying and reading the Bible. My language changed, my mind changed. One of the things I got on my knees and prayed for was that God send help to Suwannee Correctional and arrest all the officers who were beating and setting inmates up. Then I couldn't believe I kicked so many people out of my life. When I thought about it, my pride was still hard to overcome. My pride wouldn't allow me to breakdown.

The excessive use of force continued. Helicopters were landing, and ambulances were a regular. The medical staff falsified reports in order to cover for the officers. The confinement was still cold. Inmates would go up to the frozen cell window and with their fingers write "help me." I was so sad to know inmates were sleeping on steel bunks, in the cold, butt naked at times.

I was playing basketball one day and I noticed two men in three piece suits walk from the main unit through the annex. They walked alone, no escort from any employees. These two men turned out to be federal agents (FBI). They took over the inspector's office. Dozens of inmates were called for questioning. The warden was forced to make changes. After a week, the officers from the main unit were switched with the officers from the annex. The officers from the main unit were just as bad or even worse. I was amazed on what had taken place. Who was going to help us? A warning was not going to work. Those officers were so malicious and nasty, the new officers that came in would not last a month. We would bet how long it would take a black officer to quit or ask for transfer to work at another prison.

The motion for a newly discovered evidence containing Dr. Anderson's autopsy report was denied. We met the two-prong standard of: (1) the evidence was not available to the defense through due diligence. (2) The evidence may cause an acquittal upon new trial. The prosecutor argued that Dr. Anderson worked under Dr. Gore and therefore would become biased to allow Dr. Anderson's conclusion. Furthermore the prosecutor argued Dr. Anderson's conclusion was not concrete. I was forced to pay $3,000 for the initial brief appeal to the fifth District Court of Appeals. Then I paid almost $8000 for an attorney in New York to continue the appeal under a 2254 federal habeas corpus (actual innocence). All the motions whether state or federal appeals were denied. I paid my lawyer Stephenson every last drop. I have receipts totaling over $75,000. We had one more shot with the professor Dr. Shanklin if he found me to be innocent and a botched autopsy by Dr. Gore.

Meanwhile, in Swantanamo Bay Live Oak, Florida, the prison annex is getting uncontrollable. Violence among inmates spiked tremendously. Everyone was looking for a way to leave the hellhole. One morning, there was a rumor that officers would be attacked after lunch. Certain inmates were looking for a few "good men," or at least that's what the Marines would say. Anyhow, numerous shanks were made and the crew was ready for action. Everyone kept apart and quiet. Lunch seemed too quick. Recreation was called. I knew this was going to turn out ugly. Two inmates staged a fight. A female sergeant nicknamed "Monkey sergeant" pulled out a can of mace, her weapon and sneaked up to the fight and sprayed. Right behind her, an inmate with a steel aluminum lock tied to a laundry bag, swung it hard, hitting the sergeant in the back of the head. It looked like her spirit left her body. She was out cold! The tower called for help. The overweight officers ran in the yard. One by one, the inmates were stabbing the officers and fighting. The incident was not contained because the officers took control. It was the inmates who were tired and gave up the shanks one by one. We were on lock down for another seven days.

Assaults of staff were so common, I kept the extra food in my locker for lockdowns. The Florida Department of Law Enforcement reviewed the cameras. Within hours, all inmate suspects were escorted to a van and from what I understand, beaten half to death.

The year 2013 came around. By this point, I was praying for miracles. If you didn't know, let me tell you that God is amazing. Professor Shanklin did a thorough autopsy investigation and not only found me to be innocent but explained in detail how Dr. Gore botched the original report. I was interviewed by Central Florida Channel 13 News. The reporter did a good job with providing the evidence to the public and allowing Dr. Shanklin to comment on his findings. My lawyer charged another $5000 for Dr. Shanklin's autopsy report newly discovered evidence motion. He advised our trust fund account was low, and he would be charging a fee for any more hearings and appeals. God blessed me again. Remember how I wrote to the American Civil Liberties Union in New York and the answer was they would review the documents I provided about my case? It turned out the ACLU contacted Miami University Innocence Clinic and requested they represent me with the appeals. What better time. The law professor advised the court they were the lead attorneys. I went from almost losing my lawyer to having three lawyers. I was praying and thanking God for being alive and for providing a chance. Providing a light at the end of the tunnel.

There was a Haitian inmate who decided to build a .com with his wife's help. The plan was to call home every day and give full reports on the officer-inmate violence. He had an inmate who worked in confinement and provided information. He had an inmate who worked in medical and did the same thing. This is how Suwannee officially was nicknamed "Swantanamo Bay." People were reading about the brutality in the hands of the officers. The news channel reported on anything they could get their hands on from "Swantanamo Bay." It started to go viral. We never thought the FBI was reviewing all of the information placed on the website, carefully. The young Haitian inmate made one mistake that cost him some setbacks. He passed out to hundreds of inmates printed articles of the reports. When it got to the colonel's office, a search team was sent out to find the distributor. Nine times out of ten there's always going to be an inmate snitch and officials were able to get their man. "Zo" as the young Haitian was nicknamed, was placed in confinement pending investigation. There was nothing authorities could really do so a few falsified disciplinary reports were written. Zo was taken to the main unit close management for his role in what was called, inciting a riot. The administration thought nothing else would happen since Zo was locked down in close management. They sure thought wrong once again. The federal agents once again came to question this brave intelligent inmate. I will tell you what happened later in this book.

The newly discovered evidence motion with Professor Shanklin's autopsy report was denied. The prosecutors argued I should have brought that evidence during trial. That it was too late! My lawyer argued actual innocence has no time limit and the reappeal was denied. Another initial brief was prepared for the Fifth District Court of Appeals. My lawyer used up all the money in the trust fund account, and I did not have one cent to pay him with. I was stressing and praying. Stephenson told me he would stop after the Fifth DCA decision on my appeal. In other words, if the appeal had to be filed in federal court he was not moving forward with me.

The Miami University Innocence Clinic was not going to step in and spend money on my case. They only wanted to litigate in front of the judge, if it came down to it. I was in what turned out to be the Florida's worst prison. I no longer was hustling. I wasn't talking to my family. My workers out there in the streets were gone.

I hit rock-bottom in 2013 for the first time since I was incarcerated in 1999. I kept telling myself I did an extraordinary job at being able to help myself and others out in society. But I was feeding my brain with justification. I knew deep in my heart sooner or later, whether at Swantanamo Bay or on the Moon, the hustling was going to start again.

My Christian friend and I continued to pray and read the Bible. A feeling inside me was telling me to write my mom. On that same week, I received a card from my mom asking me not to be stubborn and to let her know the latest. God helped me with the pride thing, and I wrote back and sent two visitation applications. It's never been that I have any hate toward my family. We just sometimes have certain expectations with loved ones that unfortunately are unable to be met.

In February 2014, several inmates came back from the law library and gave me some good news. The Fifth District Court of Appeals reversed and remanded my case in:

Vega v. State, 135 So. 3d 382 (5th DCA 2014)

IN THE DISTRICT COURT OF APPEAL OF THE STATE OF FLORIDA
FIFTH DISTRICT

NOT FINAL UNTIL TIME EXPIRES TO
FILE MOTION FOR REHEARING AND
DISPOSITION THEREOF IF FILED

GIOVANNI K. VEGA,

Appellant,

v.

Case No. 5D13-2154

STATE OF FLORIDA,

Appellee.

_____/

Opinion filed January 31, 2014

3.850 Appeal from the Circuit Court
for Osceola County,
Jon Morgan, Judge.

Christopher M. Stephenson, of C
Stephenson Law, P.A., Orlando, for
Appellant.

Pamela Jo Bondi, Attorney General,
Tallahassee, and Ann M. Phillips,
Assistant Attorney General, Daytona
Beach, for Appellee.

PER CURIAM.

We reverse the summary denial of Giovanni Vega's rule 3.850 motion and

remand for an evidentiary hearing. We conclude, based on the unique facts of this

case, that the findings and conclusions set forth in Dr. Shanklin's report[1] constitute

---

[1] According to Dr. Shanklin's detailed report, the scientific evidence available to
the then-medical examiner, Dr. Sashi Gore, would, if honestly and competently
evaluated, establish beyond a reasonable doubt that the child victim died of meningitis,
not abuse. Subsequent to Vega's trial, Dr. Gore was disciplined by the Medical

newly discovered evidence to the extent they support an allegation that the testimony of the medical examiner at Vega's trial was knowingly and patently false (or, at a minimum, given in reckless disregard of the truth).

REVERSED and REMANDED for an evidentiary hearing.

SAWAYA, PALMER and EVANDER, JJ., concur.

Examiners' Commission for negligence and violation of professional standards in unrelated cases. As part of the imposed discipline, Dr. Gore was barred from performing further autopsies.

2

Shanklin's Autopsy Report

Aspects of the case and general medical and pathological knowledge relevant to an appeal on behalf of Giovanni Vega, #X12648. Analytic report in the matter of Xavier Collado, deceased:

Ordinarily, when a consultant forensic pathologist is asked to review a case, one turns to the autopsy report as a starting point of that reconsideration. Affiant has often chosen to do so after receiving a brief account of a case and its current issues but *in this case*, one clearly with several layers of complexity, the better starting point is to follow the matter in chronological order, from the statement of the caretaker, through the admission assessment, to the initial laboratory data, the clinical course, and then, finally, to the autopsy report and interpretative testimony from the medical examiner who was also the autopsy surgeon in the case.

It will be shown infra that there are highly relevant findings in the microscopic slides from the autopsy tissues which extend the information available in the records of the case, details not reflected in the report or the testimony of the medical examiner. These findings will be placed in the context of the clinical and laboratory findings during the brief hospital admissions of the child. The more important laboratory findings are those from the initial admission at the Osceola Regional Medical Center. This is because they reflect the condition of the child before medical intervention had a significant effect. Finally, important evidence is available in the series of photographs made available by the Osceola County Sheriff's Department, by which provision they verify the identity of the subjects in the photographs and their relevance to the issues of the matter.

The statement of the caretaker

The essential statement of the on-site caretaker of the child was this: "...the child fell in the bathtub..."

> Comment: This statement implies several things, [1] he was not immediately present when this happened and [2] likely did not know how many times the child fell, if more than once, and [3] his statement is tantamount to an admission (against interest) of inattentive, possibly negligent oversight. Since his observation had no other witness and can not observationally be contradicted or confirmed the possibility that what he said is a true account of the matter will have to be put on hold pending a determination of the effect of the medical evidence.

The initial conclusion as working diagnosis on admission at Osceola Regional Medical Center

The medical record states: "...non-accidental trauma..." at one point (Arnold Palmer Children's Hospital, Progress Notes for Endoscopy or Invasive Procedure) which is a direct follow through from the seeming conclusionary statement on the admission sheet at Osceola Regional Medical center: "Shaken baby syndrome..child assault/abuse..."

> Comment: These entries indicate several things, [1] no differential diagnosis was considered, [2] choices were made to not seek further information from certain vital laboratory tests never performed in the case, [3] treatment was afforded along lines suggested or indicated by the initial diagnosis of non-accidental trauma of an abusive sort, and [4] the treatment was not adjusted by very strong evidence from the laboratory tests that were done which gives rise to the inference they were either not read by any of the attending physicians or were totally disregarded if in fact they had been read.

-2-

The evidence for this fourth statement in the box comes from the hematological laboratory data on admission at Osceola Regional Medical Center, medical record number N00026054, time of admission: 1738 hours (5:38 p.m.) on November 12, 1999 (one record page has 1735 hours as the time of medical contact), time of blood sampling, 1832 hours (6:32 p.m.):

Characteristic reported	Value reported	Comment
Red blood cells/mm³ (RBC)	5.07 x 10⁴	Middle of normal range
Hemoglobin (HGB)	13.6 gm/L	Middle of normal range
Hematocrit (HCT)	39.2%	Middle of normal range
All three of the values above	*are against major*	*or life threatening hemorrhage anywhere*
White blood cells/mm³ (WBC)	35,200	Very high increase in circulating WBC
Segs or neutrophils	74%	Principal sign of major infection
Bands or immature neutrophils	16%	Confirmatory of major infection
Lymphocytes	4%	Low value due to increased neutrophils and bands; otherwise OK
These laboratory values are	*not reflected in*	*the autopsy report*

1. Was there enough information available from which to have made a correct clinical diagnosis on admission to Osceola Regional Medical Center (ORMC) or later at the Arnold Palmer Children's Hospital before the death of the child at 2315 hours on November 12, 1999?

    The answer is clearly *yes*. The fault for this error, or better put, these errors because there is actually a series of them in the record, lies with the clinical staff of those institutions, most particularly with the admitting physicians at ORMC.

    Comment: There are several rationales for doing "blood work" in triage, [1] to aid in diagnosis; [2] to provide a base line for treatment, and [3] to serve as confirmation of the status of the individual under surveillance as reported by EMTs during emergency transport or when transfer is made to a second hospital, one presumed by transport to have more or better resources from which to give proper treatment. Competent care requires the ordering physician(s) to study the results so that the information obtained can be coherently placed into the initial protocol for management of the case, or possibly to restructure it in some way.

    There was in the 1990s, by personal observation of affiant, a general tendency among pediatricians, emergency room medical and nursing staff, and by field investigators for child protective agencies in Florida, to diagnose and then act on an initial impression of child abuse or worse without considering various pathogenetic options. The situation is different in the early years of the second decade of this century. Twice in the past year affiant has been contacted by a senior professional for consultation in cases being thoroughly investigated weeks after the fact *before* recommending whether charges should be filed. One case deserved charges, the other did not.

155

-3-

The clinical course in continuity between two hospitals

The clinical course for this child is remarkable in one particular way: about half of the intensive care was dedicated to trying to keep the child alive, which failed, and the other half was a post mortem creation of a heart-lung preparation, ostensibly to preserve organs for possible transplant, which in reality could only have been for the kidney or heart. The main medical modalities were fluid infusion (not glucose) in a keep-vein-open mode (KVO) and pressors intended to maintain blood pressure and cardiac action. The efforts at ORMC were in part directed at stabilizing the child for transport to Arnold Palmer Children's Hospital.

On arrival at the Arnold Palmer Children's Hospital the admission note states:

"On arrival to APH / exam remarkable for diffuse bruising / ..."

This is patently false language. *Diffuse* means extensive and continuous, by which common medical dictionary definition one infers what was meant was *disseminated*, which means focal but extensive. In fact, disseminated is what is shown by the photographs. By use of *diffuse* the observer has exaggerated the finding and narrowed the search for the reasons for it, that is, the cause, to less than the pathological data actually reveals.

Despite the transfer, the continuing care was what in navigation would be called *station keeping*, with no improvement recorded, quite the contrary. No change from the initial Glasgow Coma Score assignment on admission at ORMC, a score of 3, with fixed pupils, was observed.

2. Was there enough antecedent information for the second group of physicians to change the operational diagnosis and to institute treatment for infection and disseminated intravascular coagulation?

The answer again is *yes*. By not doing so the second set of medical attendants merely gave false confirmation to the working diagnosis of major post traumatic injuries.

3. Apparently, from the lack of notation in the record, there was no recognition that the moribund state of the child on first admission could have only one outcome: death.

> Comment: Viewed from the distance in time and place today represents, at least in part, what was done for and to the child on November 12, 1999, should have been guided by a better application of the principles of triage. Among the many articles and reviews written in the 1990s on the subject, the two part review by J. M. Davies and B. M. Reynolds, The ethics of cardiopulmonary resuscitation, *Archives of Diseases in Childhood*, 67:1498-1505, 1992, stands out for close reasoning and clinical pragmatism. The articles emphasize cardiac arrest as a starting point but slowing pulse, bradycardia, is prefatory to arrest and general biological principles would apply. One has to know when to quit. After going through the medical record in this case, perhaps a dozen times, affiant gained the sense this reality was very slow to be understood, just now, 2012, realized.

Further statements on the vital signs and other presenting attributes of the case are later in this report.

The post mortem exercise prior to autopsy

Since the recorded clinical time of death, 2315 hours (11:15 p.m.), November 12, 1999, a Friday, was followed by an extended period of "life support" with the intention of preserving the vitality of some organs for possible harvest for transplantation, 4 hours and 47 minutes to be exact, both the effects of this medical intervention and the antecedent clinical care of the infant have to be taken into account in order to correctly interpret the recorded findings and conclusions of the medical examiner.

-4-

The *maintenance of central vital signs for putative organ harvest* was concluded at 0402 hours (4:02 a.m.) on November 13, 1999, just five hours prior to the start of autopsy MEH-2963-99 performed by Shashi B. Gore, M.D., M.P.H., Chief Medical Examiner, District Nine, State of Florida, per the face sheet of the said report initialed by Dr. Gore.

> Comment: If the total record is accurate on this specific point, in Dr. Gore's favor, is the account that he was asked to grant permission for organ harvest roughly an hour *after* death and he refused. This was after post mortem infusion measures had been instituted and it is far from clear how this was done and on whose authority. Despite his apparent refusal the measures were maintained for several more hours. Affiant was quite taken aback on reading this part of the chart the first time, wondering whether this was tantamount to desecration or worse. What has to be understood, however, is that these measures compromised the status of the body such that when Dr. Gore came to perform the autopsy, the attributes of primary disease and the principal care afforded would now be overwritten by zealous fluid infusions and more vasopressors.

Dr. Gore and the forensic autopsy

The comments and observations in the paragraphs infra will demonstrate this: the autopsy report by Dr. Gore as formulated and written, and as used in evidence, does not pass critical muster. Over the scope of time it may have reasonably represented forensic attitudes on comparable findings as of the end of the twentieth century and, accordingly, the art and practice of forensic pathology in free standing offices of coroners or medical examiners. One can doubt whether the conclusions would have been the same had the autopsy and the investigation been conducted in a forensic unit which was a component of a university medical center.   Affiant by experience is well acquainted with both venues. But the autopsy and its interpretation are products of when and where the record shows them to have occurred. There was medical knowledge available then to conclude otherwise but very likely not within the common purview of many medical examiners of the 1990s which has since been expanded and replenished in such a conspicuous and thorough manner as to be part of laymen's awareness in many instances and the common experience of many persons and families.

The ideal and the proper starting point for reassessment of the forensic cause of death as reported is the autopsy diagnostic sheet from the medical examiner for the 9th Judicial District of Florida. This will be followed by examination of the complete autopsy report, and the available microscopic slides from the autopsy. Study of the hospital record indicates that in part, if not in whole, Dr. Gore was much influenced by the pre-mortem interpretations and conclusions of the emergency room and intensive care unit physicians. Dr. Gore was, accordingly, seeking to confirm their opinions in the performance of the autopsy, perhaps to the exclusion of a different mode of consideration.

Dr. Gore's recorded cause of death (autopsy report and death certificate) is:

"Subdural hemorrhage, due to closed head trauma, due to blunt force head trauma"

The summarized litany of diagnostic findings under the heading "Autopsy Findings" directly relevant to the described intracranial hemorrhage is:

"II. Closed head trauma with a fresh contusion on the right forehead.
   A. Subgaleal hemorrhage, thick layer and contusion of the deeper layers of the scalp.
   B. Subdural and subarachnoid hemorrhage, bicortical.
   C. Cranial bones intact.
   D. Severe brain edema."

-5-

These components of the report of the medical examiner constitute a progressive selection by the medical examiner as to the aspect he concluded was the medical cause of death.

The detailed description of the subdural hemorrhage in the context of its immediate environment is on page 5 of the narrative autopsy report:

"When the cranial cavity is opened and the brain exposed it is noted that there is no epidural hemorrhage, however there is considerable subdural hemorrhage on both cerebral hemispheres. The total quantity of the fluid hemorrhage on the cerebral hemispheres is approximately 35 ml."

The exact extent of this subdural hemorrhage, a little more than an ounce, left to right and front to back, is not recorded, but one gains the impression it covered a majority of the available external surface of the brain. If so, then it was less than 1.5 millimeters thick from this equation:

Assume a circular hemorrhage 18 cm in diameter over the surface of the brain, thence:

Area = radius^2 x π = 81 x 3.1416 = 254.5 cm^2
Thickness = volume/area

35 cm^3/254.5 cm^2 = 0.1378 cm = 1.378 mm thick

Simply put, this is not a space occupying subdural hemorrhage which pressures the underlying brain in the ordinary meaning of the pathological term. Interpretatively, it may be a marker for some other process, but its size and distribution are significantly less than what it would take to cause death independently and solely.

The description of this lesion in the text in the *microscopic examination* is:

"Section of the dura mater shows evidence of subdural hemorrhage."

The structure of this sentence is pathologist's jargon for there being microscopic hemorrhage on the subdural side of the dura mater but is not a description of a collection of blood which fits the definition of the hematoma necessary for pressuring the brain on its surface. Accordingly, one could or perhaps should say the details of the autopsy report do not support or confirm the diagnostic conclusion as to the cause of death. If infant Xavier Collado did not die from the malign effects of a subdural hemorrhage, then what was the cause of death? The answer will be found in cross correlation between the autopsy findings and the clinical and various laboratory assessments during the two hospital admissions.

Before analyzing in detail those findings, it is important to dispose of one detail of the testimony of Dr. Gore in his capacity then as the medical examiner and as the pathologist who performed the autopsy on Xavier Collado. This item is a metaphor for the scope of the purported injuries.

In the description of the gross autopsy examination but not deemed important enough to appear on the summary face sheet is a notation on page 3 as follows:

"When the upper lip is everted it is noted that the frenulum is lacerated and shows a *minute* (emphasis supplied) hemorrhage in that area."

Thence, in depositional testimony on May 9, 2000, page 6, Dr. Gore stated:

"Now, that fold is called a frenulum. Now that fold is normally injured or lacerated whenever there is injury to the area of the face when there is injury to the area of the face including the lips and nose."

Question a little later (by attorney Louis Davila): "All right. Well, wouldn't that

-6-

injury also happen if somebody fell down?"

To which, later, Dr. Gore replies: "But this facial - - - tearing of the frenulum is *always* considered as *child abuse* (emphasis supplied). The reason is that it does not occur as a result of a fall."

The transcript contains other parts of this Q&A on the subject but that supra is the essence of the conclusion rendered by Dr. Gore. In other words, Dr. Gore uses this finding and interpretation to validate his conclusion as to the modality which yielded the cause of death, namely: "Blunt force head trauma."

The trial transcript conveys the same essential conclusion, pages 523-524, except that Dr. Gore allows for a torn frenulum in a baby being fed by formula bottle if the bottle is forcefully put in the infant's mouth (page 523, line 25 through to page 524, line 11). In this testimony Dr. Gore rules out a nursing bottle injury, on grounds of the age of the child, namely, three plus years.

The assertion that only a blow such as might be presumed to come from an abusive event could tear the frenulum is patently false, since all kinds of impact injury can result in this finding. There is in fact abundant public information available at:

www.utahmountainbiking.com/firstaid/mouthcut.html

Accordingly, any comparable fall from a child's bicycle or tricycle can result in the exact same injury. Or, obviously, just a fall of similar vector and force against an unyielding object. In addition, given the probative importance placed on this finding by Dr. Gore, remarkably, it does not appear in the structure of his *Autopsy Findings* pages issued pursuant to the post mortem examination performed on November 13, 1999.

The provided copy does not give a date of report completion (by which to judge when components might have been added, e.g., the belated cutting of the brain, commented on later in this report). A fall on the face in a bathtub which tears the frenulum is quite sufficient force to case nasal bleeding, also described. Thus, young Xavier Collado likely sustained a bloody nose by such a fall.

The assertion the other contusions and hemorrhages are due only to abusive physical contact by an assailant ignores part of the history given by the caretaker (which, however, is neither corroborated nor contradictable given the evident location of the persons involved in the events at the time, i.e., there is no witness either way), namely, *the child fell in the bathtub.*

Affiant has now investigated a number of bathtub incidents involving children of several sizes and have found bathtubs to be especially dangerous places, capable of inducing the most incredible array of surface injuries on children. Think of the protruding hard devices, spigot handles, the water spout and the occasional handle for activating the in line stopper. Add to this the edges and corners of built-in soap dishes and the lip of the tub itself, and one quickly comes to understand the rich possibilities by which a child can sustain physical trauma with no help from anyone else. A fall on the bottom of the tub, without hitting any of the protuberances, is a fall against a hard object!

Forensically, specific investigation and measurements of the putative bathtub were not recorded.

-7-

The laboratory data soon after initial admission in Osceola are dramatic and clear; the child was admitted with an acute systemic infection of a life threatening type. Moreover, the onset of this infection is clearly placed by the values for the white cell count (WBC) and the proportion of mature neutrophils (segs) and immature neutrophils (bands) as 24 hours earlier, more or less, but clearly well prior to the timing of the bathtub incident as asserted by the caretaker.

These lab values are compelling evidence for infection as a major pathological condition in the tissues of Xavier Collado, deceased. The autopsy report by Dr. Gore treats this tangentially and very briefly, not at all in his diagnostic summary, but only in the microscopic findings section as:

> "Lungs: Several sections of lungs (n.b., there is actually only one section of lung in the 16 slides of autopsy tissues and organs)...show...scattered areas of bronchopneumonia."

There is pneumonia in slide B which has one section of lung on it:

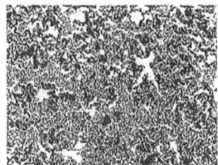

Slide B, autopsy ME99-2963, H&E routine stain, original magnification, 100X. The inflammation is in the distal airspaces and is not seen in bronchioles, other than a few secondary infiltrations of mucosa by the acute inflammatory cells, with some loose intralumenal exudate (part of the process of spreading of the pneumonia) so the term *bronchopneumonia* is not fully precise (see next photograph).

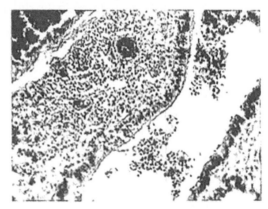

The clear spaces in the epithelial lining of this bronchiole contain a few neutrophils and the lumenal exudate is a mixture of mature neutrophils and band forms. This exudate dates from before the admission which lasted almost 5.75 hours before the original clinical declaration of death at 2315 hours, November 12, 1999. The interval from admission at Osceola Regional Medical Center to the discontinuance of attempted organ support was 10.5 hours. The oldest

-8-

component of exudate is approximately 24-30 hours old, that is, it was in place in part before the alleged bath tub incident and collapse of the child and from the continuing stimulus of the true underlying condition, an active pathological process at the time of clinical death. The laboratory findings do not allow for further interpretation during or at the end of the attempted organ support protocol. The aggregate of lymphocytes to the left of the mucosa is an expected structure in the lung and is not pathological.

The details of age of the inflammation, the pneumonia are shown at higher magnification (250X):

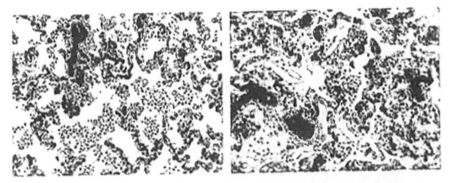

There is some edema fluid with the exudate which is beginning to show degeneration of the neutrophils which is a marker for an age of the initial infiltrate as much as 30-36 hours. Of course, any feature more than 12 hours old would be a marker for infection antecedent to the timing of the alleged physical trauma. Such lesions of early pneumonia are readily enhanced and spread around by ventilatory assistance such as was provided in this case shortly after admission.

The high white blood cell count (WBC = 35,200/mm³) is strongly reflected in some peripheral blood vessels, especially in the brain (all three photos, original magnification at 400X):

The reaction is occasionally more intense, with small clusters of coagulated platelets marking the onset of disseminated intravascular coagulation (DIC), commonly a component of the reaction of the body to severe sepsis transitioning into septic shock (all three at 400X original magnification) as shown on page 9:

161

-9-

These three photographs reveal neutrophils in various stages of maturation and degeneration from the adverse effects of the cytokines (small proteins) stimulated by the sepsis and the bacterial toxins themselves. The irregular darker acellular pink areas are the coagulated platelets. This aspect had not been sufficiently advanced at admission to yield a low platelet count but a later blood sample would have shown whether they were being consumed in a major way. Similarly, a block or two of the bone marrow would have revealed the effects of sepsis on the source of both the white cells and the platelets, but none was obtained at autopsy by the medical examiner in the case.

There are other aspects of the initial laboratory determinations of direct relevance to the case. The first is a blood glucose level of 551 mg/dL in the sample drawn at 1832 hours, the same timing as the sample for assessment of the blood cell counts. This value exceeds the standard critical value and was, accordingly, called to the clinical staff ("Elizabeth") at 1920 hours and the results were properly rechecked and verified. Close examination of the care record from 1735 (or 1738) to the time of blood sampling at 1832 reveals the intravenous fluid therapy was Ringer's lactate or normal saline infusion (KVO = keep vein open) but no glucose component. The principal therapy was vasopressors to "maintain the blood pressure." Since no glucose was infused the very high level has to be construed as part of the underlying disease process. That process is septic shock.

Other key points in the clinical chart are [1] the pulse rate, [2] the body temperature, [3] elevated liver enzymes, in particular alkaline phosphatase. The values found for these three items were, respectively, [1] 159 @ 1740, 148 @ 1848, inter alia, both close to twice normal, a significant tachycardia; [2] temperature of 93.4 °F (equal to 34.1°C) @ 1735, a very significant low body temperature, equivalent to hypothermia; and [3] alkaline phosphatase of 248 Units/Liter versus a normal range of 42-121 U/L. Other liver enzymes were elevated into their critical ranges, SGOT/AST at 2879 U/L (normal range, 10 - 42 U/L) and SGPT/ALT at 1657 U/L (normal range, 5 - 47 U/L). These are appropriate findings for diffuse liver injury either directly infectious, as in acute hepatitis, or secondary to toxic chemicals, such as carbon tetrachloride poisoning (a once popular home cleaning fluid), and in septic shock. Microscopic study of the liver at autopsy shows no massive localized injury which implies a generalized or diffuse metabolic cellular effect capable of this degree of enzyme release on admission. The liver at autopsy also shows glycogenated hepatic nuclei, a marker for high levels of hyperglycemia (high blood glucose), viz, the swollen, clear nuclei shown here (the change thus persisted until death and beyond):

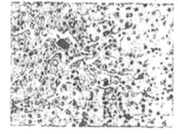

This photograph has two such nuclei, the larger just to the left of center, the smaller is in the lower right quadrant. Original magnification, 400X. H&E stain.

-10-

These chemical and clinical findings are text book classic signs of septic shock: tachycardia, very low body temperature (hypothermia), which, when viewed in light of the blood pressure despite the heavy use of vasopressors, serve to establish the diagnosis beyond reasonable doubt. For example, the blood pressures recorded after over an hour of intensive treatment, at 1855 and 1856 were 62/28 and 53/18 respectively, with companion mean arterial pressures of 38 and 31 mmHg (torr). To call these values anything other than severe shock would be a major medical mistake. The x-ray finding of diffuse intestinal ileus is typical and consistent with this diagnosis.

The alkaline phosphatase value becomes more interesting when one takes into account the fact that various strains of the gram positive bacterium, staphylococcus, secrete alkaline phosphatase which can be detected by the test for the human enzyme [Staphylococcus aureus, S. epidermidis, S. xylosus, S. haemolyticus, and S. saphrophyticus are all very active in this way; see: G. Satta, et al., Micrococci demonstrate a phosphatase activity which is repressed by phosphates and which can be differentiated from that of staphylococci. *International Journal of Systematic Bacteriology,* 1993, volume 43, pp. 813-818] Affiant would be the first to admit that this journal was not on his regular "to read list," any more than it would be for medical examiners. However, in being aware, in 2011, of the basic fact, it was easy to locate this and other equally relevant sources of scientific and medical information [See also: Smith and Mukerjee, Liver metabolism and energy production in Staphylococcus aureus septic shock in mice. *Advances in Experimental Medicine and Biology,* 1971, volume 23, pp. 253-265; Giger, et al., Comparison of the API Staph-Ident and DMS Staphy-Trac systems with conventional methods used for the identification of coagulase-negative staphylococci. *Journal of Clinical Microbiology,* 1984, volume 19, pp. 68-72]

No special stains were performed by the office of the medical examiner, and, accordingly, the quickest microscopic confirmation of sepsis was and is not available. Detailed study of the 16 slides which are/were available did reveal some findings suggestive of gram positive cocci of which staphylococci are an important component. These can be found in H&E sections as dark blue to blue-black rounded bodies, sometimes in clusters or small groups. Streptococci will appear as short chains of small dark blue to blue-black round bodies. These are the two principal bacterial agents of septic shock in young children. The photographs provided supra of the intense neutrophilic white blood cell reaction show isolated gram positive cocci in the cytoplasm of the WBC. They are there due to the phagocytic action of the WBC, one of their main functions (phagocyte = "eats," that is, they take in bacteria and viruses):

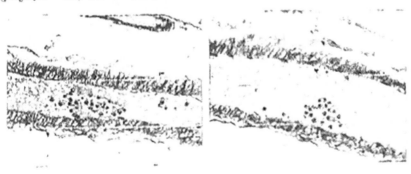

Both photographs of blood vessels and WBC are at original magnifications of 400X, H&E stain.

-11-

Other photographs show similar structures elsewhere, as in small pseudocysts or tissue pockets.

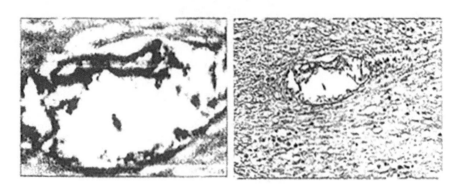

Small pseudocystic cavity in the brain with clusters (left; 1000X) and growth and spread of gram positive cocci adjacent to a deep vessel in the brain as independent cocci and some linear aggregates (right; 400X). The next two photographs are of a similar paravascular lesion at 400X (left) and 1000X (right):

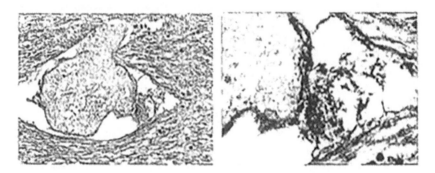

Considering the relative paucity of sections and their random selection from the brain (e.g., there are no slides of the brain stem said to have been impacted in the tentorial opening from the supratentorial pressure of cerebral edema), it is remarkable to be able to identify these definitive markers for gram positive sepsis.

A pathological question naturally arises at this point which comes close by itself to demanding an answer: "has the process gone far enough to qualify as either cerebromeningitis or meningitis?

-12-

The answer is yes:

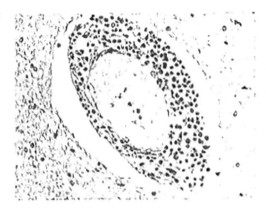

This is from Slide #4, at 400X original magnification, and is a classic, textbook illustration of bacterial meningitis which has spread deeply into the brain within the Virchow-Robin spaces, a sheath of leptomeninges (the thinner, lighter coating of the brain) which penetrates around the major blood vessels. The large number of inflammatory cells, their type and characteristics, in this location, indicate a disease formation time of several days.

The *true cause of death* is thus meningitis and cerebromeningitis most likely caused by a gram positive bacterium, which condition arose from or was simply part of the spread of sepsis and septic shock. Moreover, all of the presenting signs and symptoms of Xavier Collado when admitted to the emergency department at Osceola Regional Medical Center can be explained on the basis of these medical conditions, including the contusions. The development of DIC (disseminated intravascular coagulopathy) makes small blood vessels prone to injury from even the slightest, often a caring form of contact. Unfortunately, meningitis is seriously underdiagnosed in emergency rooms and other triage situations. This fact has been brought forcefully forward in the past decade as has the great attention now being paid to MRSA, an acronym for methacillin resistant staphylococcus aureus, a highly significant health problem both in hospitals and other health care facilities as well as in the community at large.

Additionally, all of the pathological findings in this case can be derived from septic shock plus the fact of nearly five hours of post mortem cardiopulmonary support for possible organ transplant harvest. A point emphatically made in the autopsy report was the swelling of the brain with what is called tonsillar herniation (the inferior part of the posterior fossa content, brain stem and the central and inferior part of the cerebellum, are pushed downward into the foramen magnum through which the spinal cord and the lower brain connect [page 5, autopsy report, ¶ 2, lines 8-11]).

Most of this is due to the post mortem effort to preserve some of the other organs for transplant harvest; in this wise the cerebromeninigitis has altered the water balance of the brain and the high volume intravenous intervention has compounded the issue. Moreover, from classical forensic neuropathology, most cranial blows are focalizing in the cerebral hemispheres, with herniation at the level of the tentorium cerebri, much higher in the cranial cavity, and often unilateral. The extent of edema in the brain stem and the cerebellum, from the recorded observation of the herniation, might be presumed to have diffuse and disseminated cerebral edema to a degree shown for the cerebrum in the foregoing photographs, but the absence of any slides from that part of the brain requires this statement to be provisional although probable. Two questions remain: [1] are there other findings which may have contributed in a material way to the rapid spread of bacterial sepsis in this child, and [2] what was the likely source of the infection?

-13-

Firstly, the autopsy record indicates that Dr. Gore did not weigh the adrenal glands but did measure or estimate the cortical thickness as 2 mm (2.0 millimeters). This is thin and the slide with adrenal on it (Slide F) confirms a pathologically thin cortex:

This photograph, at 250X original magnification, adds the detail that the arrangement of the cords of adrenal cells is haphazard rather than regular and the cells are small, respectively a marker for poor development and depletion of steroid reserves. The size of the gland is not always a marker for functional competence but cellular depletion is a state identifiable by appropriate microscopic features. In this case the duration of septic shock indicated by the extent of bacteria and the high WBC count are consistent with the depleted state of the adrenal cortex, and vice versa.

Slide E is of the pancreas and the islets of Langerhans, the source of insulin and other hormones, are few and far between. This would also contribute to a poor metabolic response to sepsis, but neither this factor nor the adrenal depletion can be construed as causes of death per se. They are part of the systemic response to the challenge from the infection. An isolated pancreatic islet is on the far left side of this photograph and a smaller one near the lower edge to the right (250X):

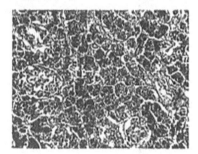

Secondly, the source of the infection is apparent in the photographs provided by the Osecola County Sheriff's Department. These are pictures of the sister of the deceased child. It took some effort to first get hold of these photographs and then to identify the child shown thereby. There is one set of critically probative photographs (five views, total: #138 - two views, 139 - two views, and 141 - a single view).

·14·

#141:

#138:

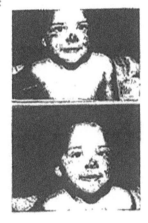

#139:

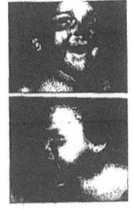

What are these lesions on the face of the sister? These are convincing images of impetigo, a highly contagious infection most commonly seen in preschool children. In the vernacular the disease has been referred to as *school sures*. The severity of the infection, the sepsis in the decedent, points to the greater likelihood the bacterial organism was *Staphylococcus aureus* rather than *Streptococcus pyogenes* but from the standpoint of etiology and pathogenesis either will do. Since the incubation period can be less than 24 hours, rapid progression can occur. The medical reason the decedent boy developed widespread sepsis rather than superficial facial lesions is not made clear by the record but such transformations easily can and do occur. Moreover, neither the emergency room medical staff nor Medical Examiner Gore took any cultures of blood, nasal secretions, cerebrospinal fluid, or bronchial secretions by which to investigate whether infection was part of the scenario surrounding the death of the child. It seems the medical attendants here, both before and after death, were locked into the simplistic interpretative equation "...bleeding and/or contusion equals trauma..." when there are dozens of well defined medical causes for both beyond this linear thinking.

167

The irony is compelling, in fact, because on a hand written page labeled "Autopsy notes" for the section titled "head and neck" is the entry:

"Both sides of face, multiple pinhead size contusions"

A more accurate description of capillary petechiae (very tiny hemorrhages) which are a hallmark of disseminated intravascular coagulation (DIC) could hardly be imagined. This is confirmed by the admission note at APH which states: "petechia ove(r) both pinna [ears]"

These almost astonishing entries fit precisely into one other set of laboratory tests apparently done after the transfer to the Arnold Palmer Children's Hospital:

At 2300 hours, or 11 p.m. on November 12, 1999, an progress note entry provides this laboratory information:

Fibrinogen <50 (mg/dl)
FPD >1280 <2560
PT/PTT 21/37

No laboratory report form is in the record for this data and this progress note entry may have been due to a telephone report. This mirrors an earlier entry at 1902 hours at Osceola Regional Medical Center for coagulation factors with both PT and PPT very high (38.4 and 75.6 seconds respectively) but suspect due to hemolysis of the specimen, with the indication, "suggest recollect." The sample was one of many drawn at 1832 hours.

What they reveal is that the child had well developed DIC (disseminated intravascular coagulation) on admission beyond what physical trauma could induce in this time frame.

The final distinctive point from the information in the record is the gain in weight through the large volume of intravenous fluid administered. What share is due to treatment before death and what share during the organ maintenance phase can not be ascertained but from the admission weight and the autopsy weight, the child gained 1.3 kg of water, exactly a 10% increase in less than 12 hours, which is approaching the physiological limit the human body can contain. The water has to go somewhere and that is usually to tissues or compartments capable of taking up a lot of fluid, lungs, body cavities, the circulatory system, and the brain troubled by meningitis.

Procedural concerns and comments

To repeat the essential questions:

1. Was there enough information available from which to have made a correct clinical diagnosis on admission to Osceola Regional Medical Center and the Arnold Palmer Children's Hospital and/or before the death of the child at 2315 hours on November 12, 1999?

   The answer is clearly *yes*. The fault for this error, or better put, these errors because there is actually a series of them in the record, lies with the clinical staff of those institutions.

2. Was Dr. Gore unduly influenced by the premature (and pejorative) designation of the cause of injury by those clinicians when performing and interpreting the autopsy?

   The answer is, *yes to a reasonably high order of possibility*, even probability.

3. Was such a mixture of presumptive clinical diagnosis and ready if superficial concurrence by a medical examiner or coroner from a free standing investigative

-16-

agency a commonplace in the 1990s, including 1999?

Unfortunately, the answer again is, *yes to a reasonably high order of possibility*, even probability.

From affiants more detailed assessment of the record over the past seventeen months, a sort of a slow rolling graduate seminar exercise on his part, then the answer to all three questions is regrettably yes. But at the time that degree of assessment and consideration did not happen and such an exercise (even in an intellectual short time frame) was outside of the operating modalities and styles of most emergency rooms and free standing medical examiner services, not to mention the operational attitudes of many pediatricians and social workers of the day.

    4. Have the intervening years brought a change in procedure or appreciation of knowledge which requires the advanced treatment of the facts of a case to be more throughly examined, both clinically and forensically, and if so, how?

Yes. Firstly, pediatric emergency care has made remarkable strides in the past twelve years. One clear indicator of this progress comes from Children's Hospital of Philadelphia (Pennsylvania), known in the medical profession as CHOP, one of America's leading pediatric hospitals, in their intensive fellowships in Pediatric Emergency Medicine which require young physicians to have completed their board requirements in pediatrics in order to be admitted to the fellowships. Affiant mentions this particular program because of personal friendship with a recent graduate of that fellowship and not to single it out to the exclusion of other similar and equal programs.

Secondly, the operational field of forensic analysis has matured, especially in regard to study of the deaths of children, and the current standard would be to obtain other kinds of information during autopsies as well as to garner all available clinical and environmental information before making a determination as to the cause of death. As to the former, the regular culture of available fluids for any agents of infection is always, at a minimum, a check on the too ready assignment of cause to trauma. It is similar to certain forms of possible drug toxicity and some aspects of genetic disease for which sampling of the vitreous fluid from the eyes is now mandatory.

Medical examiners have since learned to make their own *independent* investigation in similar cases of the deaths of children in recognition of their public responsibility to ascertain at a professional and scientific level the real facts of the matter prior to making a legal determination. If Dr. Gore is blameworthy in this case, it would be for not exercising that independence which could have or should have prompted a more detailed examination of the pathological materials produced by the autopsy he personally performed.

There was diagnostic error in late 1999 in this case and the significance of it a subject for discussion at one level but the change in procedural approaches in these cases now known to be critical raises these issues to one of primary competence rather than situational or administrative. The current standard does not allow for incomplete work like this based on triage hypotheses. There are so many aspects of the steady changes in the developing body and physiology of the human child which make for a shifting platform from which to determine disease versus trauma that a strong sense of caution is more valuable than a quick answer.

The answer to point #4 is yes, the passage of time is important, but not just the passage of time, but the increase in awareness of the complexities of these matters and what it takes procedurally and technically to negotiate effectively toward the correct answer pathologically.

The onset of severe antibiotic resistance of many common disease causing organisms has served in one good sense, namely, forcing forensic analysis as well as clinical diagnosis and treatment to raise the level of commonplace practice to the plane of genuine scientific investigation. Bad people do bad things to innocent children, and that is a fact of human existence, likely never to be eliminated from modern society, but diseases also do bad things to children and the professional error is to reflexly assign the outcome to the former without fully examining the latter and conclusively eliminating that as the cause of death. Affiant has also seen over his long career the value of progressively more detailed sampling of tissues at autopsy and their more thorough investigation microscopically and by other available means. These changes mean longer reports, as a rule, and sometimes in longer time intervals by which to render a report, but the risk of not doing so is all the greater when someone else is considered the cause, the agent of the findings, when in fact he or she is just as much an innocent bystander as the even more unfortunate victim of any severe rapidly evolving infection. Nature often seems constantly ahead of us in many of these matters, but that should not discourage professionals to try to do better by learning more about that which will confront us next.

In 2011-2012 the public at large has become aware of the problems with MRSA, methicillin-resistant-staphylococcus aureus, originally hospital based in the mid-2000s and now community based. ER doctors, pediatricians, pathologists, and medical examiners are now all aware of the problem and how to identify it in their regular practice. I doubt whether Dr. Gore or any of the others responding to the scenario of November 12, 1999, if they remain in practice, can claim to have never heard of it, and even if they are no longer in practice, the same. Affiant knows of a serious case of pneumonia in a four year old girl due to MRSA, the daughter of one of his recent fellows in Memphis, which was caught at a useful time in September 2011, and was immediately treated for sepsis, and has survived intact. The gain in knowledge in such cases is palpable.

What likely happened on November 12, 1999

The medical story actually begins a number of days before the 12th when Xavier's sister developed skin surface bacterial infection. By the usual close proximity of children of their ages, the bacteria jumped to the boy but not as a direct skin contact, more likely inhaled desquamating bacteria from her weeping lesions. If the adrenal and pancreatic development shown by the slides were also reflected in low functional competence, then aspects of the defenses of the child were inadequate and severe systemic sepsis became established, with the commonplace sequels of meningitis and cerebromeningitis. Even if their role is small, infection became established. The degree of infection in this brain is more than enough damage to make a small child unsteady on his feet, through loss of equilibrium from nerve injury and malfunction. Thence, flopping around and trying to gain vertical status, the encounter with the bathtub added to the medical presentation by acquisition of surface contusions while the bacteria were doing their thing in the brain. The boy was unfortunately terminally moribund on admission judging by the extent of the central nervous system disease which a more thorough review of the autopsy findings at the time would have revealed, as they now have come to light. There was no crime here, just rapidly advancing infection. The then young man serving as caretaker for the child, not being medically trained, could not have recognized the basic problem, and with the collapse of a young child ostensibly under his watch, would panic and fear for the child and for himself. That might have been reasonable in 1999 given the atmosphere which surrounded comparable events but should not obtain in 2012. Much if not most of the autopsy findings beyond the evident septic shock are due to the high fluid measures instituted after death in the spurious plan to salvage organs for near future transplantation. It is a good thing that did not happen because the infection would have been transplanted along with the organs, a startling phenomenon this affiant has seen more than once.

Respectfully submitted,

D. Radford Shanklin, M.D., F.R.S.M.
Emeritus Professor
University of Tennessee, Memphis
2 April 2012

C Stephenson Law, P.A.

NORTH ORANGE AVENUE, SUITE 500, ORLANDO, FLORIDA 32901
EL. 407-841-3361   FAX 407-843-3391
info@cstephensonlaw.com

January 31, 2014
Giovanni Vega, X12648
Suwannee Correctional Institution Annex
5964 U.S. Highway 90
Live Oak, Florida 32060

Re: Update on Case Status

Mr. Vega,

I've tried calling classifications at Suwannee CI this afternoon without success, so I am sending this in case I do not speak to you before you are able to receive this. I'm very pleased to let you know that the 5th DCA reversed and has mandated an evidentiary hearing in your case. The opinion was just emailed to me today from the 5th, and it does not become final and binding until the passage of 15 days without a motion for rehearing by the Attorney General's Office. If a motion for rehearing is filed, I will let you know.

I have contacted the Miami Innocence Project and Dr. Shanklin in anticipation of moving forward once the enclosed decision becomes final.

I will attempt to set up a phone conference with you, but again, in case this is able to reach you more quickly, I wanted to make sure to get it out to you as soon as possible.

Thank you and congratulations. We still have a battle in front of us, but this is a great step.

Sincerely,

Christopher M. Stephenson, Esq.

CS/ss

Enclosures: Decision, dated January 31, 2014 from 5th DCA

I arrived in Clermont once again. It was early 2014. All I kept thinking about was the reverse and remand for the evidentiary hearing by the Fifth District Court of Appeals. My lawyer, Stephenson, had already given me the bad news that Prof. Medical examiner Dr. Shanklin passed away. I was remaining as strong as I could. But deep down, I had a feeling the court would railroad me once again. The only evidence I was working with was Dr. Shanklin's autopsy report.

Lake Correctional was completely different. It was now a 90% white administration. I knew this from the minute I got off the Bluebird bus. There were three white sergeants looking for trouble. If I remember correctly, twelve of us arrived from different prisons. One Hispanic inmate got smacked up for complaining about the tight leg irons and one black inmate was smacked up for sucking his teeth. As I walked through the middle of the prison near the medical department, I noticed a big change. Restrictive movement, yelling at inmates, and no recreation. Inmates started to tell me stories of the excessive use of force and the white administration. I was not too worried because I was on my way to court, and I was closer to my mom's house.

A couple of inmates that I know from 2009 to 2010 were still there shaking and baking. Still had their connections. Everything was done more carefully and smoothly. I was going to the law library every day and attempting to learn cases that would help during my upcoming hearing. I got a little brave and started to draft a motion concerning a new law the governor signed July 1, 2013. For many years, Florida would allow any expert to testify for prosecutors with little or no experience on the issue being testified about. The new law requires the expert to have education in the specific area of testimony. I figured, since Dr. Gore was not a board-certified pathologist, the standards were lowered twice in order to make Gore chief medical examiner, and his degrees were from India and not accepted anywhere in the United States. I could file a motion based on this new constitutional change in law. I also included a Brady vs. Maryland claim. This means I accused the prosecutor of withholding evidence favorable to the defense. Specifically that the prosecution knew all about the corruption and investigation that was taking place in the Medical Examiner's Office headed by Dr. Gore from 1995 through 2002. I was incarcerated in 1999 and went to trial May 2001. I definitely fall in between that time.

Could you imagine if my trial lawyer would have presented this information to the jurors? No one on this earth would find a person guilty with the Medical Examiner's Office mixing evidence in hundreds if not thousands of murder cases. After doing a wonderful job on the motion, I filed it to the court under a 3.850 (b) (2) new law. Since the motion was filed pro se, which meant an inmate filed it, not an attorney, it would take a year or better to hear a response. When an attorney files motions, it takes a few months in Osceola County Florida. I wonder why? Could it be that prosecutors don't give a shit about inmate appeals? On the news channels, they sure act like they do!

I also decided to file for a change of sentence with the Florida government. Something like a clemency but different. The packet required me to write a paragraph or two about why I should be eligible for a change of sentence. I wrote my case was reversed and remanded by the fifth DCA based on a malicious, negligent medical examiner with a degree from India that could very well be fake. I then attached a copy of the University of Tennessee Medical Center, Dr. Shanklin's autopsy report as evidence. I wasn't supposed to attach the legal documents. But I know Florida denies 98% of all clemencies and sentence reductions anyway. It would not matter if I paid a lawyer $3000 to prepare the packet or if I do it myself. One day, it will surely be denied.

Does anyone know how the parole system operates in Florida? Anyone that was locked up prior to 1995 is eligible for parole. As the years pass by, inmates eligible for parole have passed away. Some were paroled, finished their parole, and moved on to the states. This has brought down the number of parole eligible inmates to less than three thousand. What would happen if the state were to release those inmates and keep a few hundred? Some people would be without a job right? So now you must be asking yourself, what if the inmate is not eligible for parole due to his sentence? Well, let me put it like this, I know men who have been down since the 70's and haven't received a written disciplinary report in over twenty-five years. Men who have successfully completed fifty programs and are ready to die in prison right now. If being clean for over twenty years is not enough, then what is enough? You have to draw the line somewhere. We are humans, not dinosaurs.

I decided to talk with Cynthia in person. I didn't want to speak about how much money she kept from me, but I just couldn't do it. It was hard to come to any agreement. She was upset because I didn't fully commit myself to her. I did not trust her one-inch. We decided to put a few things into work out there in the streets. I had to be careful and nice at the same time. Cynthia didn't need me, I needed her. The truth is she opened up a business in Ohio and was doing okay. She felt a little guilty about her actions and decided to give it a try. Not give *us* a try, only business a try. This would help me with the upcoming hearing.

Meanwhile, I started to deal with cigarettes. One carton of 305s would cost me $100. I would turn around and sell three packs for $100. The last pack I would convert into food. This was very little money compared with what I made years before that, but it was something! I thought I could slowly save and eventually have enough to defend myself in court. Out of the blue, I was picked up by the private transport officers in route to the Osceola County Jail. I had no clue as to why I was going to court. My understanding was that the evidentiary hearing had not been scheduled. This meant I left a lot of contraband behind. It was another loss.

The county jail is very different. The sheriff doesn't run the jail any longer, it is the commissioners. And those people make sure the jail is high and tight! They no longer attempt to talk when an inmate is being disorderly. Now they bring in a gun that looks like a small bazooka with three chambers. The gun shoots tear gas and rubber bullets. I was like, "Wow!" The commissary, as it is called in county jails, was super expensive. Ramen noodle soup was $.80, a small pouch of tuna $3.10 and a chili with beans is now $11.25 and once was $3.75. The county charges each inmate $2.00 each day for housing. Where's all the taxpayer's money going? They were selling Angus burgers for $16. I ended up spending some of the money I saved up at Lake Correctional, which wasn't much, and my mom ended up helping me with money for food.

I contacted a few news channels. Some gave me an interview, a chance to prove my innocent and explain how the justice system was treating me. Central Florida Orlando weekly newspaper published an article. Univision television reported on my case also. Channel 13 news was back and asking questions again. It was now time for the hearing. I knew I was down to one lawyer because the professor of law and director of the Innocence Clinic in Miami had backed down. They claimed no additional funding was available to continue with my representation. I asked them for help with other legal issues and they didn't give me a chance. Stephenson, my lawyer, advised I ask the judge to moot the reversal. That would have meant to leave it undecided while I spend thousands of dollars hunting down a medical examiner not scared to testify against the people who pay them—the state.

Where was I going to get money? I didn't have a team out there to help me and it would have taken me a little while before I could even start to form such a team. I told Stephenson he was fired. He asked me not to fire him, that he would withdraw himself. I responded by advising that if the judge asked me questions, you're fired! Period! The judge accepted Stephenson's withdrawal and I requested the right to be represented by the public defender's office. The judge looked at me as if I was crazy, but the news channels were there, so he appointed me a public defender. I was in the county jail waiting for my new public defender to visit me. My mom called and found out his name was Ochoa. He explained to my mom that he had a lot of cases and would visit me shortly. He went on to say, "Giovanni has a complicated sexual charge." And he had to study the case. My poor mom must've snapped over the phone when she explained her son was charged with murder! It was a bad start already!

I immediately looked up state law on attorney-client regulations and wrote Mr. Ochoa a letter. A week later, we were sitting face-to-face. I was nice and respectful. I provided him a copy of the 3.850(b) (2) motion I filed and requested him to adopt the motion, to put his name on it. Mr. Ochoa refused. As he read it in front of me, I realized he had no appellate education. I started to throw case law at him in regard to my reversal and he was in wonderland. I became upset but kept my cool. Mr. Ochoa and I couldn't agree to anything. He said the judge would not order the public defender's office to provide funding for a medical examiner. That the judge would set the evidentiary hearing sooner than expected. At last, Mr. Ochoa advised he would pay me a visit in a few weeks.

I went back to my assigned cell in the county jail and filed two handwritten letters to the judge requesting state funding for an expert under Ake v. Oklahoma and an extension of time for the hearing. The judge granted both. I guess they treated the letters as motions, and it did the job. I was transported back to Lake Correctional. I couldn't hustle too much because I was in the law library and attempting to learn more case law and rules of appellate procedure. Mr. Ochoa was not communicating with me, and I decided to file under Nelson v. State. I was asking the judge to have Mr. Ochoa withdraw from my case and appoint new counsel. I was transported back to the county jail, and in front of the judge I was again. The judge was upset, and you could see it in his face. When I was given a chance to explain in detail the grounds of violations Mr. Ochoa was guilty of, the judge would cut me right off. I quickly realized I was in a no-win situation and was trying to squeeze in as much as I could.

The judge ruled it was "premature" to fire Mr. Ochoa. I lost the first battle. Back to Lake Correctional I went. I continued the fight with the public defender Ochoa. This time, he was refusing to hire Dr. Anderson. I had to write a letter to the judge claiming constitutional violations. Doctor Anderson was hired! I filed a complaint with the head public defender and explained how I'm more professional than his employee was. This caused more tension. I was not getting any help from anyone in this world. I was stuck filing motions on my own and in a confrontation with Mr. Ochoa.

Then I filed under Nelson v. State once again. This time, the judge wasn't just looking upset, he was acting upset. As I pleaded my grounds to have Ochoa fired, the judge cut me off and refused to assign different counsel. When I sat down in the seats where inmates are called by turn to see the judge, the female inmate in front of me exploded with tears. She turned around and told me that I sounded like a lawyer explaining my grounds. That any other judge would have given me a good appellate counsel. What the female inmate said next is what shocked me cold. "That trash of a lawyer, Ochoa, represents me also and I am here to fire him. I have no chance."

I didn't know whether to feel bad for her or to feel bad about what I went through that day. A public defender that was there representing other defendants, came by and whispered in my ear, "Good job." I begged the public defender to take my case but it was not possible. Especially with the judge refusing. The female inmate went in front of the judge, broke down crying and explained the lawyer wasn't doing anything to help her. Denied! Then I watched a sentencing hearing. A young married man with two newborn children was charged with trafficking methamphetamines. His first offense. The pastor from his church came to give testimony of how the young Hispanic was a member of the church and was a great man who made a mistake. The mother gave a testimony of pure tears and suffering. The wife cried to the judge explaining she needed him to work and help with the bills or they would lose their home.

This young Hispanic male even had his boss come in and speak highly of his work ethics. Finally the young defendant testified he became desperate and made a quick dollar. He went on to say he was working while out on bond. I quickly analyzed a charge, the testimony, and the fact it was his first case. I made an approximate guess somewhere between ten and twenty years' probation. Maybe if the judge was still upset, he would get three to five years prison followed by probation. I almost fainted when the judge sentenced him to thirty years in prison.

When I was transported back to Lake Correctional, I found out 250 inmates were transferred to different prisons. They did these mass transfers on the regular basis. The administration was changing also. I started to see more Hispanic and black officers as I did the first time I was there. Things started to calm down a little better as far as officers abusing mentally, physically and emotionally. I was going to church every week and praying that God would send me help. All the court proceedings really broke me down. I was depressed and aggravated. I didn't want to lose my hope, my faith in God and the upcoming evidentiary hearing.

One day, I went to pick up some cigarettes. I had all of the packs sold but didn't see my client. I was forced to hide the cigs in some potato chip bags, sealed. As I was taking a shower that night, the K9 dog and his pal came into the quad I was housed in. The search was light, and I was thinking I was going to pass. The K9 officer yelled out, "Who lives in 4012?" I got out quickly and said it was me. The officer asked who else lives in the room, and I said my bunky had nothing to do with his discovery. I told him to take me to confinement. It is what it is! I will never take anyone down with me.

In the disciplinary hearing, I pleaded guilty and was sentenced to thirty days in confinement. I appealed the disciplinary report on a technicality. It took two weeks, and the disciplinary report was overturned. I thought I was going to be released when I received the grievance answer and it didn't work out that way. Classification went by my cell and told me I was pending transfer. I couldn't believe it. For cigarettes? Inmates get caught with ounces of K2, cell phones, shanks and come right out of confinement to general population. I get caught with cigarettes and it's a transfer? Wow. I automatically knew someone went to the administration and spoke lies about me.

When people owe money, are trying to get you out the way, or get jealous, they do chump moves like that. The truth is, I have seen with my own eyes the biggest haters and lowlife snitches in the prison system. Believe me when I tell you, dudes walk around acting hard and tough, meanwhile, if it came down to it, those same dudes will turn on their grandmother in for a reduction in time. I spotted one in the captain's office pointing at inmate mug shots on the computer. When we confronted the inmate he answered, "The captain is my friend and we're only looking up other old friends." Really? This same inmate ended up telling everything he knew and not about inmates, but what officers were doing.

Sometimes I wish I could be moved to an island by myself where no one is around, and I could go fishing until I die. Then I snapped back to reality and continued to be in the struggle. I was in the Lake Correctional confinement until the last week of November 2014. On the day of my transfer, I looked at the files and discovered I was being sent to Bowling Green, Florida, once again. I got a little nervous because of the fallout I had with the property sergeant and all the BS I went through in 2007 while at Hardee correctional. Nonetheless, I was on my way.

G. K. VEGA

Giovanni's Court Battle

November _____, 2013

Chairman, Medical Examiners Office
P.O. Box 1489
Tallahassee, Florida 32302

Re: Dr. Shashishekhar Bhasker Gore
License #ME31791   MEH-2963-99
Official Complaint

To Whom It May Concern,

On November 13, 1999 Shashi B. Gore, M.D. performed an autopsy on Xavier Collado, wherein he attributed the cause of death to subdural hemorrhage, due to closed head trauma, due to blunt force head trauma, and the manner of death a homicide. This complaint surrounds the autopsy report and procedure as well as Dr. Gore's testimony and role in the connected criminal proceedings...

Enclosed to this complaint in the form of a professional autopsy review by Professor Douglas R. Shanklin M.D. Are copies of the autopsy report, Central Florida news channels reports. New State of Florida law signed by Governor Rick Scott, HB 7015 regarding expert testimony. (July 1st 2013). It is alleged that Dr. Gore performed a substandard autopsy, cross-contaminated data and relied only on the Osceola Medical Center opinions, provided numerous erroneous facts and false testimony in a first degree murder trial...

Dr. Gore's neglect, errors, false testimony and malfeasance performance led to a wrongful conviction, placing an innocent man in prison for life. Moreover, he caused severe mental, emotional, and financial harm to an already grieving and traumatized family...

The following are medical examiners, attorneys who have reviewed the materials within this case and assert Dr. Gore's negligence, as well as the serious and grave questions surrounding the integrity of Dr. Gore's autopsy and testimony:

1.   Professor Douglas R. Shanklin M.D., F.R.S.M.
2.   William R. Anderson M.D.
3.   Attorney- Christopher M. Stephenson
4.   Attorney- Bernard V. Klienman
5.   Attorney- Craig Trocino Miami University School of Law Innocence Clinic
Recently reviewing materials in order to provide expert testimony are the following:

1.   Jane M. Orient, M.D. Executive Director of the Association of American Physicians and Surgeons
2.   Jennifer Turner, ACLU

Also inclosed is an article which reports on an internal investigation which reveals that, among other things hundreds of cases in the Medical Examiners Office were cross-contaminated as early as 1994. This article points out that Dr. gore is not a board certified forensic pathologist. Another article indicates ethical misgivings surrounding Dr. Gore. Governor Rick Scott's new signed law, HB 7015, is clearly a move by the State of Florida in order to prohibit false testimony by non board certified medical examiners. Enclosed is the news article on the action taken by the MEC in revoking licenses as soon as HB 7015 was signed into law.

Our team is pushing for an F.B.I. Investigation concerning allegations of Dr. Gore receiving funds and other material goods from central Florida prosecutors in exchange for botched autopsy, false testimony leading to wrongful convictions. (Dr. Gore was already guilty of receiving payments for private work at the county morgue. A clear and direct violation of MEC chapter 11g-1.002(10)(a)(b)

180

"Medical Examiners shall not utilize a business or professional association in which he, his spouse or children has a business interest for any services, including secretarial, labatory, courier and investigate"...

Based on the enclosed information, it is clear that an exhaustive and extensive independent review of Dr. Gore's role in this case be examined and proper action be taken towards a new trial in Osceola County, Florida. Dr. Gores incompetence was and still is a liability to Orange/Osceola County Prosecutions. 95% of Defendant's across the State of Florida whom Dr. Gore handled autopsy's and other evidence's pertaining to criminal accusations, are not aware of these horrible actions by Dr. Gore and prosecutors botching autopsy's and false testimony. Many Defendant's are poor, unable to read, definitely will never understand the law and/or its corruption within state employee's. It is also noted that Central Florida Channel 9, Channel 13, are reporting on the case. Dateline, 48 Hrs., and 60 minutes are presently being contacted in order to let the nation know what has transpired in the State of Florida Medical Examiners Office, Orlando. The elevates the need for exhaustive review to the level of great public importance...

(Note) We are working to provide evidence which will find Dr. Shashi Gore guilty, among other charges, of obstructing justice and perjury. Claiming he held a board certification in pathology and other degrees from universities while providing testimony in Case# 1999-CF-2565 Osceola County Florida. Dr. Gore does not hold any certifications from specialty boards recognized by the Florida board which regulates the profession for which he is licensed. The practitioner has not verified the information provided to the Florida Department of Health concerning degrees at numerous universities...

Dr. Shashi Gore's corruption falls in violation of Rick Scoot's new law HD 7015. Senator Tom Lee, Rep. Larry Metz, Rep. Matt Gaetz, Tom Feeny CEO-AIF, and Vincent Degennaro M.D., all have praised new HD 7015...

It all starts with former District Attorney Lawson Lamar's influence to lower the hiring standards for Chief Medical Examiner position. Dr. Shashi Gore then proceeded and acted in the color of state law. Therefore, The State of Florida is responsible for his malpractice...

Thank you in advance for your assistance within this matter.

cc.   District 9 State Attorney

F.B.I.

Channel 13/ Channel 9/ Dateline

United States Attorney, Orlando Division

U.S> Department of Justice   _____

June 30, 2015

Honorable Judge Jon B. Morgan
2 Courthouse Square
Kissimmee, FL 34741

Reference to: **CASE #1999 CF 2565 Giovanni Vega**

Honorable Judge Morgan,

Sir, at this time, I respectfully request for the July 20th 2015 2:30pm, Evidentiary Hearing to be re-scheduled 30-days or as your Honorable court may find adequate. I request a Nelson Hearing in order for me to demonstrate ineffective assistance and prejudice from counsel.

The Florida Rules of Court, clearly state in **Chapter 4, Rule 4-1-3, "A Lawyer should pursue a matter on behalf of a client despite of opposition, obstruction or personal inconvenience to the Lawyer and take whatever lawful and ethical measures are required to vindicate a client's cause or endeavor."**

For the past few weeks, I have mailed, attempted to call land mailed the public defender forms to Attorney █████ Chavez, requesting that he have both medical examiners Dr. Stephen J. Nelson and Dr. Jon R. Thogmartin subpoena/or hired in order to testify for the defense. These testimonies will be crucial because it will be part of the reverse and remand from the 5th DCA.

My mother has also e-mailed Mr. Chavez with no response on his behalf! I am claiming a constitutional violation because I am being denied access to material evidence favorable to my defense. Due process clause of the Fourteen Amendment and (through incorporation) in the Compulsory Process clause of the Sixth Amendment.

Love v. Johnson, 57 f.3d 1305 (4th cir.1995) "Counsel Failing to call particular expert medical examiner"

Lebron v. state, 100 So.3d 132(5th DCA2012) "Counsel Failure to call witness to strengthen credibility"

Mcclellan v. state, 112 So.3d 754(2nd DCA 2013)"An indigent defendant's right to the assistance of an expert at state expense is rooted in the 14th Amendment, guarantee of Fundamental Fairness"

Mcdonald v. state, 101 So.3d 914(5th DCA2012).

Respectfully Submitted,

Giovanni Vega

Case # 1999 CF 2565

August 10, 2015

Honorable Judge   **RE: Case # 1999 CF 2565**
Jon B. Morgan
2 Courthouse Square
Kissimmee, FL 34741

Dear Honorable Judge Morgan,

Please do not schedule the **Evidentiary Hearing** and do not allow for a transport order to be filed until the 5th District Court of Appeals reviews the February 2nd 2015 and the July 27th 2015 Nelson Hearing Transcripts. I stand by my ground that an **Evidentiary Hearing** without both Medical Examiners to testify about Dr. Gore's discipline, Dr. Stephen J. Nelson and Dr. Jon R. Thogmartin will be in violation of my 14th Amendment Constitutional Right, "Fair Due Process".

I now request for Former Coordinator Office Manager to Dr. Gore, Ms. Sheri Blanton, District 9, to be subpoena or hired by the public defender's office. Ms. Blanton has valuable information concerning Dr. Gore and his work ethics, etc....

I am willing to stay in prison as long as it takes to better prepare a defense for this hearing. It was under the understanding that equal justice was also for individuals who are poor. Unfortunately, that has not been the case! We are talking about a corrupt Medical Examiner who Botched Autopsies, falsely testified at trails which gave people "Life" in prison, maliciously changed death results so that Orange County is free from paying millions of dollars in wrongful death lawsuits and most severely, he was not qualified to testify at anyone's trial.

Always, Thank You for your Patience.

Respectfully Submitted,

Giovanni Vega

G. K. VEGA

August 10, 2015

Law Offices of Robert Wesley   RE: CASE # 1999 CF-2565
Public Defender, Mr. ▓▓▓ Chavez
435 N. Orange Ave. Suite #400
Orlando, Florida 32801

Mr. Chavez,

Please be advised, I am requesting that you hire or subpoena former Forensic Coordinator from the District 9 Office. (Ms. Sheri Blanton)

At a Deposition, question her about the investigations that took place at the District 9 Medical Examiner's Office and its **Mishandling of Evidence in hundreds of cases.** Ms. Blanton was Dr. Gore's Office Manager and has a lot of information pertaining to Dr. Gore and all his **corruption.**

A failure to hire or subpoena Ms. Sheri Blanton will be a violation of my *Sixth Amendment Constitutional Right to "Effective" Assistance of Counsel and 14th Amendment Right, "Fair due Process"*.

My case has been a miscarriage of Justice. At this point, I can only prepare of the 5th DCA and PRAY that the appeal judges determine that my rights have been violated and reverse for a new trail.

Love v. Johnson 57 f.3d 1305 4th cir.1995

"Improperly denied access to material witnesses favorable to Defense".

Respectfully Submitted,

Giovanni Vega

Cc: Honorable Judge Morgan

August 25, 2015

Mr. Chavez,

Sir, please be advised, I have filed three letters with the 5th District Court of Appeals requesting for a review of both "Nelson Hearings", dated February 2nd, 2015 and July 27, 2015. I explained that my Sixth Amendment Constitutional Right has been violated because you, Attorney ⬛⬛⬛ Chavez, refused to hire and or subpoena former Chairman of the Medical Examiners Commission, Dr. Stephen J. Nelson and former Board Investigator, Dr. Joh R. Thogmatin. Dr. Nelson handed down the discipline on Dr. Shashi Gore in 2004 and Dr. Thogmartin was in charge of the misconduct investigation ...

I explained to the 5th District Court of Appeals that if the Evidentiary Hearing is held without "all" experts and witnesses, I'm requested, that this hearing be held in *Violation of my 14th Amendment Constitutional Right to a "Fair" proceeding* ...

Last week I mailed Judge Morgan and you, Mr. Chavez, a letter requesting for you to hire and or subpoena former Forensic Coordinator and Office Manager to Dr. Shashi Gore, Mrs. Sheri Blanton. Mrs. Blanton is very well aware of the corruption of *"mishandling of evidence"* within the Medical Examiner's Office from 1996 through 2002. (Mrs. Blanton is material witness)...

At this time I am requesting for your Public Defender's Office to subpoena, Ms. Iris Soto and Mr. Sipriano Reyes. Both Mrs. Soto and Mr. Reyes statements are enclosed with this letter. The statement evidence has never been addressed to the court because Attorney Christopher Stephenson failed to do so. Both statements are material evidence and should be allowed at the hearing to better prove that I have been wrongfully convicted.

With all due respect, Sir, as of today, I have basically informed you of all the finding of witnesses. You are maliciously denying my right to better prepare a defense. Obviously, your actions show, you could care less if I lose this hearing! For the record, there is a total of (five) material witnesses that I have requested for your office to hold depositions on.

Respectfully Submitted,

Giovanni Vega
Giovanni Vega

Cc: Honorable Judge Jon B. Morgan

Selina (Sister), Aurora (Mom), Zinia (Fiancé),
Gio, Richard (Mom's Husband), Raquel (Sister)

I arrived in Hardee correctional in the first week of December 2015. I was told the old Philippine property sergeant had died a while ago. The searching of my property and intake was easy. I did not hear any officers screaming or harassing inmates. The officers were mostly white but civilized. Hardee is a good prison for those trying to lay back and do time calmly. They offer classes from the University of South Florida in entrepreneurship. There is a great gavel club and music band program. The normal General Education diploma classes and the Life-Path group dorm. The Life Path are classes of self-betterment. Things like, character qualities, brotherhood series, anger management and more. The visitation park is really tricky. There are about twenty cameras watching everything. But the officers do not harass the visits. What they began to do was considered harassment. This was to pick out visitors and inmates to search during the visit. I think they got way out of hand on that one. Overall it was not bad.

My evidentiary hearing was scheduled for January 15, 2016. I was not preparing anymore because I knew that hearing would be a negative outcome. I managed to have the judge allow Dr. Anderson's testimony but the state would cry Dr. Anderson's autopsy report was denied in 2010–2011. My mom was starting to gather up family members in order to attend the hearing. I told her my chances of winning where little. I did not have a good appellate lawyer. Dr. Shanklin passed away. The public pretender was not going to represent me correctly.

When the private transport officers picked me up at Hardee, I was thinking about the long trips they take me on. They handcuffed me with a black box, Daisy chained down to the leg irons. The back of the van is exactly like a dog cage. I could barely put my ass on the steel seat it was so small and cold. Bowling Green to Osceola County is about one hour and a half. I left on a Monday morning and did not reach Osceola county jail until Wednesday night. We stopped in what seems like every county jail down to Miami. The handcuffs were killing me. They cut my skin and made my fingers numb. I met a man who was picked up in Oregon. They drove to Montana and back to Oregon. Then they flew him to Arizona. From Arizona the transport company kept driving him until he reached me in Florida. He was passed out sleeping, dirty on the van floor with handcuffs and lesions. His destination was Missouri. The transport officers promised he was going to Orlando International Airport in order to fly to Atlanta. Crazy!

The way the private company transports results in cruel and unusual punishment. I can't believe no one has stepped in and penalized the transport company for holding inmates in custody way too long. They feed us exactly $2 of McDonald's or Burger King for breakfast, lunch, and dinner with water. As the years have gone by, some employees of the Osceola County Jail have retired, quit, or change jobs. Very few remain. Most of the few know me from when I was young. I showed the reversal from the Fifth DCA to those officers, and they were amazed. A lot of people could not believe I was still locked up.

January 15, 2016 finally comes around. The news channels were parked behind the Osceola County Courthouse. Reporters were ready to hear what the judge had to say. My mom, her husband, my sisters, niece and nephew, aunts, cousins and my old roommate, Maurice from Suwannee correctional, were all there showing support. It was nice to see everyone together. At least for that little while. Before the hearing started I told the public defender to go over and ask the prosecutor for a plea deal. The answer was no! They were ready to drop the charges if Dr. Shanklin was able to testify. But since Dr. Shanklin passed away, why would the prosecutor offer anything?

The hearing consisted of my testimony and Dr. Anderson's autopsy report conclusion. It was not enough for the judge. The prosecution claimed he had a constitutional right to cross-examine Dr. Shanklin and it wouldn't be right to proceed with the case. I was broke down completely. I was so hurt that I gave up on praying and having faith. I could not believe God allowed me to go through such a devastating day. When I lost trial, I was messed up. When I was sentenced to life, I didn't eat for almost two weeks.

After the evidentiary hearing, I gave up on everything and everyone! However, I was not giving up on trying to be free. You would think my family would visit me more often and help me with the emotional part. My mom still was visiting once a month and to get one of my sisters to visit, it will take an act of God. At the end of the day, it's no one's fault that I am in prison so I have to move forward. When I was being transported to Hardee Correctional, I only had one thing in mind, money. By the time, I reached over sixteen years in prison and my youth going down the drain. My only true chance at freedom is through a lawyer and lawyers do not work for free anymore. We live in a world where money talks and bullshit walks. Especially with the Florida Justice System. Why do you think millionaires can be charged with murder and 95% of them will not do any time? They touch the right pockets with the right amount of money. The other 5% come to prison with 3% coming right back out on appeal. My trial judge, the same one who gave me life, used his influence so that his nephew got three years in prison for a string of armed robberies. This kid had seven punishable by life felonies. No one can tell me otherwise because I was in the same quad at South Bay with this kid, looking through his photo album with my judge at a barbecue. I wasn't hating or mad. I was just wishing I would have been in the same shoes.

Every government in other countries are corrupt as well. The United States is not the only one. When it comes to Florida, this state is on another level of blind justice. I immediately started to contact old friends and was doing everything possible to make new friends. Cynthia didn't like how I was thinking or talking, so she decided to turn her back on me once again. She took the little money I had saved up and probably used it to catch-up on all her bills. I never talk to her again! I should not have given her a second chance at business anyway. Maybe it was because at the moment I was attempting to come up and make it happen anyway possible. A prisoner who is smart can do anything from this place. Anything! It just takes longer than being out there free and able to move quicker. Some inmates are blessed to have a mommy and daddy that will do anything in the world to help. Some inmates have aunts and uncles who will sell a car or boat to help. Some inmates have grandparents who will sell a piece of land and help. I didn't have such blessings. For thirteen years straight throughout different prisons, I had to feed myself. Experts, lawyers, and private investigators I had to hustle and pay myself. Was I wrong?

Hold up. Did you want me to sit back, and give up, and smoke K2? Did you want me to chase female officers with sexually transmitted diseases? Did you want me to settle for being gay? Or maybe I should have been a model inmate with the Bible on my arms going to the chapel five times a week satisfied with the writing materials they received? I am not cut from that type of plant. You could put me in the middle of Thailand, and I will find a way to provide for myself. In 2013, while I was at Swantanamo Bay, I had to swallow my pride, asked my mom for a few dollars every two weeks in order to not relapse and possibly get killed by officers for flooding the prison with drugs.

Back to Hardee 2016. I was housed in gangland, Charlie dormitory. The perfect spot to serve these men with synthetic heroin, K2, and cigarettes. I met someone who was on the same level as I named "Trick." We helped each other as much as we could. All our business deals were on point and straight! This man out of Pensacola, Florida, has been down since 1989 and deserves his freedom. He wasn't walking around acting hard-core or foolish. All he wanted to do was send money to his daughter and have food to eat at night. I respect that! Trick and I were trying to get all the $50 and $100 sales as we possibly could. I know that little sales here and they were not going to help me fast enough. I had to find outside help, and I had to do it fast.

I was introduced to a young Mexican female named Ines. After talking over the phone, I decided it was time to see what Ines was all about in person. She turned out to be a very nice person. Briefly, her story was that she came from Cancun, Mexico, in search for better life. She had two kids while in the United States and the children's father turned out to be a bum. Ines worked in a tomato factory, which meant she was struggling. Really struggling! No family in Florida and depending on the church to help her with any major needs she ran into. This meant I had to teach Ines a thing or two in order to make good money. It was not going to happen from one day to another. She didn't even have a computer in the mobile home/trailer called home for the time being. What caught my attention was Ines told me she had some relatives living in the border of Mexico and Texas. If I pay for the trip, the pounds of weed would cost $150.

While I was at the visit one day with my mom, a Cuban inmate walked up to me and explained his wife has a sister in the table who would like to speak with me. The young Cuban female named Adianez who's humble and caring. I could not believe what I heard when she told me she had looked me up on Google and read articles about me. Adianez expressed her thoughts over my conviction and wished for my freedom. I thanked her, and we spoke a few times over the phone. Nothing ever turned out as far as business because she lives with her mom and dad at the age of thirty-six. Adianez will never have the courage to bust a move on the street.

After another visit, a friend of mine named Flaco told me he knew of a female, early forties, who grew up in Cataño, Puerto Rico, with him. I ended up talking to Dalniliz, and we kicked it off nice. I explained what I had to get done and also that I knew a few things that could help us both make money. I was unable to see Dalniliz right away because she had to remove herself from Flaco's visit list and then wait six months to fill the application and get on my list. While we waited, I was sending all the money I was making to her. I took a risk. But I had to because I didn't have anyone else trustworthy of holding money. I knew people, but those people could have very well stolen my money and not talk to me again. The risk paid off. Dalniliz never took a penny from me. Instead, she opened a PayPal account and had my money available when needed.

There wasn't a lot of money at Hardee. That prison is a dump when it comes to making money. However, I had to feel and know that I was doing everything possible to help myself. A friend of mine put my photo on a dating site and within a few days I meet a Cuban female named Isis. We must've talked one time, she looked me up, and told me all about my own case. Isis did not want a relationship with me nor did she want to hustle. At least she never told me. Isis has a brother in prison that was wrongfully convicted also! The story with the dude is that he had a female with a young daughter. After some years of relationship, he separates from the female. Upset with his decision, the female coaches her daughter to say she was touched inappropriately. I am not going to write about whether Isis's brother is guilty or innocent. I will advise that I have seen with my own eyes these same cases, turn out to be the mother mad and desperate to damage a man's life. This happens more than anyone can imagine. When I went to the Osceola County Jail in 2014, I met an older man accused of sexual battery on his stepdaughter. The mother didn't allow doctors to examine the ten-year-old claiming the incident took place weeks prior to the man's arrest. This was all hearsay! I sat down with the older man and asked if he was truly innocent. I went on to advise him about what to have his lawyer do in order to prove his innocence.

When I was studying the three credit hours psychology books from Ashworth University, I learned that children would tell a lie and believe it themselves. Especially if the mother coaches and does a good job in convincing the child. The lawyer has to get the judge to give an order to the Department of Children and Families to question the little girl without the mom. This can be done with the mom standing outside of the room. Children and family counselors, or the defense lawyer, has to buy a McDonald's happy meal and feed the child during questioning. I watched the old man pack his stuff and leave the county jail. The alleged victim confessed her mommy made up the story and she did not want to lie anymore.

I had my friend put a photo again on the Internet. This time, I looked through the ads and saw the beautiful smile I will never forget for the rest of my life. I sent out a hello! No response. The next day, I sent another short message. This time I got a response. The first time Zinia and I talked will be something special to remember. When I explained about my incarceration, Zinia snapped and was acting like she was going to turn me in or something. She demanded my full name in order to look me up and find out all about me. She acted so aggressive that I almost, and I mean just barely hung up and gave up on her. I was all in already, so I continued to give her the information of the news articles, motions and anything else I can possibly think of my case.

When we finished talking that day, I was asking myself what I got myself into? No one I ever met had been like Zinia. For a minute, I thought she might have been a former police or something. We talked the following day. I guess you can say I was interrogated. The more we talked, the more I found out how exactly the same we were. My birthday August fourteen, and her birthday August nineteen. Both Leos, both really clean, both have to finish things we start, both have strong characters, both nonjudgmental. We both have good hearts. Both are precautious. We both like to travel. Both like strawberries. I felt like it was too good to be true! To be honest, it was like my spirit came out of me and connected with hers. And we hadn't met in person yet!

I felt super good about Zinia. But while this was going on, in the back of my mind I knew I had to keep myself focused. I continued to sell and make a little money. Zinia had been praying asking God for a husband prior to meeting me. I'm sure she must have asked God 1000 times whether it was me, Giovanni? Why would God bring an inmate to her? Why would God bring someone with a life sentence who has been in prison for so long? Most people look down on anyone who is locked up. Most people would not even speak to someone in my shoes. Zinia did what many people wouldn't do. She went to church on the regular and prayed.

On November 16, 2016, I met my baby in person. Everything was automatic. As if we knew each other for twenty years. We talked about everything. I explained how down I felt when I lost the evidentiary hearing and the reason I gave up on faith. I went on to express that I didn't want to fully commit to God and then be dropped off again. I was still hurt emotionally. Calmly and slowly she started to read Bible verses to me. I don't know how, but we began to pray each night together. I even enrolled in the University of South Florida classes at Hardee. Eventually earning credit hours in entrepreneurship. I also ended up moving to the Life Path group dormitory. There, I earned a couple of certificates and character qualities and brotherhood.

Hardee got a new warden and with a new warden comes change. New administration, new rules and regulations. Three dorms were closed and 400 inmates transferred. We were getting searched twice per week. On one day, fifty-three rapid response team officers and ten K9 dogs searched until they were tired of searching. They found cell phones, knives, drugs, and other petty contraband. During that time, I paid an attorney named Morris $2,500 to review my case. I was robbed! The same way when I was at South Bay, and I paid $3,500 to a lawyer named Conception. Legally robbed!

Anyhow, I was happy that I was not transferred. I wanted to stay at Hardee. One hour away from Zinia. On top of that, Hardee was not a bad prison. I only saw a few officers assaulted and inmate use of force. The prison had some asshole officers but overall nothing serious. If you responded with yes sir, no sir, it was all good. I received a letter from an appellate lawyer assigned to handle the evidentiary hearing appeal. The lawyer claimed I did not have any issues to raise and therefore filed for the appeal to be denied. I ended up doing some research in the law library and filing myself, pro se. I was denied faster than a person receives a light bill. That's how they play.

In 2017, I asked Zinia to marry me. Not only did I fall in love, but in my heart and soul I knew my soul mate would come only once in the lifetime. Never did I think I was able to cry in front of a woman. I didn't even know what it felt like to accept your partner as is! I always found faults in my past relationships. I never found not one problem with Zinia! We bumped heads a couple of times here and there but nothing out of hand. Everything was perfect with my lioness.

Classification denied our request to marry stating Zinia submitted the visitation application with the relationship as cousin. We both explain to the supervisor it was a mistake and that Zinia could refile the application with the change in relationship. Can you believe this nasty, no-good, unprofessional lady suspended my fiancé's visit for six months? Further stating the original visit application was fraudulent. I now had to start the grievance procedure. And when we file grievances you never know how long it will take to get relief or denial. The informal grievance was denied. The formal grievance was denied.

Over two months went by, and I finally was able to file the last grievance to Tallahassee. My fiancé was filing complaints to the regional director's office and the warden. On the fourth month of the six-month suspension, I had Zinia e-mail the head of classification. She asked if it was possible for her to refile the visit application. The supervisor accepted and the very next morning classification received the faxed visit application. We waited two weeks and then Zinia called to check the status. My classification officers said the assistant warden had to approve the visits again. One week later, Zinia called again and was told the warden had to approve the visits.

I knew they were 100% full of shit then. In total, we waited five months for approval once again. Do you want to know what was really unprofessional and malicious on behalf of classification? I never received a grievance response from Tallahassee in the mail because all along it was approved. I slowed down with seeing other people at the visits. Eventually, I was only visiting with my fiancé and my family. I received a visit from my first cousin Nathan after not seeing him for almost twenty years. It was a great visit. As I write this book, I'm waiting to see him again. My mom brings her in-laws sometimes, and I enjoyed visiting with them very much. My mom's husband also visits me from time to time.

In December 2017, right before New Year's, I was sent under investigation. A so-called friend of mine passed me an MP4 Music player with videos in it while officers were searching for music players with videos because they were not authorized. I get caught with the MP4 player and housed confinement. I thought I would do fifteen days in the box and get out with no problem. They accused me of being involved with the computers in the chapel and distribution of videos. You already know they were wrong because I never went in the chapel, not one time. So how was I involved with computers? One thing I have learned from the Florida Department of Corrections is officials will falsify anything in order to mess with your time.

Before I went under investigation, I paid a good appellate attorney named McLain. The Osceola sheriffs altered/damaged the interrogation tape and convinced the judge I did not request an attorney during said questioning. McLain was able to locate the tape within the courthouse, sat down with an audio video expert, and recorded a copy for further review. Two different audio video experts concluded I stated the following, "You said I can talk to a lawyer, can I talk to a lawyer?" The detective responded, "Do you wish to continue to talk to us?" Upset from the beating the sheriff gave me and all the blood in my face and shoulders, I yelled back, "I just told you, man, I just told you, bro."

On February 4, 2018, I had to hear on the radio the Patriots versus Eagles. I could barely get the station because the confinement was surrounded by cement walls. By the third quarter I knew my patriots were going to lose. I believe the defense was not able to execute at full potential because Butler did not play at cornerback. That's just my opinion. Either way, Brady seemed to be in his prime throwing the football. The defense did not make the one important stop that would win the game. The G.O.A.T. has won five Super Bowls and lost in three, for a total of eight. If that is not the greatest of all time, what it is?

My mom and fiancé were calling classification and asking if I was going to be transferred, and to please keep me in Central Florida. The lying witch of a classification officer I had, assured them I would stay in Central Florida. On February 6, 2018, I was on my way to

Central Florida reception center East unit. I asked the bus driver officer where I was going, and he said, Okeechobee. Okeechobee is in Southeast Florida and the route comes out of South Florida Reception Center. This goes to show you these Departments of Correction officials will lie in a heartbeat. They don't care about the inmate or the families. To make matters worse, I was transferred because of an MP4 with movies in it. Are you serious? The MP4 even had the other inmate's name in the memory. The sergeant who found it knew it wasn't mine, but he lives to harass and punish inmates anyway he possibly can.

IMPORTANT INFORMATION ABOUT
YOUR DRINKING WATER

Martin Correctional Institution Has Levels of Total Trihalomethanes (TTHMs) and Haloacetic Acids (HAA5s) Above Drinking Water Standards

The Martin Correctional Institution water system has violated a drinking water standard. Although this is not an emergency, as consumers, you have a right to know what happened, what you should do, and what we are doing to correct this situation.

We routinely monitor for the presence of drinking water contaminants. The latest test results we received in April, 2009 show that our system exceeds the standard or maximum contaminant level (MCL) for Total Trihalomethanes (TTHMs) and Haloacetic Acids (HAA5s). The standard for TTHMs is 0.080 milligrams per liter (mg/L). The running annual average concentration of TTHMs in the water is 0.142 mg/L. The standard for HAA5s is 0.060 mg/L. The running annual average concentration of HAA5s in the water is 0.072 mg/L.

You do NOT need to use an alternative (e.g., bottled) water supply. However, if you have specific health concerns, consult your doctor.

This is not an immediate risk. If it had been, you would have been notified immediately. However, *some people who drink water containing trihalomethanes in excess of the MCL over many years may experience problems with their liver, kidneys, or central nervous system, and may have an increased risk of getting cancer. Some people who drink water containing haloacetic acids in excess of the MCL over many years may have an increased risk of getting cancer.*

The Florida Department of Corrections (DC) has completed a modification of the water treatment process to reduce the concentration of these parameters below their MCL. DC placed the modified treatment process in service in June, 2009. We expect the results of the analysis of the samples collected next calendar quarter will be below the MCL for both contaminants.

For more information, please contact ▓▓▓▓▓▓▓▓ at (954) 202-3933.

6-30-09

PWS ID Number: __4434406__   Date Notice Distributed: __June, 2009__

DRINKING WATER WARNING

Hardee C.I. Well # (4) Tested Positive for Fecal Indicator and E. Coli

Our water system detected fecal indicators (Total Coliform *E. coli,*) in our well #(4). As our customers, you have a right to know what happened and what we are doing to correct this situation. On 19 May 2017, we learned that our assessment samples for the month of May were Total Coliform and E.coli positive. As required by EPA's Ground Water Rule, one of our follow up steps is to shut down Well # (4) and collect additional samples from well starting 22 May 2017 to determine if we continue to have a water quality issues. This sampling will occur on 22 May 2017-26 May 2017.

What should I do?
Nothing at this time. The well in question has been taken out of service on 22 May 2017 per D.E.P. instructions, follow up sampling has been scheduled and we are monitoring disinfection levels throughout the day.

What does this mean?
Inadequately treated or inadequately protected water may contain disease-causing organisms. These organisms can cause symptoms such as diarrhea, nausea, cramps, and associated headaches. *Fecal indicators are microbes whose presence indicates that the water may be contaminated with human or animal wastes. Microbes in these wastes can cause short-term health effects, such as diarrhea, cramps, nausea, headaches, or other symptoms. They may pose a special health risk for infants, young children, some of the elderly, and people with severely compromised immune systems.* These symptoms are not caused only by organisms in drinking water. If you experience any of these symptoms and they persist, you may want to seek medical advice.

What is being done?
We will keep you informed of the steps we are taking to protect your drinking water and will provide information on any steps you should be taking, until this issue is identified and corrected.

For more information, please contact ~~███████~~ Vocational Instructor III F/C (water/ Wastewater) at (863) 767-3056.

Please share this information with all the other people who drink this water, especially those who may not have received this notice directly (for example, people in apartments, nursing homes, schools, and businesses). You can do this by posting this notice in a public place or distributing copies by hand or mail.

This notice is being sent to you by Hardee C.I.
State Water System ID# 6254754   Date Sent: 22 May 2017

UNIVERSITY OF
SOUTH FLORIDA
SARASOTA-MANATEE

The University of South Florida Sarasota-Manatee

proudly recognizes that

Giovanni Vega

has successfully completed

Introduction to Entrepreneurship

Presented this Tenth Day of April, in the Year Two Thousand Seventeen

Jean D. Kabongo, Ph.D., Associate Professor
College of Business

James M. Curran, Ph.D., Dean
College of Business

James M. Orcholski, Ph.D., Assistant Professor
College of Liberal Arts & Social Sciences

Jane A. Rose, Ph.D., Dean
College of Liberal Arts & Social Sciences

The LifePath Group Project

This Achievement Is Proudly Presented To:

GIOVANNI VEGA

DC#X12648

The above participant has completed the LifePath Character Qualities class, which explores and develops many different character elements that make up who a person is. This 30-hour course that is certified by the Florida Department of Corrections enhances interpersonal interactions and helps one to grow into a more mature responsible human being. This is the very fabric of being a LifePath Man.

Character Qualities Class
Awarded on October 03, 2017

A LifePath Man:
Mentors Advocates Networks
Permanent, Positive Change for Success – NOW!

G. Hendrix
G. Hendrix, LifePath Sponsor

HARDY CORRECTIONAL INSTITUTION
2016-2018

TOMOKA C.I. 2018

On February 15, 2018, I arrived once again at the old and broken down Tomoka Correctional. I did not have any of my property with me because the officer at the reception center sent it to the South Florida Reception Center. My fiancé was forced to file a complaint with the inspector general's office concerning the officer misconduct. Tomoka changed completely. The handball courts were torn down. The softball field closed down. The recreation yard fenced in half. The kitchen was rebuilt. Yellow lines were painted on the

201

grounds so inmates are obligated to walk in a straight line (better inmate control). The tennis court was tore down. Two out of three basketball courts were closed down. Fences were put up within the prison as if we walk from one cage to the other. Junkies and violent inmates are still being housed in bravo dormitory. On the other half of the prison, there're two dormitories set up for faith-based/character-based programs.

The officers who work the visitation like to harass family members by asking them to change their clothing while there is a three-hour wait to finally reach the inside visit part. The administration changed also. A lot of new officers and very few that have been working at Tomoka for many years. One female captain apparently retired. A few weeks later, she returned as the institution librarian. I'm guessing her retirement was not paying off because she began to smuggle contraband. One day, the former captain came to work with the book cart full of cell phones, K2, and cigarettes. The inspector and the assistant warden were waiting for her inside the library. Before it was all over with, she was arrested and escorted out of the prison. This same former female captain was the same one who in 2008, housed me in confinement under investigation.

Every year, the Daytona 500 NASCAR hires temporary correctional officers for security. The male colonel of Tomoka correction was one of them. According to the news reports, the colonel was stealing thousands of dollars of NASCAR merchandise throughout the years of employment. He was arrested and also fired by the Department of Corrections. Judges always go super soft on law enforcement officers, so the former colonel received a probation sentence. It was not long before he was employed for Walmart. Sticky fingers became brave again and arrested for stealing Walmart merchandise.

As of today, the overweight colonel is serving a seven-year sentence within the corrections department. He is either a minimum custody facility or shipped out of state. Allowing for the former colonel to live in general population would be suicide. Most of the programs available in 2008 are now gone at Tomoka. The few that are left are, Masonry pride, waste water management and general education diplomas are still available. But the inmate has to be short in sentence to enroll. The recreation time is the most horrible I have ever seen in any prison. On average, seven to ten working days may go by before officials will allow a couple of hours of exercise. Inmates are sitting around most of the day looking at each other, coming up with ways to get high, rob someone or steal from the kitchen.

Throughout the years, I have changed a lot. One of the things I stopped doing recently is hustling. My fiancé and I read the Bible together during visit and pray each chance we get. I really have committed myself to our relationship, and I will not do anything to jeopardize it. Because I welcomed change, I requested to be housed in the faith-based program. Delta dormitory is clean, laid-back, and has mandatory classes each week. If an inmate wants to better himself, this is the program that will definitely help. I fit right in perfectly or at least I thought I did! I was completing all the homework assignments and began a Windows 7 computer class. We prayed as groups each night, shared with one another and watched educational biblical movies. How much better can I have been doing my time? This faith-based program was one of the best decisions I made within this tour.

Then all of a sudden, the devil made one of his moves. On a Tuesday, one sergeant and two officers were ordered to search my property. I was placed in handcuffs and placed in a room with no windows while they were looking for contraband. Besides my pet spider, I did not have anything they were apparently looking for. That night, I spoke to my fiancé and explained something was going on. I was told the officers were reading all my paperwork. I automatically assumed they were looking for chapters of this very book I'm writing.

Two days later, Thursday, another sergeant was ordered to search me and three other inmates. The sergeant did a thorough search and found nothing! I called my fiancé and explained things did not seem right, something is going on. The next day, Friday, I was handcuffed and escorted to the front of the prison in order to be questioned by two inspectors. I was asked if it was okay to be recorded, and I cooperated fully. After all, I did not have anything to hide. The inspector to my left asked if I knew why I was being questioned. "My book," I answered. It turned out the inspectors did not care about my book and I was there because someone gave information that I wanted to start an uprising on slavery. They asked if my fingerprints were on a knife and if I would be willing to take a stress test. I offered to take any test they may have and assured them my fingerprints were not on any knife.

The inspector went on Google and showed me some articles I never read before. They were about the 13th Amendment Constitutional Rights to be freed from slavery. Now I understood it all! An inmate, probably to get my lower bunk, gave false information that three other inmates and I were conspiring against the administration or the officers. I'm still not sure what exactly was told to the inspectors. After answering all questions, I was allowed to go back to the dormitory. I quickly went on the kiosk machine and e-mailed my fiancé to call before she traveled to come see me.

The same Friday, May 18, 2018 at 3:40 p.m., the captain and a group of sergeants entered Delta dormitory and ordered every inmate on their bunks. The captain started to call out names. Three other inmates and I were escorted to confinement under investigation. The captain explained the inspectors ordered for us to be housed in confinement. I knew it was bullshit because I already talked to the inspectors and they told me everything was okay, I would not be under investigation. So who is full of shit? The administration or the inspectors? That Friday night when I laid down on the bunk to sleep, roaches started to crawl up on my hand and neck. I was under attack! The next morning, I got up, soaped up my washrag and began to scrub the entire cell. It was filthy. Tomoka echo dormitory is so old and outdated, I can't believe health regulators haven't condemned the building and closed it.

My appellate lawyer filed a manifest in justice motion on April 25, 2018. One of the grounds argued is that I have provided two medical examiner autopsy actual innocence reports to the courts and no justice has been given to me. The other ground is the Miranda rights violation concerning my request for counsel during interrogation. All I can do is pray. Tomoka painted two sets of footprints next to the wall in each confinement cell. When a high-ranking official comes into the building, they call inspection and we have to be fully dressed, bed made, health and comfort items on the bed and standing right on top of the footprints. Officials do this military time drill so that we are unable to ask questions when they do their rounds. The steel bunk is two inches thick. The mattress I was sleeping on, one inch thick. When I lay down to sleep, I touch steel right through the mattress. A dog sleeps better in your backyard than most of us in here in prison. But it's supposed to be cruel and unusual punishment in prison right?

My fiancé and I waited for our marriage to be approved at Tomoka Correctional. I filed a grievance complaining about the amount of time authorized for the ceremony of fifteen minutes. The chapel employee at Tomoka has been rumored to dislike inmate marriages and therefore will do everything possible to delay another human being's happiness. Unbelievable!

While in confinement under the investigation, an inmate nicknamed Joker who works for the institutional maintenance squad explained the following: the state authorized for the old kitchen to be torn down and the new kitchen built. A certain amount of money was taken out of the budget to pay for construction crews to handle the job. However, inmates tore down the old kitchen and build the new kitchen with a few officers pointing their fingers on what to do. Inmates did the entire work for an extra bag of lunch containing two peanut butter sandwiches, an orange and a cookie. My question is where did the money to hire the construction crews go? Could it be that legislators have realized the corrections department has been frauding for centuries and are now cutting back on funding?

When an inmate is housed in confinement, the dormitory officer must search the property and deliver hygiene products like soap, washrag, towel and toothpaste. The officer that packed my property didn't have the common sense to deliver my deodorant. My armpits were red from using soap as deodorant! I could barely keep my arms down! We are given three showers a week while in confinement. My cellmate and I had to complain about the temperature of the water at over 110°. We could not get under the water! I showered from far away and was looking like a red shrimp when finished. I cannot believe Tomoka doesn't care of the burning water showers after the state was forced to pay millions of dollars to the family of an inmate burned to death.

At Dade Correctional, officers placed the inmate in the shower, turned on the water 160° to 180°, and let the inmate burn alive. A couple of months ago at the regional medical center in Lake Butler, an inmate was housed in confinement for refusing to eat breakfast. Officers beat the inmate to death. The autopsy report did not indicate any foul play. The family ordered an independent autopsy report and it revealed the inmate was killed. All for not eating breakfast? Wow! Because of all the deaths throughout the years, someone ordered for all confinement across the state of Florida to have full audio. This has helped in certain prisons. Now officers can't lie and accuse an inmate of banging on the cell doors. Officers have to be careful with what they say and how they handle inmates in a cell. For the most part, prisons from Ocala Florida going south, have slowed down on the excessive use of force. From Ocala up, it's a different world. Cameras might not work when needed for review. Officers will have spots where they can beat an inmate and get away with it. Throughout the years, prisons change due to administration changes.

Overall, the worst prisons in the State of Florida that have always been known for officers killing inmates, violence and corruption, have been: Century, Santa Rosa, Walton, Holmes, Washington, Jackson, Calhoun, Liberty, Gulf, Franklin, Taylor, Hamilton, Mayo, Suwannee, Cross City, Columbia, Union, Florida State Prison, Okeechobee, Charlotte and Martin. If you look at a map of Florida, you will realize 21 locations I have provided, only three are in South Florida. I have to call it how it is! The Florida Panhandle is where 80% of Ku Klux Klan members live because Central and South Florida are full of minorities. In the country, those hateful people can hide and do what they want to do. They make sure their children don't interact with minorities.

One day I was standing in front of the music kiosk waiting for my turn to plug in. I had my headphones on as if I was listening to music but really I was listening to the two officers talking. One officer said, "I moved to Kissimmee with my wife and teenage daughter," one officer told the other. "I immediately move up to Live Oak when

I caught my daughter in the car with a Puerto Rican. I couldn't lose my baby to those people." I wanted to say something, but I kept my cool. The Florida Department of Correction breeds officers like this, and it would be a waste of time to say anything. The further we are in the panhandle, the more likely we are going to experience racism. I have even met black folks that are racist in Florida. One thing I will never understand is when inmates say that an officer is "straight" or "down." In some prisons, officers will whisper lies in one ear and another lie in the other. Then they allow the inmates to fight each other. Officers will sit back and laugh at how foolish inmates can be. After the fight, the inmate would say, "Sergeant was straight for letting us fight."

The Department of Corrections is attempting and most likely will cut the visitors hours and days. The regular schedule has always been on weekends and holidays, 9:00 a.m. to 3:00 p.m. From what I read, first, they wanted to change the visits to every other weekend. Then I read another article that said every other weekend but for only two hours. Whatever the case maybe, it's all a big mistake on their behalf. Visitation is by far the best rehabilitation any prisoner in the world can receive. When visitation is taken, prisons will be more violent and officers will have their hands full. Very full! Why on earth does this state pretend to care about the officers but then put them in tight situations? You're supposed to make the corrections department better, not more dangerous.

Chapter 20

Orlando, Florida

When the going gets tough, the tough gets going! After a total of five baths in fourteen days, while under investigation, I was kicked out of Tomoka Correctional like a bad habit. I filed a grievance explaining the allegations were false but it did not work. How does a so-called professional state employee believe one inmate over the other? With no evidence? I was doing good! The faith-based program was really helping me with a closer relationship with God. It was good rehabilitation in a time where the corrections department is cutting more and more programs.

Speaking of reducing or cutting, on May 25, 2018, a hearing was held in Tallahassee, Florida, concerning numerous proposals the corrections department will eventually implement on visitation. Lately, prisons throughout the state have already canceled weekend visitations claiming they do not have enough staff or their favorite excuse, too much contraband. Everyone on planet Earth knows when family members take time to visit the loved ones in prison, it helps with the emotional and mental part of transitioning back into society.

To make inmates calm and not worried about these huge changes, the corrections department signed a contract with JPay in order to install kiosks in every quad dormitory. Both the state and JPay will make millions of dollars profit while charging us $.44 an e-mail, $1.76 for a thirty second video, and $.44 for an E-card. Let's see what the state does with the money. For now, how does someone explain to a five-year-old child that he or she can no longer see their daddy each weekend? Or explain to an eighty-year-old mother, about to go to heaven, she can no longer touch her son every weekend? I see all these changes causing more violence and heavy lockdown situations. It's all okay, because after all, we're prisoners right? We deserve to starve, get beaten, mistreated and our families can just deal with it right?

I arrived at the Central Florida Reception Center on May 31, 2018. I was then housed in gulf dormitory 311-low. The officers here get away with murder, literally. Young and old men, mostly young though are fresh from County Jail and are not educated in the title thirty-three laws governing the Department of Correction. The officers use profane language on the regular. The counts are almost two hours long. Food portions look like a McDonald's happy meal. I'm sorry, I take that back, a happy meal is way better than most of the food trays served. The food service directors here at CFRC must be getting fat bonuses!

Everyone else frauds across the state, one more won't hurt! I was told that recreation was for twenty minutes, once every other week, wow! Are other state corrections doing these malicious acts on inmates? Someone tell me that in Texas, inmates only get one hour recreation every 10 days. So I can feel better? Someone tell me that in New York, you can only receive two hour visits, every other week, so I can rest calmly? Someone have the heart to tell me in California inmates pay $16.80 for a twenty-four pack of ramen noodle soups so I can tell my family their hard-earned money is put to good use?

I went from being attacked by roaches at Tomoka to being attacked by one-inch mosquitoes at CFRC. All the cell windows have no screens and are broken, torn apart. I can stick my hand out, reach next door to the next cell and get a book. It rained hard and kind of sideways, upon entering my assigned cell, there was a half an inch of water on the floor and my bunk was all wet. Do you think the sergeant gave me dry sheets and a blanket? Maybe you would be civilized enough to give an inmate a dry area to sleep in. But remember, we are inmates, we are supposed to have nothing! Right? Hotel dorm at CFRC has a chunk of roof hanging, cracked down the middle. When it rains, it's called "wet and wild!" It's been nineteen years and I have yet to see state inspectors shut down in a prison.

In the past few years, God himself sent a legislative man who has seen for himself how corrupt and destroyed the Florida Department of Corrections truly is. Because of this angel from heaven, we now get toilet tissue as needed, not every 10 days. We now get a toothbrush as needed, not every three months. We now get a "motel soap" as needed not once every week. If you happen to read this book, sir, please do not have an inch of sympathy for corrections officials. If they get the chance, they won't have sympathy for you either. I received great news from a friend of mine that was at Suwannee correctional aka Swantanamo Bay! The warden we nicknamed "No neck" was forced to resign and admit allegations his prison was experiencing way too many deaths and beatings. Why the FDLE didn't put the warden in jail, I don't know. But at least something was done. Two officers, however, were taken into custody and charged with aggravated battery.

Now let me tell you about the Florida governor before he leaves office soon. It's no secret, "Mr. Clean," as many of us call him, eats in a Disney restaurant with his family and grandchildren. The restaurant reserves a corner blocked away from everyone else. That's understandable. Only one waitress can serve Mr. clean and his family. On this particular day, a white-skinned female waitress appeared to be doing a great job serving the governor almost formally charged with a 300-million-dollar medical fraud scandal. "Where are you from?" asked Mr. Clean.

"I'm from Puerto Rico," the shy young waitress answered. Five minutes later, the manager had an American white-skinned female waitress serving our honorable governor and his loved ones. The manager threatened to fire any employee who said anything to the public. Help me to understand this: Puerto Ricans are not worthy of tips from high-ranking officials? I'm wondering how Mr. Clean felt when our last president elected the first Puerto Rican United States Supreme Court Justice?

My mom gave me a visit while I was at CFRC. She has been more understanding with me as time goes by. I guess it might be that she will be sixty years old in October. Or maybe she feels sorry for me and whatever I say goes in through one ear and out the other. Almost nineteen years and counting of being in prison can damage anyone mentally. My mom knows this, and at the end of the day, she just wants me home. Even if I get out institutionalized. I am super happy for my sister Selina and her recent 16-year marriage anniversary. My niece and nephew are beautiful and looked like they grew up on steroids. What do they feed those kids out there? My other sister, Raquel, is doing great! Living her life responsibly while earning her master's degree out of the University of Central Florida. I'm super proud of my sister! My family has, however, let me down in many ways and at the same time, I let them down also by living a teenage life of crime. How long will it be before they forgive me and start to act like sisters? You would think maybe five years? Maybe ten years? Okay, fifteen years? Eighteen and a half years in prison as I write this book, and apparently, I will remain, out of sight, out of mind. We don't know the future and people do change, as I am living proof of it.

The central Florida Reception Center, South unit, was built to house inmates who are on their last days of life from cancer, aids, and other medical reasons. Every time I have been through CFRC, I requested to become a palliative care orderly. It's a tough job, which no one wants. However I would be willing to help in those inmate's times of suffering. The last time I was at CFRC, June 2018, I had my fiancé call classification in Tallahassee, the medical department, offering my name for the palliative care orderly job. They want to force an inmate to do the job instead of accepting the one who wants to help. It's the reason everyone quits, and medical departments are short staffed all the time. In the corrections department, everything works the opposite. If an inmate wants to stay close to this family at one prison, he gets moved to another. If an inmate wants to transfer to be close to home, they do everything possible to keep him. It's crazy! The mentality of corrections employees is to punish and punish some more. Limit what is sold to inmates at triple the cost. Where else on earth could someone pay $70 for a pair of Riddell shoes and almost $9 for a plain white Riddell T-shirt? I want the readers of this book to know that my purpose is to give the public and inside eye on how the Florida Justice System truly works. Also on how the Florida Department of Corrections truly works. Regardless of whether we are guilty or innocent, we are all still God's creation. If you are the victim of a horrible crime, any crime recently or in the past, do not hold your anger within. Can't you see that everyone is a sinner? Because you've never been to jail, you are now better than a prisoner? Rich people commit murders! Music artist commit armed robbery! Movie actors commit sexual assaults! Adult female teachers have sex with twelve-year-old male students! Maybe you've frauded within your job? Even if you are a supervisor for a corporation and you sit back all day buying things on eBay, you are a fraud. You get paid to work and not to shop around. Are you eating candy at the store you're working in without permission? The list goes on. Society has a really bad picture of people in prison.

For years, the TV channels and the law enforcement will say anything about us to make news. As bad and as negative these prisons can be, I believe with outstanding educational courses, certifications and training, a better percentage of inmates can remain home. If you provide intense education, some of the most brightest minds will come out of prison. Period! I know this for fact because I have talked with individuals with mastermind business plans who only need one chance. Just one opportunity to be a productive citizen and enjoy life.

Have you ever asked yourself what would be the correct amount of time one should serve based on a specific crime? Should arm robbery be life in prison? Should grand theft auto be five years? Should trafficking cocaine be fifteen years? Should murder be punished by death or natural life? When you see the accusations on TV, the first thing people usually scream is "put him in prison forever." It is easy to judge someone right? You sit back on your couch and point the finger like you're an honorable judge.

One of the jurors at my trial said, "If he gets put in handcuffs, he's guilty." I was like, really man? What if this person who committed arm robbery had been addicted to heroin or crack? Then what? It's not worth giving a human being a chance? What about the person who was raised by his dad to steal cars? Do you think allowing him into the United States Military wouldn't work out? Or would five years wasted doing nothing in prison be better? My female cousin who I call Jo-mama is now serving fifteen years for trafficking heroin (pills). She gave birth to twin boys a month before trial and left a five-year-old daughter behind also. She met some chump of a man who manipulated her into making deliveries. Never been in trouble in her life. Does she deserve the fifteen years? Or would it have been better to sentence her to a few years of being in a drug offender facility that allows for her to rehabilitate and show she made one mistake? Jo-Mama Is not worth saving? Now here comes the real hard part. Murder. Four young adults walk in a motel at gunpoint, demand the money out of the register. One of the perpetrators fires a shot, kills a woman behind the counter. Do all four deserve life in prison? My friend Orlando, presently at Everglades Correctional, was not the shooter but was sentenced to life. Get ready for this, he was locked up in 1974. I wasn't even born yet! The Florida parole board keeps throwing his date back and back because there are less than 3000 inmates eligible for parole and if they let them out, a lot of people will be without a job! I am not saying that everyone deserves a chance. I'm in here around a lot of sick-minded individuals. I know some people do not want to change! It took me a lot of years to realize and change. I learned the hard way and have matured. Becoming a much better person while being considerate toward others.

Chapter 21

Regional Medical Center 2018
"Wild, Wild, West"

This book has officially become dangerous for me to write. I'm glad the first nineteen chapters are already home. The Tomoka CI inspectors had fun reading about how corrupt the Florida Department of Corrections is. Now things will be changing for the worse. Classification at Tomoka or central office (same bull-s), decided to send me to Apalachee C.I., Sneads, Florida. Once I'm there, I will be five hours from my loved ones. The distance is bad. What really bites is the entire area, panhandle, is home to the Ku Klux Klan. Back in the days, years ago, Klan members had strong chapters in South Florida. The population grew with minorities therefore running most of these hatred groups away. There are still some left in South Florida, but they don't function as they really want to. Central Florida had chapters all over also. One of the main ones, St. Cloud Manor and Narcoossee, Florida, have been dismantled due to the Puerto Ricans buying all the land. Them damn Puerto Ricans are like termites! Slowly the Klan members have been moving on up and up Florida. Anywhere from Ocala north is still home to many active Klan chapters. The police departments know what takes place but will never do anything about it because, unfortunately, law enforcement officers are Klan members also. It has always been like this in Florida when it comes to corrections and officers who arrive at your front door when you dial 911 for help. Ouch! You would ask yourself, why these people with cruel and angry hearts work in law enforcement to begin with?

When I was in high school, my dream was always to become a firefighter. I wanted to save people no matter what age, race, or color. Ever since I could remember, I have looked at people the same. I learned to stay away from foolish people and treat everyone with respect. I can't understand why certain individuals want to "protect their race" by hurting the next man or woman. When we get cut, we all bleed the same. When we die, God will not discriminate us based on our skin color. What we must truly worry about is living righteous. I know we were born into sin, we are not perfect. I sure can't say I've been a role model citizen! That's for sure! Why so much hate though? Was me being born in Lawrence, Massachusetts, to Puerto Rican parents cause for anyone to fall? Why look down at me because I have light brown skin color?

I went to eat today and counted thirteen officers standing inside and outside the dining hall. That's a little bit too many if you asked me. This is state funding that could be going somewhere else for good use. My question is, why doesn't the administration at Central Florida Reception Center open the recreation yard every day, twice?

Not enough officers? It is just crazy and really unprofessional how correctional officials are allowed to get paid to sit back and scream profane language at inmates. When I mailed other book chapters home while I was at Tomoka C.I., it really didn't matter because Tomoka has plenty of minority officers who could care less what I have to say in my book. However, I'm not going to be able to mail the recent chapters home freely because I will be in Ku Klux Klan land. There's not one prison in the Florida Panhandle that doesn't have several Klan members working. Not one! I'm going to either mail the recent chapters to my lawyer or figure out another way to send them out. When I get to Apalachee correctional, those country folk better have the institution running in tiptop shape. You can call me whatever you may want to call me, private eyes, sneaky or what else? Just don't call me late for dinner!

I was thinking maybe officials would retaliate and move me out-of-state? I am not a present security threat. I am not gang related. I have no violence on record. The only cheap excuse officials can use is this book has caused officers to become upset and my remaining time here in Florida would pose a threat to my well-being. Yeah Right! Sure! I feel like the author of the famous book, *Behold A Pale White Horse*. The author was in navy intelligence and all of a sudden began to reveal government secrets. An attempt on his life by the CIA did not stop him from publishing the book. The second attempt, however, was deadly. The author sacrificed life in order for the public to know the corruption within the United States Government. My respect goes out to Mr. Cooper. May you rest in peace! If there're any civil attorneys willing to represent me in case the corrections department retaliates, please contact me as soon as possible.

As of right now, I am being represented by an intelligent and great attorney, but he is handling my criminal appeal! Proverbs 3:24–26 confirms, "You can go to bed without fear; you will lie down and sleep soundly. You need not be afraid of sudden disaster or the destruction that comes upon the wicked, for the Lord is your security. He will keep your foot from being caught in a trap." When Mandela was in prison, did anyone have any idea he would influence not only Africa but the world? When Hopwood was serving time in prison for robbery, did anyone ever guess he would become a highly respected Georgia town university professor? When Allen served time in prison, did anyone ever guess he would get out and become a movie star? Allen even had his own show called *Home Improvement*. Remember?

The day our Lord blesses me with freedom, the chance to be next to my loved ones, I plan to establish a website containing information directly from prisoners. Not only in Florida, but across the United States. You don't think there is corruption in other correctional departments? I want the website to be connected with the federal government and news channels. This way everyone knows what truly happens in prisons. It will be something that I would owe to myself, and to all those who have shed blood and tears within prison walls. How would I be able to go home and forget everything I went through? I might wake up scared in the middle of the night calling out my inmate number, thinking I wasn't ready for count!

People say we are lost souls. Society doesn't want anything to do with someone who is locked up! They say we are shit, and we are bums. I say, don't let us burn in the fire, instead, extend your hand out and help! You don't have to put money into an inmate account or even send a book of stamps. Become involved in any type of prison reform. Demand to know exactly how your taxpayer money is being spent. Before you vote, e-mail the candidate and find out what changes, if any, he or she will push for once in office. Volunteer for religious or mental health counseling. Help us fight against the reducing of visitation hours. You don't think it's important for us to hug and kiss our families? I have even seen people out of the blue, sponsor an inmate's college education and or certifications. That's super big! If you really feel funny about dealing with an inmate, then send an e-mail of encouragement. You never know whose life you might impact and change! Have you ever heard about the famous Puerto Rican Prison Ministry of Pastor Avila? His daughter was killed and the murderer was doing the sentence here in Florida. Can you imagine how mad he must've felt? That's a hard pill to swallow. Mr. Avila knew he would never be able to enter the kingdom of heaven with his anger in his heart. So he prayed! One day, he flew into Florida and gave the murderer a visit. They both talked, cried together and the rest is history! Could you begin to imagine how much patience and understanding one must have to even attempt to sit down with the man who killed your relative? That's deep shit right there!

We now know that Okeechobee CI went from six-hour visitation on Saturday and Sunday, down all the way to a disrespectful two hours every other week. Apparently, officials promised a bigger visit park and while construction was underway, two hours every other week would be appropriate. The construction is now over and they still have a two hour visits every other week. Officials do not have any consideration for the families who have to board an airplane and fly in to Florida, rent a motel, rent a car and pay for the inmate to eat. Everglades CI went down from six hours on Saturdays and Sundays to six hours one day per week. Officials there claimed the inmate population at 1725 is too much and brings in too many visitors. You build a prison in the middle of Miami Florida and forget to build a big enough visit park? Really? We just got word that Dade CI is "trying out" this same visit schedule as Everglades CI. For those who don't know, Dade CI is in South Miami and for many years never had a problem with the amount of families visiting inmates. What is the difference now? The Florida Department of Corrections has it all figured out. In the panhandle where families visit less because of the distance and having to deal with racism, officials can't claim visit overcrowding. What they have been claiming is the contraband is out of control, cancel visitation. Officials are focused on the wrong thing. They need to be worried about these long roaches running around like they came straight out of an African jungle. Last night I had to cover myself with a blanket from head to toe because the mosquitoes were flying around the cell like I was in the Brazil Amazon Jungle. These eighth amendment constitutional rights violations that amount to civil lawsuits are the things the correction department needs to be worried about (cruel and unusual punishment)! They don't care about payouts because it doesn't come out of employee pockets, it's taxpayer money. What civilian taxpayers don't know about, won't hurt them! That's the outlook!

I have a question. Why is it that regional directors and central office advise the institution of the date and time and inspection will be conducted? The wardens quickly have the inmates paint the dormitories, fix the doors, fix the windows, fix the benches, wax floors, fix the bunks, fix the lights, fix the plumbing, give out new T-shirts and boxers, fix the water fountains and my favorite one is serve the food trays with hot "correct" amounts of food. You have to do like the legislative man out of Miami does. Creep up to the institutions at midnight unexpectedly. Officials received good benefits and good paychecks. Where else can you get a babysitting state job starting at $15 an hour? Where the training academy teaches you to mistreat inmates at all costs and not worry about the consequences? Where else can you live in a mobile home or apartment for $40 a month with all utilities paid? It makes me sick to my stomach when I hear of the correctional employees crying about their job. This place is a big piece of "cake" that officials all eat from. But you always have a group of officials who want to eat and keep the "cake" to themselves.

Now I just wrote the word "cake" and most of you thought about a "cake" at a supermarket you buy for a wedding or birthday party, right? Don't lie, you know you did. I utilized the word "cake" to signify money. *Dinero*! You couldn't bring me one warden, regional director or central office official that hasn't figured out how to make "bonuses." Why do you think it is really hard to have a warden arrested when he or she allows federal civil rights violations at the institution? It is not that the FDLE can't arrest them because they truly can. It's the consequences of the arrest that the department is worried about. A warden will scream and point fingers like a Florida Mockingbird! The corrections department has been under investigation by the United States Department of Justice for the many inmate deaths and corruption. Do you think they can stand more? Even the federal government goes light on the Florida Department of Corrections. The FBI had to investigate Suwannee Annex several times before making the warden resign. This same warden I wrote about nicknamed "No neck" had a buddy he promoted from colonel to assistant warden and then licked someone's ass to make warden at Hardee. This all happened in less than two years! Then at

Hardee, he terrorized! One of the foul things the new warden did was have groups of inmates packed all their property into bags, carry the bags while walking around the middle of the prison for hours! If the inmate resisted, officers were ordered to beat you up on the way to confinement. The rookie warden was asked to resign after a record-breaking use of force was discovered under his administration. He is now a sheriff in the Midwest.

One problem we have encountered here in prison has been obeying the "class A" rule, Monday through Friday, 8 a.m. to 5 p.m. This means we have to be fully dressed in the nylon blue uniforms. No one out there in society will ever know how hot the blue uniforms are. What I can explain is the dormitory quads can get 93°, add full clothing and we are quickly gasping out for air, soaking wet in sweat! I have filed grievances raising title thirty-three which clearly states inmates can be in "class C"—shorts and T-shirt during the day unless the inmate has to work. All the grievances have been denied! Here's some food for thought: Florida law requires dog pounds to house dogs in 83° or less temperature. So dogs get treated better than us?

Today we were told officers are wearing body cameras at Sumter correctional. It's called a "pilot program," just to see how it works out. I know the officers hate it! Audio-video will record all profane language, any schemes, any abuse and all other misconduct. I'm willing to bet, however, there's going to be many cases where the video and audio "didn't work" when someone is killed or beaten. Happens all the time! I do believe many officers will quit and the excessive use of force will slow down. They need to start in the panhandle first!

This chapter is titled *shout-outs* because I feel it is important that I pay respect to everyone who has previously encountered hate, racism, discrimination, disrespect, lies, and any other malicious acts on behalf of the state and county employees. My heart goes out to you all!

1. To all the family members that travel from out of state for hours to see your loved one in prison, only to be told to change clothing because the state employee felt it was too tight.

2. To all the inmates and their families who were stalked and harassed by state employees during your special visit time.

3. To all the females who were sexually assaulted while being searched by state employees as you enter the prison to visit your loved one.

4. To all the family members who call the department of corrections classification department and we're told lies in order for them to pursue wrong toward an inmate.

5. To all the family members who lost a loved one in prison while state employees called to notify the death a week later. Trying to clean up their mess.

6. All inmates who wait one year clean to submit a good adjustment transfer, then, turn around and wait two to four years to actually be moved closer to home. Some didn't make it because a nasty officer wrote up disciplinary report. Keep your head up!

7. To all inmates to have been sick from eating the soy patties. Who were about to eat the salad on the tray only to discover a roach.

8. To all inmates who slept on cold steel in boxers or naked, for days at a time.

9. To all inmates who have been physically abused, spit on, lied on and anything else in the hands of state or county employees. Stay strong! Educate yourselves!

10. Rest in peace to all the thousands of inmates killed by the Department of Corrections employees. Violence is not and will never be the answer.

11. To all the prison ministry volunteers who were disrespected by state or county employees when all you we're trying to do was provide counseling for inmates. Thank you!

12. To all family members who have waited hours just to visit your loved ones. (Tomoka three-hour wait) Don't be discouraged!

13. To all family members who drive across the state in your late-model vehicle 1996 Camry, scared it might breakdown but nonetheless need to embrace your loved one in prison. God Bless you with wealth!

14. For all the defendants who stood in front of a racist judge while being represented by garbage public defender. The justice system is a joke!

15. To all inmates who have been incarcerated for years. To name a few, my friend Jerry, almost fifty years. Orlando, almost fifty years. Johnny, almost thirty years. Felix, almost forty years. You men truly deserve to be free already!

16. To all inmates who gave up and committed suicide. Especially my good friend Lázaro after forty years of torture. No one can judge your actions but God himself. I know it's superhard, sometimes I don't know how I, myself, remain on track.

17. To all the families who sat in a courtroom and watch their loved ones be sentenced to thirty years, sixty years, eighty years and even life. We are not dinosaurs! My mother suffered and cried while I was sentenced to natural life in prison. Basically sentenced to die in prison. I love you, Mom! I pray for you every night no matter what.

18. To all the inmates who have become mentally challenged due to correction employees prescribing medications as if they were throwing pills at birds. Sad but true!

19. To the very few and I mean very few officers who just wanted a paycheck, were mistreated, and discriminated against by high-ranking officials. Now you see what the Department of Corrections is about. Why don't you tell the world about your experience?

20. To the secretary of the Department of Corrections for doing an outstanding job by having corrupt officials arrested when you first came into office. However, you took your foot off the gas! You don't kill the snake by the tail, you chop the snakes head off! My opinion with all due respect is you have the heart and mind for change but now realize complete change is way out of your reach.

If I left out any shout-outs, please forgive me. Ideas, concerns, news, comments and opinions, go to JPay.com, Click on Florida, my name is Giovanni Vega #X12648, set up the free account, download the app, utilize the option to e-mail a message. Let me know how you sincerely feel about the book and whether I should write a part two? (All feedback accepted.)

Chapter 23

Testimonies

In this chapter, I will have either the initials to their names or write their nickname, in order to provide a detailed story about any incidents encountered with law enforcement officials. It can be upon arrest or during the correction tour. I will be unable to question most people because Florida has way too many institutions and only God knows what has occurred in those places. Some prisoners will refuse to tell their story, fearing retaliation. Others will hope for their voices to be heard through this book. I have good judgment of character. Therefore, I am asking prisoners who carry themselves with respect, dignity and maturity. The last thing I want is a clown to just write anything! Although many people have recommended for me to write a book about my life, I never took the time and effort to do so. Deciding to write this book happened from one minute to another. Since I am and always will be a God-fearing individual, I pray each day for our father God to bless this book. This means I have to make sure the contents are truthful.

1. I, "DJF," on or around May 17, 2017, was at CFRC east unit. In the evening meal and was returning to my dorm when a sergeant pulled me out of the line and began to curse at me and use threatening statements toward my well-being. I stated I was not a problem inmate after being there one-year disciplinary report free. Another officer arrived. The sergeant who started the altercation grabbed me by my throat while the other officers sprayed me with chemical agent. Out of fear for my life, I hit the officer's hands-down away from my throat. Another officer arrived and tackled me to the ground and administered restraints

(cuffs) on my hands. Once I was face down on the ground, the sergeant who began the altercation hit me in my right eye very hard. The blood vessels ruptured and I have vision problems today. I served sixty days in confinement and my visitation privileges suspended. The sergeant submitted false information, and I lost the investigation.

2. My nickname is "El Profeta," and I have a twenty-five-year bid. In November 2011, I was dropped from close custody to medium custody while at Hardee CI. Later that month, a K9 officer conducted searches in A2-dormitory. Forty grams of a "leafy substance" was found at the corner of the wall close to my bunk. It was not in my possession or locker. I was given ninety days in confinement followed by 180 days loss of game time. I had been clean for eight years. By my fourth year at Hardee, 2011, I was considered a model inmate. Gang members and officers were asking how I got such a disciplinary report. I contested my innocence surely knowing more than twenty inmates had access to throw anything around my bunk, my grievance failed. I served Christmas and New Year's in confinement. This injured my family's trust of whether I was making a sincere change or not.

3. My name is "KP," I've been in prison two years on a violation of probation. The day the VOP took place, Titusville, Florida Police Department tried to come in contact with me but I fled. I was tased in the back. Once I surrendered, I was tased again in the back of my head. Me being six feet three inches tall, the officers had plenty of areas to tase me but proceeded to tase me in the head instead.

4. My name is "BT," while at CFRC, on a Sunday 12 p.m., during count time, I was notified by the dorm sergeant that I had a visit. "You didn't know that?" the Sergeant asked. This indicated I was supposed to be notified of my visit earlier. I was escorted during count time to the visit park. (No one is supposed to move around during count.) They bend the rules when it's convenient. Once I saw my mother

upset I asked how long she had been waiting. She said one hour and then asked the visit officer to speak with the captain. When the captain showed up, my mom asked for his name and a number to contact the warden. On Tuesday, I was approached by the major who threatened me by saying that if my family calls CFRC again, I will be transferred to a place I do not want to go. If I write her up, she will lock me up in confinement. I called my mom and explained what happened. My mom complained to the warden again. Thursday I was placed in confinement as retaliation for reporting the major.

5. My name is "DF," my father died in August 2008 while I was at Taylor Correctional, a work camp. My family notified the institution of my father's death and no one told me about it. I called home and my girlfriend gave me the news. I was upset. The next day while I was at work, a captain and major ordered me to go to classification. A chaplain told me he was not doing anything about it because he felt my family was lying. The chaplain said his vacation was more important than my family notifying me of my father's death. I had community custody and requested to see my dad be buried. I was upset and exchanged a few words with the officer. I was threatened by the officers and housed in confinement for ten months.

6. They call me "Ty," I have been in prison since 1998, for home invasion robbery and a slew of other charges. These charges were fabricated by The Miami-Dade Police Department. I have always maintained my innocence. But due to my social background and my education, I became another victim of the corrupt justice system. Miami-Dade police planted evidence in order to help the prosecutor during my trial. During my time in prison I have seen a lot of abuse from correctional officers and other prison officials. For example, on or around October 2017 at Columbia correctional, ten officers beat an inmate inside the cafeteria. Just because the inmate would not "cuff up." This justified a

reason to beat the inmate unresponsive with blood all over the floor? This is one of the many examples of this corrupt Florida Department of Corrections.

7. They call me "WC," I've been down for almost five years out of Pasco County Florida. On May 5, 2013, I was arrested and charged with grand theft auto. The car belonged to my girlfriend. While I was on the ground, handcuffed, the arresting officer took out his gun and put it to the back of my head. The Pasco County sheriffs looked around and told me, "I'll blow your black ass away if you even think about moving." The sheriff then pistol whipped me in the back of my head. Later, I woke up in the back of a police car. The sheriff claimed I had a gun; however, no gun or weapon was ever in my possession recovered.

8. My name is "Bolito," on May 8, 2018, I was transported from Pinellas County Jail to central Florida reception center. As I was bending over to put my shower slides in the plastic bag, an officer slapped me really hard across my face for not putting my clothes away fast enough. The guy next to me was punched by the same officer and his left ear split open. Blood was all over his neck. Hours later, the inmate was complaining he might have suffered a concussion, but the officers ignored his request for medical.

9. The name is "Warlock," I was at Taylor correctional in July 2006. I was taken to confinement accused of spoken threat. In a thirty-day period, I was sentenced to close management level two. On the way up to the administration building, two officers beat me unconscious while I was handcuffed. They put me in a holding cell until I woke up hours later. I was then moved to Santa Rosa CI.

10. People call me "Easy." Around September 2011, I worked in the Franklin CI confinement passing out food trays. I observed an inmate in a cell that was under heavy medications. He couldn't get out of bed. This sergeant was telling this inmate to make his bed. Two days later, on a Sunday, the sergeant opened the food flap and sprayed the inmate

with chemical agents. This sergeant attempted to empty the can. The inmate couldn't walk to the shower or medical because of his health condition. Later that day, about three or four hours later the inmate died. I knew he would die because the officer put him right back in the same cell with all the chemical agents everywhere.

IMPORTANT INFORMATION ABOUT YOUR DRINKING WATER
Contaminant: Haloacetic Acids (HAA5)
MCL Exceedance at Northwest Florida Reception Center

Our water system recently exceeded a drinking water standard. Although this incident was not an emergency, you have a right to know what happened and what Northwest Florida Reception Center is doing to correct this situation.

We routinely monitor for the presence of drinking water contaminants. Testing results from July 2017 – June 2018 show that our system exceeded the standard, or maximum contaminant level (MCL), for HAA5. Compliance is determined by the locational running annual average (LRAA) at each monitoring location. If one or more LRAA exceeds the TTHM standard of 80 parts per billion (ppb) and/or HAA5 of 60 ppb, an MCL violation is incurred. The level of HAA5s averaged at the Warden's House location was 66.5 ppb.

What should I do?
• There is nothing you need do. If a situation arises where the water is no longer safe to drink, you will be notified within 24 hours.

• If you have a severely compromised immune system, you may be at increased risk and should seek advice from your health care providers about drinking this water.

What does this mean?
This is not an emergency. If it had been an emergency, you would have been notified within 24 hours. TTHMs and HAA5s are organic chemicals which form when disinfectants react with organic matter in the water.
Some people who drink water containing haloacetic acids in excess of the MCL over many years may have an increased risk of getting cancer.

What happened? What was done?

To mitigate Haloacetic Acids (HAA5) from forming in the water distribution system, the following steps have been taken with satisfactory results:
1) The water distribution system at NWFRC was flushed clean by opening the appropriate fire hydrants. This is done to insure that the disinfectant that is used does not have a prolonged residence time inside the distribution piping. (Prolonged residence time in the presents of certain disinfectants can cause Haloacetic Acids (HAA5) to form.)
2) A flushing program has been adopted to insure that long residence times cannot occur in the water distribution system.
3) The disinfectant that is used in the NWFRC water system will be applied at the most optimum rate to insure no Haloacetic Acids (HAA5) can be formed and that the drinking water is maintained at its safest level possible.

For more information, please contact: ████████████ (850) 326-0733

This notice is being sent to you by the Northwest Florida Reception Center

Potable Water System ID#: 1670733

Date distributed: June 11, 2018

Chapter 24

Transport

You're driving down the highway and see a Department of Corrections bus aka "Bluebird." Do you think it would be interesting to know firsthand what it's like to be transferred from one prison to another? You have to bear with me because I have been transferred so many times, I lost count. What I'm going to do is write this chapter as I'm being transferred, live, with the day and exact times. I could easily write exact names of officials and locations, but I'm not going to do so. I know some of you people out there are like, "F-the police," but this book is bigger than just the names of corrupt officers. We want change from the top to the bottom! People out there in society have to vote for men and women who are not intimidated by Tallahassee officials and will not stop until justice is served.

The date is June 7, 2018 and the time is approximately 2:45 a.m. I heard the cell door open and I already knew what time it was. I brushed my teeth, put on my blue uniform, shoes, packed my property, stepped on a one-and-a-half-inch roach and now I'm sitting on a bench in the day room waiting. I had a feeling that I was on my way because I saw several carts full of folders as I walked back to this dormitory yesterday. Three things can happen today. One, the bus goes six hours directly to North West Florida Reception Center, Washington CI, Chipley, Florida. Two, the bus stops at regional medical Center in Lake Butler, Florida. I then board another bus to NWFRC. Or three, the bus stops at RMC and I stay there until another day of transport. I'm going with number two. It's now 3:00 a.m., the female officer and female sergeant were walking around with their flashlights doing security checks. The officer becomes excited and screams to the sergeant, "The inmate in cell 1107 has black underwear on!" The females put on their latex gloves, radioed the cell to open, and demanded for the inmate to give up the black underwear. Without resisting, the young man turned over the underwear. I watched as a female officer exited the quad with the underwear in hand and a big smile on her face. She felt like it was a big sting or something. This sergeant should've explained to her that work release inmates come through this reception center with colored underwear. It's no big deal, lady! Do you think that heavyset female officer is going to take dirty underwear home? That's a possibility I would not be surprised about.

As I write this, I can see the female officer talking on the phone is happy as can be. Probably telling her friend she made a smelly underwear bust! It is now 4:00 a.m and I'm still waiting to be called. The female sergeant gave me the old "hurry up treatment," and then "hurry up and wait." If only corrections department hired people with common sense, this place would be much better. I ate breakfast and went to transfer and receiving. Names were called as officers separated us by bus. A total of forty two of us were standing in the bus sally port waiting to be searched. Piece by piece, all our clothing was taken and we stood butt naked, "Grab your ___? And separate it from your __? Turn around, bend over, spread your cheeks and cough." It is now 7:30 a.m. All forty-two of us are on the bus en route to RMC, Lake Butler. It is hard for me to write because I am hand-cuffed with daisy chains all the way down to the leg irons around my ankles. My left hand, around my wrist is numb from the hand-cuffs being way too tight. I told the officer about it, and he laughed. "You're in prison," he said. We are now on toll road 528. There are all types of exit roads I never saw before. I did see Orange Blossom Trail which runs through the middle of Orlando, Florida. I believe we will be getting on the Florida Turnpike heading north. Orlando looks beautiful! But I would say the same thing about a farm way out in the country. I am looking at the windows noticing the new cars and trucks. Most people look desperate, like trying to get somewhere fast. Rush, rush, rush! Out of the forty-two on this bus, three of us have been down 18 years or more. The remaining thirty-nine are directly from County Jail. The new generation looks beat up. All they're talking about is K2, money, and sex. What ever happen to power through education? We are now going past Ocoee, Florida. The houses look big and very nice, but I wouldn't spend my money on a sheet rock home. Plus, the houses are built too close together. We are now passing the exit to Wildwood, Florida. Most prisoners are complaining about the handcuffs cutting into their wrist. At one time, we were only required to wear leg irons. Those people in central office should get cuffed up like I am right now, carry property, walk on the stairs of the bus and stay on the bus for two hours. Everyone wants to get paid for calling the shots but don't have a clue about running a corrections department.

We got to Lake Butler West unit at 9:45 a.m. My wrist is still swollen from the tight handcuffs. To my surprise, there are a lot of black employees. You can tell the difference when exiting the bus they talk shit, but they ain't going to beat you for fun. Not too many of them anyway. I do see some old school rednecks separated, standing by the dining hall. This place has been investigated by the FBI so many times, officers have to be very careful. Killing inmates around here is an old habit officials can't stop. Go to Google and look up, "Inmate death at Lake Butler, Florida," or "Inmate death at Regional Medical Center, Lake Butler, Florida." Grab a bite to eat because you will be reading articles for a while. It's 8:20 p.m. count time, the dormitory sergeant conducted count and gave everyone the following speech, "You will not fight, fuck, get high or run tattoos in my dorm. You will respect the older inmates and definitely not steal. If you get caught doing any of those things, I will gas you, and my friends will punish you on the way to confinement." I am not too worried about the threats because I am not living wrong like that. What I am asking myself is whether this sergeant is a type that looks for action when there was never any action to begin with?

I don't know what it is but the further up north Florida the prison is located, the more they cut on the quantity of the food. The mashed potatoes today look more like powdered milk. I counted two small pieces of cabbage and the food service inmate worker warned me not to eat the coffee cake because it's a week old. I did not have a single food item to eat in my locker, so I ate it. Can anyone tell me why South and Central Florida prisons feed bigger portions of food than the prisons in North Florida? Can anyone tell me why inmates get physically abused more in North Florida than the South? I know the answer. I will let you figure it out for yourself. Remember how I wrote about the living conditions at Central Florida Reception Center? I have discovered in this regional medical center/reception center that there are no screens in the windows. Bugs fly in and out of the dorms as they feel like doing so. The fans are super dirty. I've been sneezing since I came into this dormitory. There's no exhaust fan in the bathroom. It's broken, I guess! The water fountain is broken also! Once again, I was burned like the color of shrimp because the water in the shower is flaming hot. I should allow for the water to burn me and then tell a lawyer to visit me and take photos. They are lucky that I am not living foul like that! Catch me ten years ago, and I would've let it burn the skin off me.

A ninth circuit Federal judge in 1988 stated, "If the government, police, and prosecutors could always be trusted to do the right thing, there would have never been a need for the bill of rights."

Today was a short bus trip. I will pick this chapter back up tomorrow and also when we go to NW Florida Reception Center. The trip will be three or more hours long. The time is 10:45 p.m. and this day is officially over.

June 8, 2018, 7:30 a.m. I woke up to hear a speech an officer said to the entire quad. "If I come on this side and smell any cigarette smoke or K2 smoke, I will shake this mutha-f'r down starting with bunk one." The officer sounded like he has never been out of this area. I immediately look out the window and realized this would be what we call the Trump administration. Yesterday, apparently, was the Obama administration. At 8:15 a.m., the same officer comes in the quad to look for an inmate in bunk 1106-low and smells cigarette smoke. No one stands up and admits to smoking a damn cig. While the officer is searching the first bunk and property, someone confessed. The officer threatens again to search the entire quad even if he has to stay overtime. I am looking at this officer like, really? Overtime to do some searches? As I look out the window, I'm noticing controlled movements. Basically, get from point A to point B and shut your mouth. The officer is walking in and out of the quad frequently. These men haven't realized he is looking for some action. It is now 10:30 a.m., everybody is in the dorms locked down. No recreation and no canteen. There is a group of officers standing in front of the captain's office doing absolutely nothing! But yet they cry about not getting paid enough money! Maybe they should come and fix the front door to the dormitory. It has a three-inch gap between the floor and the door. Now I see why this place is full of rats and mice! The only water to drink right now is a faucet water. Do you think they can take a few minutes and find out why the water fountain is broken?

At 11:30 a.m., we went to go eat sloppy macaroni. There were five officers in the dining hall looking like they wanted trouble. One inmate had his pants sagging, and the sergeant told him, "Pull your pants up, boy, before we make an example out of you." What the sergeant didn't know and didn't take a few seconds to find out was that the blue pants were issued too big. To make it even more interesting was the inmate is completely psyched out! He walks around like he is in outer space, talking to himself.

At 12:20 p.m. count time. There is an inmate high on K2 to my left that looks like he might not make it. His hands are stretched out and I think he is not breathing. Any minute, the officers will come in the quad to count. Another inmate just pulled him up and slapped his face a few times. He is in another zone! The officers did their count and the inmate fell out again. He now has until the next count to snap out of the high or go through the same risk. Based on what I've seen, I am willing to bet in an hour he will smoke another stick and go back to the almighty game of "risking your life." K2 is killing inmates all over state prisons. Men are dropping like flies! Everyone is looking for a mental escape out of prison and those new synthetic drugs are our number one choice. I want to get out of here and give testimony to the youth about the things I have seen in prison. I know that I can change a lot of lives!

At 3:35 p.m. count time. I haven't smelled any cigarette smoke but the sergeant apparently has. "I'm coming back tomorrow to search everyone's property and take as much as I can," the sergeant yelled out. I have come to the conclusion that most of these officers are barbarians. Everything is said through a threat! Everything is retaliation or malicious. Why are they worried about cigarette smoke? I do not smoke and when I smell it, I walk away from it, simple as that! I don't see a logical reason to search eighty inmates' properties over cigarette smoke. Guess what? You're not going to believe this. I just saw the first Hispanic officer. Actually, he is a sergeant, wow! There is a Hispanic family around here! Or maybe he drives every day from Jacksonville. First, a lot of black employees yesterday and now one Hispanic employee. Regional medical center is making progress, somewhat.

If I were a millionaire, I would build an apartment complex in Lake Butler, Florida, and move a few thousand Puerto Ricans. (Housing free for the first five years.) I know my people. We will spread out and buy everything around here quickly. Klan members would be forced to move further north, to the panhandle again. Puerto Rico is a US territory so there is no deportation or immigration process. We are born with social security numbers. Best of all, Puerto Ricans come in all types of shapes and colors.

At 10:20 p.m. roster count. The night shift is much smoother than any other shifts thus far. Leave us alone, we leave you alone attitude. Overall I have seen some improvement here in Lake Butler, RMC. May all the glory be to God.

June 10, 2018 3:43 p.m. Just when I was writing about the improvement in this reception and medical center, the truth once again comes out. My fiancé drove three hours to visit me. We spend the day talking, eating and walking. As I get up to say goodbye, we started to kiss when a short female sergeant yells across the visit room "hey!" We looked at the sergeant surprised not knowing what she was talking about. I said goodbye again and walked toward the inmate search room. I looked across the visit room and saw the female sergeant telling my fiancé something. I wondered what it is this sergeant is complaining about. A minute later, the sergeant walked over to me advised me she will make a report on the computer. I asked her ten times, "What did we do?" Finally, the sergeant said there's no tongue kissing. I didn't argue, I know she was wrong. The rule is brief kissing coming in and one coming out. Nowhere does it say in the rule that there is no tongue kissing. These types of unprofessional actions, misconduct and malicious ways on behalf of the officers is why families now call the inspector general's office. It's like the female sergeant can't get any attention on the streets or something. A warning would have been good enough from the start! I don't mind following made-up rules by officers but only if you let me know ahead of time! My opinion is, the sergeant walks bowlegged, so it is a big possibility she rides horses. If she rides horses, she's country. Being country doesn't make you a bad person. I'm country myself. But there's a big chance she is country around here where the Ku Klux Klan breed! She came to talk to me with evil talk and evil eyes. I saw hate in her soul! That's a problem!

June 12, 2018, 4:15 a.m. Over 100 inmates were woken up in different dormitories. Same thing as CFRC, hurry up and wait. We ate the watery grits, two pieces of white bread, small piece of sausage and mayonnaise potatoes. I already knew at Tomoka Correctional that I am on my way to the panhandle (Apalachee CI). A lot of other inmates, however, do not know.

At 7:00 a.m., our properties were checked by the X-ray machine and we were given opportunity to utilize the bathroom. The bus ride will be three and a half hours long. Lake Butler Reception Medical Center to North West Florida Reception Center.

At 8:00 a.m., just as my wrist was starting to feel better, I am back in full force restraints. The handcuffs are going to cut my wrists if I'm not careful. We are riding out of Lake Butler, Florida, with nothing but cows, mobile homes, ranch homes and land. (A lot of land.) I didn't see any major stores like Walmart or Target. Only small gas stations.

At 8:20 a.m., we are now headed toward I-10. There's a few pick-up trucks at the gas station, two of them sitting up high with mud tires. The back roads thus far have been two lanes (going and coming). You're not going to believe this: the bus has stopped right in the middle of the railroad tracks. I'm not going to start imagining how dangerous this can be. We are on our way anyway! After a quick left turn, we are now on I-10 heading west. I read a sign indicating there is an exit road to Valdosta, Georgia, coming up ahead. For those who don't know, I-10 starts in Jacksonville, Florida, and ends up in Los Angeles, California. This means I-10 shoots across the top of the state of Florida (panhandle).

At 9:25 a.m., I woke up from the loud laugh of the man sitting across from me. I realized that I am tired because I drooled on my shirt. Nonetheless, I sat up straight and will remain awake. Perry and Greenville exit sign is the latest I've seen. This should mean we are riding on the top of Taylor County, Florida, and maybe about half an hour from Tallahassee. We have two more hours to go! We arrived at N. Florida Reception Center at 11:25 a.m. It's my first time in this part of the panhandle. This is home of the "Chipley five." Five officers including one captain were arrested for beating and spraying inmates on the regular. Authorities now did a good job in changing this around. Remember how I arrived in Lake Butler and was surprised to see the Obama shift? When I got off the bus today, again I was surprised to see an Obama shift. The state of Florida's answer to stop officer misconduct is "higher black folks." I'm not going to lie, mixing the shifts with minorities was a very good idea. It's a good start. What else will the state do to stop excessive use of force here and everywhere else?

June 13, 2018, NWFRC. I was told today if I don't leave tomorrow morning, it will be on Monday. This place is a dump! The shower water comes out as if someone was taking a piss on you. There is a big shortage on the portions of food. I can't believe some people feel comfortable here! There is absolutely no way that I could stay and do time in this isolated depressing place. A Cuban who told me he has been down for over thirty years came to my assigned cell and asked for me to go and buy a sack of K2 for him. He had a pack of batteries as payment. I looked at him like he was stupid! The Cuban went on to explain the dope man gave him too many deals and he didn't want to ask again. I told him I was sorry and I was not involved in any of those things right now. Much less, go and buy pack for anyone. A few hours went by and the Cuban, feeling guilty, comes up to me again and explaining how he is a big dope dealer, he does this and does that. He is waiting for some material and smokes on the side. I responded by congratulating him and his story. I told him I don't care who he was or what he is trying to be. I haven't been a saint all my life but right now my mind and heart is on my freedom. While I've been in prison, I never hustled to look good. I hustled to pay lawyers, experts and private investigators. As the years went by, I became more embarrassed of the things I did. I know that sometimes we have to do what we have to do, but I now stay away from that life. I move with respect and want the same respect in return. The word within the prison population right now is the corrections department will be closing an institution down and filling it back up with close management cases. This is bad because officials will decide to send inmates with petty infractions to those punishment institutions. Many years ago, a lot of institutions housed close management inmates and it was a mess. Someone filed a lawsuit and a federal judge ordered there could only be three institutions housing close management cases with one overflow. Currently, those institutions are, Santa Rosa Correctional Main Unit, Suwannee Correctional main unit, Florida State Prison and Union Correctional. Allowing the corrections department to go back in time would be devastating.

June 18, 2018, I woke up at 3:30 a.m. to the sound of the door opening. I knew I was transferring. Eighty-four of us ate two small pancakes, a banana, and dry cheerios. The milk was flavored nasty water. Two buses, forty-two of us per bus. One bus, going to Jackson Correctional and the other bus to Apalachee Correctional. I was in leg irons, daisy chain and handcuffs once again. This time the cuffs were not too tight. The ride was less than an hour, thank God. I was glad to leave North West Florida Reception Center but when I arrived in Sneads, Florida, Apalachee Correctional, I wanted to go back!

Chapter 25

Medical and Mental Health

The Florida Department of Corrections mental health care system is beyond broken. With budget cuts on the rise, the third largest prison system in the United States is headed straight down to hell! It has been reported half of the 100,000 inmates have hepatitis C. Psychiatric patients roam around prisons mistreated by both officers and our fellow brothers in blue uniforms. I will question these men and attempt to provide the reader with an inside look at this health-care crisis.

1. Mr. JW (b/m): came into the system in May 2018. In Tampa, Florida, doctors recommended that JW have reconstructive knee surgery. He was born in 1948. JW walks in pain and requested for the institutional doctor at Central Florida reception center to prescribe medication and or new pads to help with the pain. The doctor at CFRC refused treatment and did not document JW's condition.

2. Mr. Al (b/m): came into the system September 1989. Al is from Jacksonville, Florida. Medical conditions Al suffers from hepatitis C since 1997, he believes. High blood pressure, low back pain and muscle pain. Doctors at the reception medical center advise Mr. Al he would be receiving Hepatitis C medication a month ago, and he hasn't received any yet. Al explains the doctors at Tomoka correctional knew about his medical condition since the late 1990s and kept quiet. Al is being denied any medications for low back pain and is receiving high blood pressure medication. Al advised doctors in 1989 he was going blind from his right eye and today is unable to see from the right eye. Al tells

me his left eye is almost gone also! Al has complained to the nurses about his condition and has been denied any relief. Al was born in 1955. Al's teeth are all broken and is in pain as he answers my questions. Al looks completely broken down!

3. Mr. RH (h/m): entered the system in May 2018. RH was born in 1971. RH told doctors about his hernia while at Central Florida reception center. RH became dizzy and fell back and fractured his skull. The Department of Corrections medical department has not treated or attempted to treat RH for the hernia. RH gets dizzy even when he is laying down. RH is being forced to climb up to an upper bunk although suffering from the hernia pains.

4. Mr. NM (w/m): Born in 1984. NM came to prison in 2015. NM began to take psychotropic medication for schizophrenia in 2006 while living in Tallahassee, Florida. Doctors within the Department of Corrections prescribed Risperdal and gave him shots of Haldol. NM is walking around attempting to come back to earth! He is borderline zombie/normal. NM seems to be a nice person. NM Is scheduled for release in 2025.

5. Mr. FA (w/m): was born in 1959. Came to the system in 2012. FA Brought in medical records from his clinic in North Carolina stating he suffers from degenerated disks #4 and #5. FA requested help. FA was prescribed ibuprofen, a bottom bunk pass and back brace. In 2017, a nurse at Tomoka correctional recommended for the pain medications, back brace and bottom bunk pass to be taken away. FA Walks around in pain and at his age, it's extremely hard to climb up to an upper bunk. Medical charges $5 each time after time to "fake," like they will help FA but at the end of the day, FA is in serious pain and risk. FA should not be charged $5 for visits to the nurse for the same condition he has complained about for years.

6. Mr. PB (w/m): Born in 1985, came into the system in 2017. Upon entering the Reception Medical Ctr., Lake

Butler, PB advised the doctor he suffers from asthma and the doctor told PB it would be documented. While at Hamilton, PB suffered an asthma attack. The nurse provided a breathing treatment and prescribed asthma inhalers. However, six months ago, while at NW. Florida Reception Ctr. Main unit, a nurse advised PB he has no documentation of asthma and inhaling pumps. PB has submitted sick calls, charged $5 each time, with no success. PB is walking around worried he may suffer from another asthma attack. PB uses other inmate's asthma pumps when available.

7. CF is a (h/m) Born 1980: CF was being transported from a Polk county jail, (Frost proof) en route to see a doctor. The van the county jail used was the "dog cage" van. No windows, all steel inside. CF had handcuffs on only. A car hit the van on the side, the van popped a curve, skid sideways, a city bus hit the van and dragged the van thirty feet. Five inmates were in the van. Two died instantly. Three were severely injured. CF's right leg was crushed. CF's scull was opened, and he lost two of the five lobes. Too much blood! CF has big scars on his head. Doctors placed CF on a breathing machine while in the hospital. CF was in a coma, handcuffed to a bed, for one year. CF was pending arm robbery charges when the accident occurred. In 2016, CF came in through Central Florida reception center. CF advised doctors at CFRC of all his medical conditions. Doctors prescribed pain medication for sixty days. CF never received any more pain medication. CF was prescribed yellow pads, like icy hot for thirty days. CF has been transferred from prison to prison because medical departments refused to deal with his condition. CF is currently suffering from severe pain in his right leg, right hip, and he doesn't walk straight or fast. CF suffers from migraines. CF lost his taste buds, right ear hearing loss, left eye is partially blind, can't smell properly. CF's throat is damaged, he chokes on the food he eats. My opinion of CF is "someone please help him."

8. ET was born in 1968 (b/m): came in the system in 2008. While on lockdown in Franklin CI, ET submitted a sick call in order to see a doctor concerning his high blood pressure. A couple of days went by and ET was forced to declare a medical emergency. When ET was in the medical department, a nurse advised ET he signed a refusal form to be treated. ET called on the dormitory camera as a witness that he never left the dorm to sign said refusal. ET was feeling chest pains and dizziness. This occurred in 2016. ET has not been given any medications as of today, June 12, 2018. ET explains Franklin correctional was under investigation for officer misconducts and for officers filing fraudulent disciplinary reports.

9. "RAFA" (h/m): was born in 1981. He came through Central Florida reception center in February 2018 out of Tampa, Florida. RAFA takes psychotropic medications since he was a child. On the first day of reception, RAFA was punched in the face by an officer at CFRC. RAFA explains other inmates were slapped, punched and kicked in the face that very same day. RAFA assures me all he did was laugh at the officer. RAFA is another one running around psyched out!

10. MP was born in 1979: has been incarcerated since 1997 out of Osceola County, Florida. MP Has fought hard for prisoner rights. Filing grievances, lawsuits and his family members complaining from the outside in order to be better heard. MP has been retaliated against countless amount of times. Officers have put out hits against MP, housed him in confinement under investigations and have written fraudulent disciplinary reports against him. MP is currently taking medications for his depression. Counselors often cooperate with officials and allow the mistreatment.

I called Apalachee correctional "a cemetery" back in 2007 when the bus stopped here to drop off inmates in route to Jackson Correctional. What did I ever do to deserve being housed in this dump? From what I'm being told, Apalachee is one of the oldest prisons in Florida. You have to see it to believe it! Hollywood can make plenty of movies within all the old red brick buildings. There is even a fence dividing half the prison because it's falling apart. Condemned! I'm asking myself over and over how does Apalachee make it through inspection? Someone is getting paid real good money to turn a blind eye! I will definitely be looking into writing to the American Correctional Association (ACA) and asking many questions about the living conditions in Apalachee Correctional. Nothing here makes sense!

On the very first day I arrived, I submitted a transfer form. I requested the following three prisons: Zephyrhills, Marion and Lake Correctional. Any of the three will be okay. The problem is last December, I went to confinement at Hardee correctional and was hit with a minor possession of contraband disciplinary report. Technically, I'm supposed to wait one year from the time of the infraction to submit the transfer form. I tried anyway! As soon as I see classification, I will ask to be transferred to Everglades Correctional, which now supposedly offers a lot of programs. If classification gives me a hard time, I will submit a grievance stating my claim. I qualify for the Everglades program because there have been no major disciplinary reports on my record since 2008. The key is being clean of major disciplinary reports, not minor. Let's see how that turns out!

I haven't been at Apalachee twenty-four hours and numerous incidents have occurred. One inmate got his ahead split wide open with a lock. The other inmate didn't want to be placed in handcuffs and therefore officers utilize excessive use of force. A riot almost broke out after an inmate was mad over not being able to smoke K2. That's crazy! And a gang member's face was sliced open after his brother discovered he was trying to join another gang. Not bad for less than a day's time right? I will find out how the rest of the days go around here. I will continue to write about Apalachee correctional, the Florida parole system, medical department and much more in my next book titled, *Guilty by Corruption, the continuance.* Every day is another story around the corrections department.

Epilogue

It has truly been fun and exciting writing this book. I decided to name it *Guilty by Corruption* because that's exactly what the justice system put me through. I believe I did a good job in providing legal documents surrounding my innocence. Many claim to be wrongfully convicted. Very few actually can show it in black-and-white! Obviously, the justice system needs improvement from the moment officers make the arrest, to the moment a convict is released from prison. So many men and women simply do not belong behind bars. I said it before, I will say it again, "intensive counseling—group programs and education are the key and opening the door of success for reentry into society."

As of this present month of July 2018, the manifest injustice motion is still pending in the Osceola County Courthouse. The ninth judicial circuit court of Orange and Osceola Florida has to assign the assistant state attorney's handling hundreds if not thousands of criminal appeals. It's no wonder why people are denied any type of relief. They play the "rubber stamp" game with people's life.

My mom has been consistent with monthly visits, accepting my phone calls and helping with whatever she can. If only the rest of my family would do the same, I would be a little better. My fiancé and I continue to pray for God to touch the hearts of those overseeing my appeal. Words fall short of how amazing Zinia has been and continues to be.

I will remain positive, wise and creative. There has to be brighter days for me soon, right? Thank you for taking your valuable time to read my book. Don't hesitate to let me know how you feel.

"If you listen to constructive criticism, you will be at home among the wise. If you reject discipline, you only harm yourself; but if you listen to correction, you grow in understanding" (Proverbs 15:31–32).

Legal Epigrams

Retired Supreme Court Justice William Brennan:

"We do not have, nor did we ever want pure democracy. The Constitution and Bill of Rights was to protect individuals and minorities from the oppression of the majority."

US v. Doe, 860 F.2d 488 (1st Cir.1988):

"Prosecutor does not represent an entity whose interests include winning at all costs; prosecutor's client is society, which seeks justice not victory."

Arthur Hailey 1976:

"Given anytime at all, prison could only degrade and worsen him; could only increase his hatred of "the system," which had sent him there; could only reduce the possibility of his becoming, ever, a useful, law–abiding citizen. And the longer his sentence, the less likelihood there was of any moral salvage."

Henry Ford 1947:

"Capital punishment is as fundamentally wrong as a cure for crime is charity is wrong as a cure for poverty."

Louis D. Brandeis-US Supreme Court Justice, 1941:

"Crime is contagious. If the government becomes the law breaker, it breeds contempt for the law."

Anthony Hope-1933:

"A book might be written on the injustice of the just."

Friedrich W. Nietzsche-German Philosopher-1900:

"Distrust in all whom the impulse to punish is powerful."

Richard Haynes-1981:

"The men and women who do what I do are really the difference between free people and the Gestapo. I prepare every case like a Sovereign was trying to kill my client…many times, they are."

Author's Note

"I hope you have enjoyed the first book in the "Guilty By Corruption" series. Be on the lookout for Guilty by Corruption: "The Continuance," and, "Evidence speaks for itself". Thank you! And may our father God bless you always.

About the Author

Giovanni Vega has been incarcerated nineteen years battling the justice system after his case fell victim to the hardest disciplined chief medical examiner in Florida history. As an author/journalist, Giovanni has interviewed many men who have suffered severe abuse and medical malpractice in the hands of state correctional officials. Giovanni has earned multiple certifications and degrees throughout his tour of the Florida prisons.

CPSIA information can be obtained
at www.ICGtesting.com
Printed in the USA
LVHW090444060419
613206LV00001BA/150/P